Seeking History through Her Source

Seeking History through Her Source

SOUTH OF THE VINDHYAS

Edited by

ALOKA PARASHER SEN

Orient BlackSwan

SEEKING HISTORY THROUGH HER SOURCE: SOUTH OF THE VINDHYAS

ORIENT BLACKSWAN PRIVATE LIMITED

Registered Office
3-6-752 Himayatnagar, Hyderabad 500 029, Telangana, India
e-mail: centraloffice@orientblackswan.com

Other Offices
Bengaluru, Chennai, Guwahati, Hyderabad,
Kolkata, Mumbai, New Delhi, Noida, Patna

First published by Orient Blackswan Private Limited 2022

ISBN 978-93-5442-292-8

040154

Typeset in
Minion Pro 11/13pt
by Shine Graphics, Delhi 110 094

Printed in India at
Thomson Press, New Delhi 110 020

Published by
Orient Blackswan Private Limited
3-6-752, Himayatnagar, Hyderabad 500 029, Telangana, India
e-mail: info@orientblackswan.com

To

The University of Hyderabad

For the many years spent with you

Contents

List of Plates

(Inserted between p. 82 and p. 83)

Preface

All academic engagements are dialogical, and so is this one, whose origins can be located in the University of Hyderabad. Over the past decade, students under my supervision, as my research group, have engaged with historical research on regions south of the Vindhyas in an attempt to highlight the centrality and particularity of their chosen sources of study, to rethink the way the past can be recovered. This book emerges from these efforts.

As is evident, this collective endeavour would not have been possible without the energetic and enthusiastic effort of all the contributors. Originally as students, their initial journey into historical research began at the University of Hyderabad, but their commitment to continue with expanding the boundaries of historical knowledge has enabled them to seek new pastures of engagement. However, the first initiation into the field often leaves behind traces that impact all of us in unknown and intangible ways.

When my idea to put together this book came about, I was instinctively drawn to revisiting the questions and problems that I had raised in the classroom with these students while they initially tested their forays into research. That they too found it worthwhile to revisit their association with me gives me immense satisfaction, and I place on record my deep sense of gratitude that all of them immediately responded in the affirmative and have eagerly contributed to the book.

This book has brought to the forefront the issue of treating the footnote, where the 'Source' is meant to be placed, with as much care as one does the dominant narrative based on it. Indeed, we emphasise that 'History' is actually a seeker of knowledge from her 'Source', and thus, the latter's particularity must necessarily be focused upon. In particular, when dealing with regional and local scenarios, the contextuality of the source has to be highlighted, rather than merely comparing it with some benchmark of an authentic source located elsewhere. It is with this concern that the chapters in this book look internally at the nature and specificity of the intended 'Source' being interrogated by each of the scholars. This has enabled us to highlight issues of literary perceptions, fragmentary objects, pieces of writing, and scattered coins positively, rather than seeing in them a lack of authenticity and therefore rejecting them as valuable sources of information. On the contrary, looking at history from the perspective of the small, the marginal, and the rejected, these sources in fact enhance the scope of history to bring in the hidden, the borders, the stray finds, the unnoticed labels, and the like.

As a final word, we have not moved our search into an alien land that was hitherto absolutely unknown. Rather, we have relooked at the sources, some of which were known and others which had not been interpreted so far, so that the past can be retrieved in ways where the Source is given primacy and not looked down upon from an authoritarian position. We have shown history as seeking rather than grabbing the sources of information to broaden our concerns about the type of history we need to write. Hitherto, an aggressive approach has led us to only perpetuate a view of the past as seen through the narrow prism of a few who had access to the production of the sources that were being used to write our histories.

We do not see this book as the finite end of our endeavours. Nor do we see it as the last word on the subject. In fact, it is hoped that the direction set in these chapters shall enable us to probe more deeply to understand the myriad sources that have not had an opportunity to speak to us. It is intended to open up more such endeavours in other regions of the country and generate a more dialogical approach to writing about the past, which will be more encompassing, more open to accepting perceptions inherent in the sources, and more accommodative of the views of the others.

It is a tradition not to thank oneself. But it needs to be said that the calm and collegial atmosphere provided by the Sanskrit Studies Department where I am currently located was indispensable for working on the book. I refer here to both the intellectual vibrancy of its faculty and students and to the dedicated support staff—Narasimha and Mahalakshmi. In particular, my sincere thanks to Ambaji for her academic insights and in grappling with the intricacies of usefully tapping technology.

To Roopa Sharma of Orient BlackSwan, for her openness and prompt replies to all my queries, a sincere thanks. A casual but earnest question from Nandini Rao of Orient BlackSwan at a gathering celebrating books, about my next research book energised me to put this collection together, something that I was mulling over for quite some time. I thank her for her interest and I sincerely hope that what has been put together here provides a suitable ground for our continued interactions.

It is impossible to thank all those who have made it possible for each one of us to put in our time and effort to complete our respective chapters. There were many hurdles on the way and we shall remember them, only to realise that all good things reach their finality in circumstances that are challenging—that is what makes the end result satisfying, but in no way closed to receiving reactions and criticisms in equal measure.

ALOKA PARASHER SEN

Introduction

Aloka Parasher Sen

The compulsion to make the Source central to our interrogation and treat it in a more nuanced way emerged when I laid hands on Anthony Grafton's *The Footnote: A Curious History* in the late 1990s, a present from a friend. Why did she choose this book? Both of us were then trying to understand small, scattered, often unrelated pieces of information from excavations at sites, inscriptions, and texts in areas that had hitherto been considered 'backward' in historical terms as they had not thrown up monumental remains or textual canons for early periods of history as opposed to those found in plenty in contiguous regions for the same period. With concerted effort we seemed compelled, perhaps erroneously, to propel the unitary ideas of the scientific method. But Grafton had in his book unfolded a complex story to take us through a long journey of the status of history as art, as science, and as an institution. He wrote primarily in the context of Western or European historiography to show the trajectory of how the 'footnote in history' had been treated, and convincingly argue that its value and position were embedded in the power and authority given to it, depending on our respective tools of analysis (Grafton 1997: 223–235).

Writing in the context of pre-modern India, it struck me that our prolific footnotes had majorly been sourced from ancient literary texts. The ease with which we had all used these literary sources as data presenting pieces of information had led to an ignoring of the world view in which these texts were immersed in the first place. If literature is based on perceptions, then how does one use it as a proof-provider for historical events that occurred in bygone days? Furthermore, some textual sources were more comfortably used while others were rejected, since they were seen as less reliable. To add to this, many scholars wished to corroborate the literary with the so-called hard core data emanating from the archaeological, numismatic, and epigraphic records, which are also constructed with the help of scientific methods. None of these endeavours gave due importance to the nature of the footnote. Our concern in this book project is a fundamental one: How do we reconcile our tools of interrogating the past with the ostensibly irrational ideas inherent in the sources we use to write this history? The struggle over what history is and how it should be told is dependent on the footnote. This tool differentiates history as a mere narrative from one that is substantiated by evidence, and thus makes it a 'true science' purporting truth, and is therefore critical to the scientific nature of historical writing which reflects both the ideology and the technical practice of the craft. Anthony Grafton defines the task of the footnote for the construction of 'scientific history' as follows:

> Like the high whine of the dentist's drill, the low rumble of the footnote on the historian's page reassures: the tedium it inflicts, like the pain inflicted by the drill,[1] is not random but directed, part of the cost that the benefits of modern science and technology exact (Grafton 1997: 5).

History, of course, is not an axiomatic science and therefore, there are historians among us who wage whole wars against other scholars through the medium of their footnotes. The pain can be overcome if we refine our attitude to the footnote, as its very perception and use impact the understanding of history. This then concomitantly entails a moving away from a singular voice asserting history to one that is multi-vocal, throwing before us many ways of perceiving the past and, most importantly, seeking out the 'reality' of the past rather than its 'truth'.

However, history itself is embedded in its deep past. Much inspired by Clio, the Muse of History, it has evolved to be a domain of inquiry that has involved the method of science inasmuch as, when it is presented, it has all the sensibilities of art. Clio was history's patron and she was said to have not only inspired the retelling of factual accounts, but also stories in themselves. Visually, she is represented as holding an open parchment scroll or a set of tablets, seated beside a chest of books. Built around these early ideas, the Greek tradition of history writing set the benchmark of considering contemporary accounts of events as the most authentic sources of information about a historical past. Like ancient Greece, the Indian subcontinent is a land as old as time. However, in establishing elements of her historical narrative, one is often dependent on unconventional sources of information that are at variance with what are usually described as the primary records contemporary to the period being written about.

Over the years, in the practice of history writing as an academic discipline, primary or original sources came to include artefacts, documents, diaries, manuscripts, autobiographies, and other such recordings that were created in the period under study. As the scope of history writing expanded to include social and cultural aspects of life, additional sources of information became relevant. Thus, fictional sources such as novels, plays, images, photographs, sculptures, coins, paintings, and buildings created at the time came to be drawn upon. It came to be believed that literary sources usually told a story and reflected the ethos of the times, and brought to the fore contemporary attitudes. Historians also came to use epigraphic and archaeological data that ostensibly threw up tangible facts of history. In relatively recent times, oral ways of retrieving the past have come of age. In the use of these sources, it has been a common practice to use the footnote to provide a badge of legitimacy, and often the historian establishes an authoritarian relationship with the footnote, aggressively looking down on it. It is this aggressive relationship that brings forth conflicting narrations of a historical past, wherein two views may be diametrically opposed to each other while using the same source. There is a definite point in time in every society when footnotes attain a level of acceptability, so that using them distinguishes historical modernity from tradition.

When we graft these concerns on to the Indian situation, the nature of the footnote must necessarily become a subject of concern. Thus, for instance, the textual past of early India and the reliability of such texts, often rooted in mythical beginnings, are treated as less amenable to truth and authenticity compared to a more recent official record, or the more rigorous information emanating from a contemporary inscription or archaeological object. Furthermore, the power and burden of the Indological discourse is something that historians of ancient India have found difficult to escape from. We are supposed to locate all early Indian literary sources belonging to different genres as 'footnotes', to be used as 'evidence'. The footnote here is often mistaken as only of technical use, providing testimony to a past reality apparently free from a world view that was inherent to or impinging upon it. We submit that dealing with a footnote in a more nuanced way unveils a complex story that must underline the nature and complexity of the footnote as well as the reality or world view that it was supposed to represent. Scholars often do not recognise that the dominant intellectual discourses about what should be understood as history in early India looked at the notion of history rather differently than we do today (Thapar 2013).[2]

Despite this, and given the yeoman's service that went into the search for the 'fact'(s) of ancient India, different types of history writing have emerged, even though, as E. H. Carr pertinently reminds us, the 'facts' of history remain elusive! He writes:

> The facts...are like fish swimming about in a vast, sometimes inaccessible ocean; and what the historian catches will depend, partly on chance, but mainly on what part of the ocean he (she) chooses to fish in and what tackle he (she) chooses to use—these two factors being determined by the kind of fish he (she) wants to catch (Carr 1986: 28).

Nonetheless, using the generally accepted methods prescribed for writing history, the earliest modernist writings on ancient India began with the so-called 'imperialist historians', who initially lamented that 'proper' sources of information were absent in the development of a coherent narrative about the colony's past. Their enterprise of writing about early Indian history was thus always projected as lacking a historical sense (Thapar 2013: 18–28). A commonplace assumption within the dominant discourse in the early nineteenth century, for south India as well, was that 'the department of ancient history in the East is so deformed by fable and anachronism that it may be considered an absolute blank in Indian literature', and for which reason Wilks articulates that his aim is to rescue 'from oblivion (its history) before it should be lost forever…' (Wilks 1810: xv, xix). This of course, was not the view of the Orientalists, some of whom patiently and with diligence edited, translated, and explained ancient Indian texts[3] to the modern educated Indians, whose now-colonised minds permanently doomed them to suffer from a lack of self-identity and a limited sense of their past.

Apart from the construction of sources, history as an academic discipline also came to India as part of the cultural baggage of colonialism. Dilip K. Chakrabarti has aptly summarised the concomitant effect of this thus: 'The model of the Indian past… was foisted on Indians by the hegemonic books written by Western Indologists concerned with language, literature and philosophy who were and perhaps have always been paternalistic at their best and *racists* at their worst' (Chakrabarti 1997: 21). In the post-colonial world, we therefore cannot talk about our past without the essential and immediate history of the last 200 years. This has resulted in a set of complex conjunctures wherein Indians have now lost the sensibility to identify the difference between 'India's essential past' and 'its historical connection to the empire' (Dirks 1990: 28). It has been well established by scholars that ancient India was a contesting ground for some of the earliest endeavours by the Imperialist and the Orientalist writings to mould and perpetuate certain types of interpretations, for instance, the comfort with which 'India' as a total object of study was seen as a monolithic whole. More commonly, a great emphasis on unearthing only the textual traditions led to the image of a highly 'spiritual' and 'exotic' land bereft of any political or economic agency and with a lack of interest in materiality and things mundane (Inden 1986: 402, 440).

The Nationalists writing on ancient India seemed wholeheartedly indebted to the Orientalists in terms of the latter providing valuable textual sources that had been translated by them for their major thrust to depict India in glorious terms. In fact, with them, as well as with other schools of historical interpretations, the making of the historical narrative about ancient India went hand in hand with the creation of the 'source' and 'fact' of its past. For the Nationalist school in particular, this bind of history only solidified their attempts at writing about the past from the perspective of the dominant 'Self'. Our attention is drawn to the examples of men like Bankim Chandra who sought 'to graft the discourse of history on a structure of feeling indigenous in character' (Kumar 1991: 11), and by relying only on the high culture of Hinduism to retrieve this essence, lost sight of the other diverse traditions in the Indian subcontinent.

The course of the twentieth century saw Indian historians mastering the methods and techniques of a scientific writing of Indian history. This ranged from the positivist framework of analysis guarding history's individuality to more radical approaches that grappled with interdisciplinary studies. This was alongside a diminishing of rigour to analyse textual material but it was replaced by a growing interest in the use of epigraphy, archaeology and numismatics as sources of information. Despite this shift in 'source' base, most historians continued to play within the given 'rules of the game' (Kumar 1991: 5–10), which meant: (*i*) an acceptance of the fact that the ancient past of their country was devoid of a sense of 'scientific' history writing; (*ii*) an acceptance of the simple logic that the ancient past of the Indian civilisational entity was linked to the collective existence of the present, as represented through the nation-state and its institutions; and (*iii*) apparently absolute universal meanings of time, progress, humanism, and the like had to be somehow drawn upon to explore the Indian past.

The more recent interpretations of ancient Indian history have indeed recognised that conflict and the material basis of production were factors which swayed India from one phase to another, but they continued to view these in terms of the totality of agrarian systems, urban landscapes, and other structures defining the mega entity that is India (Sharma 1965, 1987).This was so because their tools of research intended them to retrieve the whole rather than the particular. Recent scholarship using historical materialism as a tool for interpreting the past established their stand by critiquing the earlier colonial and nationalist interpretations to show that the 'traditional' order of society was not monolithic in time and space. In doing so, the same texts were critically used, but based on a synthesis of opportunistically chosen indigenous texts/inscriptions, often translated by the well-known Orientalists, and other odd bits of pre-modern information suitably muffled by early British records. This trend was suddenly shaken from its stupor by very conservative right-wing interpretations that used the same methodological tools of historical authentication and tried to suggest an 'Indian' monolithism, based on Hindu cultural nationalism. The so-called conservative, reactionary or 'nativist' historians who used positivism to the hilt to generate an unquestionable, apparently indigenous version of the ancient past ironically did not talk the language of 'history', which was embedded in Indian idioms. In fact, efforts at redefining school curricula and textbooks to support them in some states of the Indian Union, at first instance during the 1990s, clearly indicate an attempt being made to impose a cultural monism on the Indian past, and displace a more liberal view of Indian culture that had been prevalent in the decades immediately after Independence (Abraham 1992: 8).

Both the conservative and liberal views in the post-modern idiom were, however, equally complicit in perpetuating historicised notions of social totality and projecting grand narratives, without even recognising that there was a historical discourse of imposition going back to the genesis of Indology as an academic discipline. The post-modern turn in the writing of Indian history began with the painful process of first providing a critique of the Indological discourse (Inden 1986: 401–446). This was to lay bare the intimate collusion between writing about the ancient past in all its hues and the power of those who controlled knowledge generation, those who disseminated it, and then imposed it as the defining characteristic of people whose knowledge it originally was. It then attempted to privilege the margins of the past which had all the elements of heterogeneity, multi-vocality, and open-endedness (Roy 2011).[4] Others trying to deal with the post-Independence dilemmas, concerned with not only generating the 'source' for writing about the past but also how the 'discourse' of history could be made more inclusive, reflected on how the enterprise of the modern writing of history was in crisis. As pointed out by Dipesh Chakrabarty, the muse of 'Indian History' was caught in the impossible situation of being able to only mimic 'a certain "modern" subject of "European" history', and was thus 'bound to represent a sad figure of lack and failure' (Chakrabarty 1992: 18–19). Despite this impossibility, all the above interpretations of Indian history 'did not simply "represent" the past as it was but in fact profoundly re-ordered it…' as well (Ali 1999: 9).

In order to shift beyond the notion of history in terms of a meta-narrative, as it is conventionally understood, with a focus only on the monumental and conspicuous at a pan-Indian level, this collection by design moves away to look at historical realities primarily south of the Vindhyas at the small, the fragment, the marginal text, and the fragmentary object in their respective local niches, so as to incorporate the history of hitherto unknown or little-known aspects of past lives, both materially and at an ideational level. As an exercise, this became necessary as writing regional and local histories threw up challenging problems, since there was often a lack of so-called official sources of information in these parts. The centrality of the local source, often in a fragment, had to be contextualised as a valid way of reading the past. Further, reflections from stories and literature located away from the region had to be sieved out carefully. Archaeological data, often believed to provide hard core facts, was in itself constructed, and usually left out the unfamiliar from its purview. These, and several other issues, had to be addressed keeping the regional dimension of case studies in mind. Today, it is well-recognised that to write history is to unravel the processes of life as had been lived, and in order to do so our dependence on a whole range of sources of information has become a necessity.

This volume of specially crafted chapters seeks ways of writing history through tapping either unusual sources of information or reading them in innovative ways. It elaborates on ways to rethink a seeking of the past that engages with how difference can be highlighted. Inherent in this task has been an attempt to dwell more emphatically on the footnote while trying to write this history, so that the multifarious ways of reading different types of sources can be adequately addressed. Furthermore, attempts have been made to highlight the ideological and material setting in which these sources were located. Eight case studies have been undertaken here that interrogate (*i*) an earlier known source—coin or inscription—which may have been rejected because it was available only in fragments; (*ii*) a written or visual source which may have been used earlier only for a particular kind of conventional history, political or monumental in nature; (*iii*) literature that had erroneously been used to cite 'facts' when it had actually narrativised perceptions of the past; and finally, (*iv*) the problematising attempts to uplift a story or a poem as a source for the historical past.

Broadly, we have placed the chapters under two sections: The first comprises those emanating from a literary perception that endeavours to sketch the past, originally drawing from an oral repository of thought and reflections that we have named 'Part I—Perceiving the Past'. In the second section are those that emerge in a contemporary context as products of an age that chose to inscribe or produce artefacts for particular needs, this we have called 'Part II—Producing the Past'.

In Part I, the first chapter titled 'The Making of Classical Tamil Literature: Multiple Sources in its Construction' is by V. Rajesh. It is important to begin with this as it raises the fundamental question of how an ancient source is usually constructed in modern times under the purview of the intellectual influences that came with colonialism. That most ancient sources were constructed is usually ignored by historical scholarship, and canons of texts have hitherto been blindly used as 'authentic' sources of information to build a variety of historical narratives. Rajesh takes up this issue to argue that it is necessary to interrogate the processes that led to their formation even in pre-modern times, as inherent biases, explicitly or implicitly, impair our understanding of the nature of the source. He begins this chapter by discussing how the making of classical Tamil poetry—*Cankam* literature—in the modern period had much to do with the emphasis placed on the print and publishing industry in the history of the nineteenth- and early twentieth-century Madras Presidency. He further points out that an earlier set of scholars, burdened by the idea of a dramatic '(re)discovery' and publication of Cankam literature in the colonial period, concomitantly nurtured a tendency to show that this tradition was forgotten in the preceding centuries by the Tamil scholarly community. In his analysis, Rajesh points out the flawed nature of this understanding since it was based only on a specific set of sources, namely the autobiography of one of the editors of classical poetry and the collections of the dominant Saiva monasteries in Tamil Nadu, which was a rather narrow basis on which to make this so-called recovery of the tradition. In the ultimate analysis, he builds on the work of recent scholarship to make a plea for examining other possible sources that went into the making of the tradition, which have hitherto been ignored by scholars of Tamil literary history. He concludes by stating the need for examining multiple sources to understand the making of Cankam poetry in the early modern and colonial period. This chapter alerts us to look at literary sources in the context in which they were produced. If not interrogated or properly put together, the sources run the risk of misunderstanding the different pre-modern periods in which they were located and continually changed as well.

From sources being constructed to them being considered 'unreliable', the next chapter by Sagnik Saha, titled 'Virtual Hegemonies and Literary Imaginings: Reading the *Jātakas* "Against the Grain"', exemplifies how popular stories, however malleable in their content, can reveal historical insights, especially with reference to everyday aspects of the life of ordinary folk. Popular stories like the *Jātakas* were edited and translated into English as a collection in modern times. Originally, these stories were transmitted orally and, as is well-known, the tenor of the messages they conveyed changed when they were actively used by the Buddhist monks to spread their teachings. Saha points out that while initially, scholars emphasised the *Jātakas* as a potential source for an alternative image of the early Indian socio-political structure, this corpus of stories eventually receded to become mere footnotes to the grand narratives of the varied stages of material culture and social formations in early India, put forth by both the Nationalist and Marxist scholars. He takes cognisance of more recent scholarship that does attempt to bring out their potential as a thematic source for mapping an alternative cosmos; however, his own engagement has been to recognise the *Jātakas* as a source to understand the subversive popular culture of early India, and thus he sets out to read them 'against the grain'. While doing so, the didactic material on the state and its ploys, gleaned from sources like the *Arthaśāstra*, provided a backdrop that Saha consciously alludes to, just so that he can present a contrary picture of the socio-political order as perceived by the peasants. Saha builds his argument by using recent theoretical models to read the *Jātakas* and interrogate the nature of the 'hidden transcripts' that reflect on different aspects of peasant life, including their attempts to protest by strategically using servile behaviour, migration, gossip, rumours, and so on, which enable them to challenge their subjective experiences. The dominant imaginings on early India that revolve around the hegemonic institutions of kings, *brāhmaṇas*, sramanas, and merchants are thus questioned by reading the *Jātakas* 'against the grain', so as to provide an alternative reading of the conditions of and agency that rested with subaltern groups. To expand the scope of history with a focus on the subordinate and the everyday, the source in this case is presented as a viable tool with which to write a more inclusive history, rather than being dismissed as mere stories and thus 'unreliable'.

If the popular story was considered 'unreliable', the literature of the genre called *Kāvya* or poetic texts was accepted, as some of the *Caritas* or historical biographies were written in this format. Overall, though, even this was considered an unauthentic source of information since it was layered with hyperbole and exaggerated claims. The next chapter, titled 'Perceptions of History in Images of Space and Power: The *Kāvya* Narratives', by Mrinalini looks closely at how fictional narratives can enable alternative ways of looking at the past. Mrinalini rightly points out that literary texts assume importance while reconstructing history because they provide a repertoire of perceptions otherwise not available in sources emanating from the state. She recognises at the outset that hitherto, scholars have pointed to the Kāvyas as being conventionally embellished and adorned with figurative speech like similes, metaphors, etc., and have categorically rejected them because it was believed that history could not be extracted from this type of literature. Mrinalini takes a different stand to show how, if carefully employed, the Kāvyas can be a valid source as they produce images of the past in which the everyday lives of people can be found embedded. The focus of her chapter is on a comparative study of two near contemporaneous Kāvya texts, namely the *Kirātārjunīyam* and the *Harṣacarita*, to highlight how the idea of space and the concept of power in controlling 'forest' zones outside a core settled agrarian tract of the kingdom were represented in these texts. The *Kirātārjunīyam* and *Harṣacarita* use different terminologies to refer to the space of the forest, i.e., *vana* and *aṭavi*, respectively. Hence, against the background of these terminologies, she has delved into the question of how the space of the forest was defined in relation to both the village and other external forces emanating from the economic and political interactions between forest and non-forest areas. Ideological intrusions by mendicants and renouncers have also been discussed to argue that these interventions broke the binary between settled and non-settled areas in the domain of the forest. Hence, through an analysis of the *Kirātārjunīyam* and *Harṣacarita,* this chapter presents the particularity of the Kāvyas as sources that provide a view of the past rooted in perceptions that were more expansive in understanding relationships, rather than merely perpetuating stereotypes of the forest as an alien wild space whose inhabitants had no contact whatsoever with the so-called civilised space of the town and village.

Part I ends with an endeavour to use poems as a way of understanding the past. This chapter addresses regions of the far south called the ancient Tamilakam, which are known to us from the corpus of the Cankam literary tradition. Sreekala M. V., in her chapter 'The Idea of Water: A Reading of the *Cankam* Poems', delves into this source that is at once about creativity and yet, entangled with it, is the desire to reflect reality. Entwined in the tropes of love and longing on the one hand and war on the other, the poems speak of polity, society, and economy. She points out emphatically that the poems do not provide direct descriptions of events, but can be effectively used to extract large-scale information about Cankam society. Much water has flown down the Kaveri and over the years, scholars have exhausted these texts for all that can be culled from them about the historical aspects of the three kingdoms that they refer to. But Sreekala focuses on the idea of water and water resources to point out that these poetic depictions take us close to the inherent images that the society found indispensable to portray, as survival depended on this resource in more ways than one. The chapter elaborates on water that was, at one level, a benign force as it provided the much-needed basis for agriculture and land reclamation, which led to the evolution of time-tested technologies that both the state and the people could use to control this resource. At another level, water as a source of fear, of the oceans, of the sea voyages undertaken depict an ambivalent attitude to these resources. In both imaginaries, the livelihoods dependent on it are vividly discussed by Sreekala. Once again, a well-known source like the Cankam poems have been read not to depict historical events, but rather to understand the different ways in which human–nature interactions have been depicted. From reservoirs being commissioned and built by rulers to their being guarded by ordinary people against attacks, as well as their overflow during the rainy season, to how the ancient Tamils coped with using the ocean and its coastline to garner its resources, all have been analysed to tell us how ancient Tamil society viewed the relevance and importance of water in their lives.

Part II, on 'Producing the Past', begins with Nairita Ghosh's chapter, 'Identities in Fragments: Early Deccan in Inscriptions'. It is ironic that this source is valuable in providing specific details such as the names of people, the places they hailed from, their kin-based relationships, their religious affiliations, and so on, but the inscriptions used to garner this information are too brief. A lot is left unsaid in them and therefore, it becomes a challenge to understand and use them to seek a past that can thus only be lived through fragments. Two hundred and seventy-five donative label inscriptions have been studied, which, according to Ghosh, can become the basis for us to rethink the writing of the social history of the Deccan from the second century BCE to the fourth century CE. She aims to see the pattern that emerges by laying bare the minutest of information that people have left behind. The chapter thus first explains this pattern to map the numerous social groups like the *gahapatis* or landlords, *sethis* or merchants, *vaṇijas* or traders, *āvēsanis* or artisans, *śrēṇīs* or guilds, administrative officials, and women through their names. Her arguments move away from what was hitherto upheld—that this data can at best be only corroborative. She has in fact made this data the backbone to then connect two issues of relevance to any social order, that is, where these people hailed from and with whom they related themselves. In other words, the geographical networks of these social relations and kinship patterns, rather than caste features, have found mention in these inscriptions. Even this limited source has enabled Ghosh to focus on the local and the individual in an interactional space provided primarily by the Buddhist ideological institutions empowering these individuals and groups to ascertain their identities in the context of a changing economic and ideological setting. Thus, men and women who travelled from their homes to make donations to Buddhist establishments across the Deccan succeeded in asserting their many identities—habitational, kin-based, class status—but not ones that defined them by their 'caste'. She concludes by contrasting this with the generally accepted ways of defining society in ancient India through prescriptive and normative texts to argue that however fragmentary, this source enables a glimpse of the social landscape of early historic times that is at variance with the one known through didactic and legal treatises.

Continuing with a focus on the Deccan, the next chapter picks up a source that can be read along with the label inscriptions highlighted by Ghosh. The local coins that Jashwanth Prasad has taken up for a detailed study also, showcase inscriptions, but they are only limited to legends displaying the names of kings on the coins issued by them. Unlike the inscriptions found on permanent structures, the local coins were sporadically distributed and scattered in terms of what has been found till date. The chapter 'Local Coins and Local Rulers: The Early Deccan' addresses the question of what is meant by 'local coins' that were issued by chieftains who ruled several localities of the early Deccan from the middle of the second century BCE to the third century CE. They provide critical details on local rulers not known to us from any other source of information. These were some of the first coins on the subcontinent to have the names and legends of local rulers inscribed on them. A point emphatically made in this chapter is that these rulers were clearly distinct from the well-known kings of the Sātavāhana dynasty, but some of them may have had a subordinate or matrimonial relationship with them. We reflect on these coins as unconventional sources that can be used to reinterpret the polity and early state of the Deccan. We first interrogate the nature of the local coins issued by such local chieftains as Gobhada, Samāgopa, Mahāsenāpati, Mahātalavara, Mahāraṭhi, Sadā, Kurā, etc., which have been extensively described to arrive at the significant conclusion that we should use them not just to write political history, but rather, place them in a transitional phase that enables us to look at significant changes during pre-Sātavāhana times. Right after the Mauryas lost control over the Deccan, i.e., during the pre-Sātavāhana phase, their continued existence as contemporaries and predecessors of the Sātavāhanas raises fundamental issues for relooking at the nature of polity in these parts. Hitherto, scholars who have worked on these local coins have isolated them from the larger polity, with pre-eminent emphasis given only to the Sātavāhanas. The enigmatic role played by these local chiefs alongside the Sātavāhanas allows us to integrate them into a comprehensive politico-economic set-up that cannot be ignored in the construction of this early period of Deccan's history.

After label inscriptions and coins, the third chapter in Part II by Aruna Pariti, titled 'Chāḷukyan *Praśastis*: Historical Consciousness and Identity', shifts our focus to inscriptions found either on copper plates or on temple walls during the early medieval period. *Praśasti* or the eulogy portions of early medieval inscriptions were an integral part, but have been largely ignored because of the exaggerated nature of their content. In the past, they were generally used to construct early medieval Indian political history. Conspicuous in these political narratives was a deliberate attempt to not use the mythical, epic, and *Puranic* portions embedded in the praśastis as they were supposedly inauthentic. Pariti's chapter counters this narrative by analysing all the praśastis of the major Chāḷukyan families that ruled over the Deccan from the sixth to the twelfth century CE to focus on how historical consciousness and issues of identity formation existed in them. This attempt then necessarily interrogates how the praśastis unveil different notions of time in its various components—the mythical, the legendary, and the historical genealogies. She rightly highlights that despite the exaggerated claims in the praśastis, accompanied as they were by high-sounding epithets, the comparisons drawn with the epic and Puranic heroes all formed part of an integrated discursive practice within the larger ideological framework of the society that produced them; they were critical to the way the ruling elite perceived its past. This source also contained within it a value that enabled the ruling elite to create and enhance local and regional identities and yet maintain pan-Indian linkages. Clearly, this was at variance with the modern way of writing about the past. But just as the modern nation-state turns to history to provide a legitimate past that can define its identity, it is argued that these families viewed their genealogical narratives as conscious attempts to enhance their respective status and provide them legitimacy. This chapter thus uses a much-ignored part of an inscription, namely the praśasti, which had however, always formed an integral part of this source. Ignoring and bifurcating the concerns of the ideological from the economic vis-à-vis the two portions of these inscriptions have, in fact, presented a fragmented picture of the total apparatus of power. Rather than reject the praśastis, in the ultimate analysis, it is presented as a critical source for the significant ways in which a pre-modern society looks at the historical consciousness pervading local sensibilities, while still being part of the larger subcontinental ethos.

The last chapter in Part II on producing the past aptly brings to our attention aspects of the survival of what was produced in the past, which is now available to us only through fragments. In this chapter titled 'Seeking History in Fragments', Parasher Sen elaborates how from the late 1990s, the history of early India has been written using different kinds of sources impacting broad-based studies on a variety of themes. Each of these sources had in them a value that also enabled a retrieval of information on multiple identities so that the trajectory of their status in society could be highlighted. It also helped to move away from a traditional approach to studying early India as being solely based on literature, a trend that had been popularised in earlier Indological studies. Thus, one now prolifically comes across emergent studies on gender history, history of environment, and everyday life and the history of marginal groups. In broadening the scope of these emergent studies, this chapter argues that a necessary focus on the history of localities and specific objects, often fragmentary pieces of information, must be taken cognisance of. Consequently, three illustrative case studies—an ivory statuette, an auspicious vase (*purnaghata*), and a sculptural panel (of Chenchu Lakshmi)—have been highlighted to suggest potential ways of doing so, and how this exercise can enable us to pose different questions about the meta-narrative of history that we are familiar with. The first of these examples is about archaeological objects and finding their location and meaning, the second about an inscription that is locatable, but speaks of something unique, and the third visually challenges our imagination. As footnotes, these have been known to us, but a central theme in Parasher Sen's argument is that the various seminal traditions of the Indian subcontinent can no longer be compartmentalised. First, their specificity has to be understood to bring out their particularity, and then they need to be looked at in terms of networks, each dynamically interacting with the other, to retrieve from the religious, the material, and the cognitive texts the textures of history about marginal social and regional groups that asserted difference while at the same time being linked to a larger whole. These networks and their sustenance, mutation, and transformation, it is ultimately argued, emerge from the site of the fragment and its meaning.

Well beyond the concerns of the early Enlightenment scholars, today the belief in a hardcore historical fact, existing objectively and independently of the historian's interpretation, is considered a fallacy, but is an idea that has been very difficult to eradicate. Carr (1986) has enabled the acceptance of the historian as being in a constant dialogue with the past. On a more serious theoretical level, Ankersmit has clarified that 'The modernist historian follows a line of reasoning from his sources and evidence to a historical reality hidden behind the sources.... In the postmodernist view, evidence does not point towards the past but to other interpretations of the past...' (Ankersmit 1989: 145–146). The two parts of this volume have addressed two types of sources, the first emanating from the written word or literature, and the second from extant remains that are broadly classified as the archaeological. To emphasise on the first, we submit that the domain of literature has an intimate relationship with our memories of the past. To substantiate this, one has drawn on ideas in some recent issues of the journal *Rethinking History*, which suggest that the 'historical and fictional can be mixed for certain literary purposes but ought never be confused' (White 2005: 153). In one such article, Hayden White, concurring with Richard Slotkin's work, quotes him to the effect that on the one hand, 'history-writing requires a fictive or imaginary representation of the past', and on the other, that 'the writing of historical fiction can be a valuable adjunct to the work of historians in their discipline' (ibid.: 154). This would indeed be the best way to recover the emotions, conversations, and feelings through historical texts that are in any case part of our collective heritage. The social identities that this would crystallise would depend on the nature of the text being alluded to. Some of these pre-modern identities would be at variance with our modern understanding of them.

With regard to the second type of sources emanating from the archaeological, there is a fervent recognition today that archaeology as a discipline has to address a host of different ways to contribute to the creation of individual, local community alongside national identities. With reference to the former, Lynn Meskell, writing of her training in Australian archaeology, notes that indigenous people had 'a clear voice in the archaeological endeavour' (Meskell 2000: 147). However, her experience in the context of the study of ancient Egypt has been that 'archaeologists…generally assume that their priorities for research should be placed in the foreground and that the considerations of the local people are secondary…' (ibid.: 147). This tendency is common in most countries where archaeology was initiated and developed in the colonial context. This has unconsciously distanced the researcher of local objects, inscriptions, and so on from the local situations they were found in. Ian Hodder reminds us that archaeologists have the sensitive task of interpreting the data found, and points out that some interpretations of the past are not as good as others and that not everything can be said with equal integrity. However, '…the contemporary social basis of our reconstructions of the past… must understand where our ideas come from and why we want to reconstruct the past in a particular way…' (Hodder 1986: 169). A special concern for us in the present endeavour has been to recognise that local memories are enshrined in the objects we study, and that they were in fact commemorative leavings of the past, enshrined in small artefacts or icons and even inscriptions in local spatial contexts, which did not neatly fit into the totalities of pan-regional or pan-Indian identities. In our opinion, they in fact constitute the primary layer of a reality. Their constitution is embedded in the subjective meanings that are reflected in the objects to which human and cultural sensitivities are attached. Having survived, often in fragments, it is pertinent for us to analyse the human imagination in them to identify the collective memory of the people at a local level. These memories cannot be detached from the particular cultural meanings inherent in them, and also from the fact that they would be histories which are different, of individuals, communities, and regions, and not of the 'nation-state' as a whole.

Scholars have indeed recognised that 'Pre-colonial forms of knowledge are too often relegated...to the happy condition of indeterminacy, diversity, holism—acting as foils for the drama of modernity. Their own conditions of production, internal structures, and agendas for power too often ignored'(Ali 1999: 9). In this volume, we have tried to address the fundamental question of treating footnotes as integral to the way the past can be retrieved within particular contexts and ideological settings. This has kept in mind the perspective and locatedness of the sources so that their use does not lead to a damage of the original context in which they had emerged in the first place. Significantly, this approach has enabled us to take small, fragmentary pieces of evidence as well as narrative accounts rooted in imagination as valid means of seeking a past that was much more inclusive than has been purported in narratives of history that have hitherto given validity to the records, texts, and monuments of only the prominent and dominant in society. Inspired by Sigfried Giedion, we hope to have shown that

> History writing is ever tied to the fragment. The known facts are often scattered, broadcast, like stars across the firmament. It should not be assumed that they form a coherent body in the historical night. Consciously then, we represent them as fragments, and do not hesitate, when necessary, to spring from one period to another... the decisive step has to be taken by the reader. In his (her) mind the fragments of meaning here displayed should become alive in new and manifold relations (Giedion 1948: 3).

Therefore, the critical point before us in this book has been to not allow the larger history of a society and a people or region to remain 'anonymous', but rather to explore how the fragment and imagination and their connectedness to a larger whole helps to bring before the reader not only the fullness of life, but also the everydayness of a period or an epoch in history.

Notes

1. The context here concerns an analogy with a dentist's drill and the pain it inflicts.
2. Thapar's *magnum opus*, *The Past before Us* (2013), elaborates a different notion of 'history' inherent in various types of texts that we liberally use as sources for modern history writing.
3. The *Sacred Books of the East* series in fifty volumes of ancient religious and legal texts from different Asian regions, translated by various scholars beginning in the nineteenth century (1879–1910) and edited by Max Müller, is a case in point. This task was then taken over by Indian Indologists and scholars of Sanskrit, as exhibited in the monumental five-volume *History of the Dharmaśāstra* by P.V. Kane (1930–1962).
4. This collection of essays edited by Kumkum Roy (2011) brings in different types of narratives and traditions to reflect on early India without seeing the necessity of writing its history in firm positivistic terms, and thus closing opportunities for further debates and discussions.

References

Abraham, Amrita. 1992. 'Textbook Controversy and the Politics of Cultural Separatism'. *Indian Express*, 5 November.

Ali, Daud. 1999. *Invoking the Past, Uses of History in South Asia*. New Delhi: Oxford University Press.

Ankersmit, F. R. 1989. 'Historiography and Post-Modernism'. *History and Theory* XXVIII(2): 137–153.

Carr, E. H. 1986. *What is History?* Harmondsworth: Penguin Books, 2e.

Chakrabarti, Dilip K. 1997. *Colonial Indology: Sociopolitics of the Ancient Indian Past*. New Delhi: Munshiram Manoharlal.

Chakrabarty, Dipesh. 1992. 'Postcoloniality and the Artifice of History: Who Speaks of "Indian" Pasts?' *Representations* 37(Winter): 1–26.

Dirks, Nicholas. 1990. 'History as a Sign of the Modern'. *Public Culture* 2(2): 25–32.

Giedion, S. 1970[1948]. *Mechanization takes Command: A Contribution to Anonymous History*. New York: Oxford University Press.

Grafton, Anthony. 1997. *The Footnote: A Curious History*. Cambridge, MA: Harvard University Press.

Hodder, Ian. 1986. *Reading the Past: Current Approaches to Interpretation in Archaeology*. Cambridge: Cambridge University Press.

Inden, Ronald. 1986. 'Orientalist Constructions of India'. *Modern Asian Studies* 20(3): 401–446.

Kane, P. V. 1930–1962. *History of the Dharmaśāstra (Ancient and Medieval Religious and Civil Law)*, 8 vols. Poona: Bhandarkar Oriental Research Institute.

Kumar, Ravinder. 1991. 'Exploring the Historical Conjuncture'. *Social Scientist* 19(9–10): 5–18.

Meskell, Lynn. 2000. 'The Practice and Politics of Archaeology in Egypt'. *Annals of the New York Academy of Sciences* 925(1): 146–169.

Müller, F. Max (ed.). 1879–1910. *Sacred Books of the East*, 50 vols. Oxford: Oxford University Press.

Roy, Kumkum (ed.). 2011. *Insights and Interventions: Essays in Honour of Uma Chakravarti*. New Delhi: Primus Books.

Sharma, R. S. 2005 [1965]. *Indian Feudalism*. New Delhi: Macmillan Publishers Pvt. Ltd, 3e.

———. 1987. *Urban Decay in India (c. 300–1000 AD)*. Delhi: Munshiram Manoharlal.

Thapar, Romila. 2013. *The Past before Us: Historical Traditions of Early North India*. New Delhi: Permanent Black.

White, Hayden. 2005. 'Introduction: Historical Fiction, Fictional History, and Historical Reality'. *Rethinking History* 9(2–3): 147–157.

Wilks, Mark, 1810. *Historical Sketches of the South of India, in an attempt to trace the History of Mysoor*, Vol. I. London: Longman.

PART I

Perceiving the Past

1

The Making of Classical Tamil Literature

Multiple Sources in its Construction

V. Rajesh

Introduction

The reproduction of classical Tamil literature during the nineteenth and early twentieth century occupies an important chapter in the history of Tamil literature of the modern period.[1] Facilitated partly by the expansion of and access to printing technology during the nineteenth century, the classical Tamil literary heritage underwent a transformation from the medium of palm-leaf manuscripts to printed books. Spearheaded by a few Tamil pundits with active patronage from Hindu sectarian monasteries and a nascent vernacular middle class, the publication of classical Tamil literature engendered a new literary and cultural consciousness in Tamil-speaking districts of the Madras Presidency. Understandably, the subject has received considerable scholarly attention among social and literary historians (Ramanujan 1999; Shulman 2016; Venkatachalapathy 2005; Zvelebil 1972). The predominant themes around which the historiography on the recovery and publication of classical Tamil literature is organised ranged from the Tamil renaissance leading to the emergence of Tamil literary and cultural sensibility, to the rise of the non-Brahman political movement in early twentieth-century Madras Presidency (Arooran 1980; Blackburn 2003; Irschick 1969; Ramaswamy 1997; Trautmann 2006). The literary and social historians of modern Tamil literature have often employed the concept of 'rediscovery' to refer to the process that involved the recovery of palm-leaf manuscripts of classical texts and their subsequent publication in print. Inherent in such an understanding is a view that these classical texts were long forgotten in the Tamil literary tradition, and that they were dramatically (re)discovered during the nineteenth century with the expansion of and access to print. While this is a dominant interpretation in the historiography, in recent years, attempts have been made to examine the continuities in Tamil literary tradition and, in particular, the question of the transmission of classical texts is receiving attention among scholars of Tamil literature and history (Buchholz 2018; Buchholz and Ciotti 2017; Rajesh 2014; Wilden 2014). Underlying these varied interpretations of Tamil literary history is the changing nature of the source that historians and literary scholars have been examining over the years. The hegemony wielded by Saivism in Tamil history had come to determine what constituted Tamil literature and identity for several centuries in pre-modern times, and its influence had a considerable role to play in the articulation of Tamil literary histories of the modern period.[2] Notwithstanding the recognition of the plural nature of Tamil literary space in the Tamil literary tradition by some scholars, histories of Tamil literature continued to revolve around individuals and institutions associated with Saivism in Tamil Nadu. The generic repetition of the term 'rediscovery' to refer to the reproduction and publication of classical Tamil literature during the nineteenth century has become endemic to Tamil literary scholarship. This understanding firmly anchors on privileging the autobiography of U. V. Swaminatha Iyer (1855–1942), the late nineteenth and early twentieth-century editor of classical Tamil texts, whose own perception of the Tamil literary tradition is reproduced in modern writings. Originally serialised in the popular Tamil magazine *Ananda Vikatan* from 1940 to 1942, the autobiography of Swaminatha Iyer is considered a valuable source of information by a generation of historians and Tamil scholars in the examination of the nature of the nineteenth-century history of Tamil literature. Coupled with the biography that Swaminatha Iyer authored of his teacher Mahavidwan Meenakshi Sundaram Pillai (1815–1876), these works have come to occupy an important place in literary histories.

The newly emerging studies provide an alternative framework of understanding the nineteenth-century reproduction of classical Tamil literature by marshalling and examining the palm-leaf manuscripts that modern editors of classics used to publish the first printed editions. This has involved examining the nature of palm-leaf manuscripts, their provenance, textual particularities, intertextuality, and so on. Such studies have allowed us to see the fascinating literary world of the *pulavars* (scholars), *kavirayars* (poets), *upadhyayars* (teachers), and institutions beyond the orbit of dominant Saivite monasteries in Tamil Nadu. While at one level this 'manuscript turn' in the recent historiography of nineteenth-century Tamil literature has questioned the dramatisation of the idea of the 'rediscovery' of classics and the role of print, it has also opened up a mosaic texture of social and cultural history that goes beyond the dominant individuals and institutions as objects of study (Francis 2017). An ethnographic study of the Tamil Jain community and their institutions has also contributed to our understanding of the literary textual culture other than what we have come across in the sources hitherto used by scholars of modern Tamil literature (Umamaheshwari 2017). There has been a spurt of studies in the last two decades on eighteenth-century Christian missionary activities in the Tamil-speaking regions of south India. A few of them have dealt with the linguistic and literary dimensions of this encounter that throw light on literary cultures. Such studies inform us of the methods adopted by European missionaries to learn the Tamil language, collect manuscripts, seek the help of local teachers, and build personal collections of texts. The missionary archive spread across institutions in Europe is a repository of personal letters, collection of Tamil palm-leaf manuscripts, diaries, and journals (Nardini 2017; Sweetman 2012). Studying the eighteenth-century conjuncture in the history of Tamil literature is necessary to comprehend the transmission of texts in the early modern period. Without attributing linearity or connection, there is a possibility to study cycles of reproduction leading to the print publication of classical literature during late nineteenth and early twentieth century. Identifying such conjunctures will illuminate the history of transmission of classics in the literary tradition. The early colonial encounter, especially in the realm of knowledge production, is yet another area of research that has seen a significant rise in the last few decades. The origins of Dravidian philology apart, early nineteenth-century Madras witnessed the coming together of colonial and indigenous scholars characterised by Trautmann as the 'Madras School of Orientalism'.[3] The product of such an interaction resulted in the mobilisation of texts and traditions of south India, whose implication for the history of manuscripts, print, and publication was significant. The early colonial archive comprised of the collections of College of Fort St. George and Colin Mackenzie, and these included a large collection of palm-leaf manuscripts from different regions of south India. The potential of this source in studying literary cultures of the early modern period is gaining attention among scholars of south India. Before we examine these sources in understanding the history of the transmission of classical texts in the literary tradition, a critical review of influential writings on the subject is required.

Historiography

In an essay that examined tradition and modernity in the making of Tamil literature, Ramanujan observed that, 'Indian tradition is not a single street or a one-way street but consists of many connected streets and neighbourhoods like that town itself', and that 'interlocking and coexistent though they are people of one neighbourhood may never have stepped into another' (Ramanujan 1999: 187). However, this recognition of the multiplicity of pasts did not prevent him from considering the autobiographical account of Swaminatha Iyer as the sole basis for commenting on the nineteenth-century reproduction of classical Tamil literature. Referring to the *Sangam* (also known as, *Cankam*) texts and the Tamil epics *Silappatikaram* and *Manimegalai*, he observed that the 'story of the rediscovery of these great classical texts in the nineteenth century is a dramatic one' (ibid.). This understanding of reproduction as 'rediscovery' in a 'dramatic' sense is largely based on the account of Swaminatha Iyer's autobiography. Noting that in Indian culture the past lives on, providing paradigms and ironies for the present, he claimed that,

> The classical Tamil tradition was not always known to the Tamils themselves, or actively present to them. In the eighteenth century, Hindu scholars, devout worshippers of Siva and Visnu, did not wish to read so-called non-religious poems and would not teach them to their pupils (ibid.: 186).

Citing Swaminatha Iyer's encounter with Salem Ramasami Mudaliyar, narrated in great detail in Iyer's autobiography, Ramanujan considered it a transformative moment not just in the life of Iyer, but for Tamil culture as well. Such essentialist readings betray the diversity of literary traditions that Ramanujan himself was referring to when pointing to Iyer's realisation during his encounter with the Tamil Jain community that the texts unknown to him were being read somewhere else. Similarly, after editing *Tirumurugarruppadai*, Iyer is said to have witnessed the recitation of the same text by the devotee of Murugan in a ritual procession. For Ramanujan, a scholar like Swaminatha Iyer was only discovering what was already apparent to others in Tamil culture. This recognition did not hold Ramanujan back from claiming that certain texts were lost or ignored in the Tamil literary tradition due to sectarian conflicts or bias. In other words, in this case the literary history was read from the perspective of an autobiography that privileged a dominant Saiva monastery.

In a more attentive and nuanced reading of literary culture in late nineteenth-century Tamil Nadu, Norman Cutler issued a warning that it 'is useful to remind ourselves that the literary culture we come to know via Caminataiyar's autobiography was the preserve of a limited segment of the Tamil population' (Here, Caminataiyar refers to Swaminatha Iyer) (Cutler 2003: 286). A shift in analysis from the history of literature to literary cultures in history enabled such a qualified reading of autobiography as representing a particular Tamil literary culture and not 'an omniscient master narrative' (ibid.: 271). Recognising the centrality of Swaminatha Iyer's efforts in recovering and publishing many classical Tamil literary texts, Cutler argued that the literary cultures of such texts lay largely outside of and predated the horizons of the literary world in which Iyer himself was raised. Alongside the biography of his teacher Meenakshi Sundaram Pillai, Swaminatha Iyer's autobiography had offered insights into the cultural and literary worlds inhabited by them. Cutler's insistence throughout the essay on the fact that the literary culture that Swaminatha Iyer participated in, in the Saiva monastery was limited, and that his early training there had no connection with the early Tamil literary culture in which many classical texts were rooted, is a timely warning against reductionist interpretations of nineteenth-century Tamil literature. Such exceptions apart, the dominant trend in historiography has been to emphasise the 'rediscovery' of Tamil classics stemming largely from a particular source.

In an article that addressed the Tamil literary canon formation, social historian of modern Tamil Nadu, Venkatachalapathy, has argued that the literary canon is not a given but the product of a specific history. Noting that there are few studies that have taken up the question of canon formation in South Asia and emphasising the need to trace the mechanics, constitution, and implications of canonisation, Venkatachalapathy's article has focused on the ways in which the Tamil literary canon came to be redefined in colonial India (Venkatachalapathy 2005). The religious and didactic literature is considered largely the pre-modern literary canon in Tamil with works like *Thirukkural*, *Naladiyar*, *Kambaramayanam*, *Prabhandams*, and *Puranams* occupying an important place in pedagogy and culture. These texts, according to him, were posited against the newly rediscovered Sangam literature and epics like *Silappatikaram*, *Manimegalai*, and *Sivakacintamani* during the late nineteenth and early twentieth century. The accompanying features of this new canon formation were the emergence of historic, linear time, and secularisation, which resulted in the displacement of the largely religious canon of pre-modern centuries. This understanding is based mostly on the self-perception of Swaminatha Iyer, especially from the much dramatised encounter with Salem Ramasami Mudaliyar narrated vividly in Iyer's autobiography. Although Venkatachalapathy has cited prevailing wider perceptions of what constituted the essentials of Tamil literature from such texts as Vedanayagam Pillai's *Pratapa Mudaliyar Charithiram*, *Tamil Navalar Charithai*, *Tamil Vidu Tutu*, and *Pulavar Puranam*, the difficulty in assigning a solely religious character to some of them is borne out by the presence of such non-religious texts as the eight anthologies and ten songs (*Ettuthogai, Pathuppatu*) in a collective sense, and the absence of the Vaisnava canon, the *Nalayira Divya Prabhandam*. Venkatachalapathy's concern over whether a non-sectarian Tamil canon existed in pre-modern times, and the nature of such a canon if it did exist, is a contentious hypothetical premise in Tamil literary historiography. Norman Cutler has the following to say on this question:

> How closely are religious sectarianism and literary culture intertwined? On the one hand, Cankam poetry is often described as secular; on the other, the canonical poems of the Vaisnava and Saiva saints and the theologically oriented commentaries on the Vaisnava poems were clearly produced in a sectarian context and have played a major role in the formation and maintenance of sectarian identity (Cutler 2003: 294).

The alleged divide between religion and secularity, sacred and historic, linear time played out in the historical process of literary canon formation. Furthermore, the centrality of print in engendering the change is highlighted by Venkatachalapathy by citing the perception of the editors of classics. In various writings, the latter expressed a sense of urgency to save the texts from palm leaves. Situated at the intersection of Orientalism and social contradictions in Tamil society, the newly rediscovered literary canon was anticipated and appropriated by the Non-Brahmin Movement in contesting the claims of superiority of Sanskrit and Brahmin domination. Moving away from such rigid distinctions as religion and secularity, recent studies have pointed out the transformation and reconfiguration of Saiva religion in Tamil Nadu during the modern period and its relationship with the Dravidian movement (Bergunder et al. 2010; Vaithees 2015). This is in contrast to the earlier strand of historiography, which attempted to point out the secular, rationalist, and anti-caste character of the Dravidian movement, in particular, the Self-Respect Movement launched by E. V. Ramasamy, thus underplaying in the process the continuities with the Neo-Saivite origins and subsequent interactions with different strands of Dravidian politics (Pandian 1994; Venkatachalapathy 1995). Even strictly within the histories of Tamil language and literature, the alleged divide between religion and secular is a complicated issue. Characterising such terms employed by Venkatachalapathy as somewhat misleading, Shulman contends that a large percentage of seventeenth and eighteenth-century Tamil literary texts in short genres, called *cirrilakkiyam* (minor literature in Tamil), were secular in nature, addressed to regional and local patrons and kings. Nor was Tamil literature secularised at the turn of the twentieth century according to him; instead, he suggests that an older and outmoded mythology was merely replaced with a newer one. Notwithstanding such criticism, Shulman speculates that there was a hiatus of a little more than a century between the time when Sangam texts were current and the moment when they had to be 'rediscovered' (Shulman 2016: 305).

Delving into the history of the transmission of Sangam texts in the Tamil literary tradition, Eva Wilden argues that the classical corpus was available for scholarly study and quotation up to the seventeenth century, with emphasis shifting towards texts like *Thirukkural* and other devotional literature. She further opines that the Sangam poems were increasingly marginalised and then virtually forgotten, although there existed separate strands of transmission of manuscripts. After carefully examining the layers of transmission of the classical Sangam texts, Wilden is of the opinion that the state of knowledge of texts presented in Swaminatha Iyer's autobiography is accurate. In general, the emphasis seems to be on the acceptance of the view that the classical Sangam poems were 'rediscovered' during the late nineteenth century, implying that the texts had been marginalised or forgotten earlier. For example, Wilden writes, 'Virtually fallen into oblivion by the end of the 19th century, they were "rediscovered" in the wake of the newly strengthening Tamil national consciousness and the gradual emancipation from colonial rule, and were edited, commented upon and re-included into the canon of Tamil literature'[4] (Wilden 2014: 7).

Critiquing the reasons attributed to the marginalisation of Sangam texts in the early modern period in literary historiography, Tieken has argued that the classical literary tradition is not totally lost and that 'to speak of a lost tradition is clearly an exaggeration'[5] (Tieken 2010: 235). For Tieken, the late nineteenth-century political climate in the Madras Presidency, especially the rise of the Non-Brahmin Movement, shaped the consciousness and attitudes towards Tamil culture and literature, where the reasons for the supposedly lost classical literary tradition were attributed to the Brahmins and Brāhmaṇical Hinduism. Other than vilifying the Brahmins, Tamil literary historiography also exaggerated the lost tradition of Sangam. Tieken has claimed that 'for most texts, manuscripts were still available and more importantly, the particular poetic tradition was visibly present in Tamil texts well into the eighteenth century', and that the 'tradition was never lost' (ibid.: 235). In critiquing the literary historiography that held Brahmin agency responsible for the marginalisation of the classical Tamil Sangam tradition in Tamil Nadu, Tieken not only claimed that the tradition was not lost, but also pointed out that 'the writing of literary histories of Tamil could do with a little less drama, passion and politics' (ibid.: 242). The 'manuscript turn' in literary history, exemplified in the work of Eva Wilden and the team of researchers at the Centre for the Study of Manuscript Cultures (CSMC) at the University of Hamburg, Germany, is a significant development in contemporary Tamil studies. Examining the palm-leaf manuscripts as objects in their own right, these studies have thrown light on the cultural history of texts. Such an approach offers potential for a new kind of intellectual and cultural history by posing questions related to the architecture and ecology of texts as well as throwing light on their content.[6]

Diversifying Sources

While the historiography on the reproduction of Sangam literature during the late nineteenth and early twentieth century focused on the lives of editors and the role of print, the sources for the study ranged from personal accounts of the editors of the classics to the early printed editions. Such studies, based on the reading of a particular set of sources, explained the social history of the reproduction of texts. While it theorised the reproduction as 'rediscovery', the arguments were largely based on the self-perception of the editors of the Tamil literary tradition themselves, and the state of the Tamil literary scholarship during the nineteenth century. The 'rediscovery' argument has also been dramatised, largely due to the perceived preservative aspect of print in light of the supposedly ever-decaying manuscript tradition. One of the issues ignored in this historiographical understanding has been the transmission of texts in the early modern period into the nineteenth century. What we term the 'manuscript turn' in the historiography of the reproduction of classics has raised new questions by examining the palm-leaf manuscript texts as objects of study. By focusing on the manuscript as the source of study, the recent trend in historiography has addressed questions pertaining to the cultural ecology of texts, and its transmission in the scribal scholarly tradition. Did this change in approach based on the examination of a new set of sources alter the historiographical position on the reproduction of Sangam texts during the late nineteenth century? While the manuscript copies have survived, the tradition was largely marginalised and, in some cases, forgotten. The argument is still in favour of 'rediscovery', although it has brought into light the much-needed histories of transmission by focusing on the study of manuscripts.

One of the ways to respond to the historiographical position on 'rediscovery' is to examine the diversity of sources, going beyond the early printed editions of classics, writings of the early editors, and palm-leaf manuscripts that constituted the source for the early printed editions. The early colonial archive is one such fertile ground to study this history. Drawing on Zvelebil's writings, Trautmann observed the following on the College of Fort St. George established in Madras in 1812: 'It was at the College, indeed, that the process of recovering and preparing the first printed editions of Tamil classics of ancient and medieval times was initiated.' Further, 'it is a great pity that we have only a sketchy and imperfect knowledge of this collection. The reconstruction of its content is a great desideratum for advancing our knowledge of the Tamil renaissance' (Trautmann 2006: 203–204). The College maintained a library, but we could not trace the nature of the book and manuscript collection due to the lack of a reliable catalogue. Rev. William Taylor's *A Catalogue Raisonné of Oriental Manuscripts in the Library of the (late) College Fort St. George*, published in 1857, documents only Mackenzie's collections deposited in the College library during September 1828. D. F. Carmichael, Secretary to the Board of Examiners' Office of Old College, Fort St. George, in a preface to Taylor's *Catalogue Raisonne* has made a reference to the pre-Mackenzie collection in the College library, which contained some 300 volumes. However, he states that the history of these 300 volumes 'cannot be particularly traced' (Taylor 1857: i–xxviii). Given that the College took the initiative to send officials to collect palm-leaf manuscripts of texts from various parts of south India, the collection assumes significance.

The legend of Sangam and the texts presented in the literary academy was articulated by Stokes, a civil servant in Madras, in his translation of the *Nitinerivilakkam* of Kumara Gurupara Tambiran in 1830. In the Preface to the translation, Stokes outlined the *Ilakkanam* (grammar) in Tamil language, constituting *Tholkappiyam*, *Nannul*, *Karikai*, *Akapporul*, and *Purapporul*. While commenting on *Ilakkiyam* (literature), he observed that 'the most celebrated are called *Sangacceyyul*, the college verses, because they were supposed to have received the sanction and approval of the celebrated College of Madura' (Stokes 1830: viii–ix). For Stokes, the principal among the literary works of the Sangam were the eighteen minor works or *Kilkanakku*. In the Preface, he thanked Tamil scholars Ambalavana Kavirayar and Muthukumara Swami

Kavirayar of Tirunelveli, Tandavaraya Vathiyar, and Muthusami Pillai of the College of Fort St. George for assistance provided in publishing his work. Similarly, in the early nineteenth century, F.W. Ellis, the Collector of Madras showed remarkable interest in Tamil language and literature. His translation of the *Thirukkural* into English stands out as an important classical Tamil literary work published during the early nineteenth century. In this work, Ellis demonstrated his mastery over a wide range of Tamil literary works, including classical works like *Purananuru*, *Patinenkilkanakku*, *Tholkappiyam*, *Silappatikaram*, and *Tirumurugarruppadai*, apart from works like *Sivakacintamani*, *Sutamani*, *Kambaramayanam*, *Thiruvasakam*, and numerous *Purāṇas*. The verses from these works, cited by Ellis in his illustrative notes to the *Thirukkural*, have never appeared in print.[7] Ellis was drawing on the verses from his study of these classical works in the palm-leaf manuscripts. It is a matter of speculation whether these palm-leaf manuscripts were part of the library collection of the College of Fort St. George. Ellis has not provided any information regarding the provenance of the manuscripts he consulted for his notes to the *Thirukkural*.

One of the underexplored sources in dealing with the late eighteenth and early nineteenth-century context is the catalogues of books collected by Colin Mackenzie from various monasteries in south India. One such collection, titled 'Local History', has been found in the Walter Elliot papers at the British library. It remains unclear how a small part of Mackenzie's collection landed among Walter Elliot's private papers. However, in this collection we discovered a few catalogues of Tamil literary works compiled by the collector himself from palm-leaf manuscripts. One such catalogue was titled 'List of Eminent Tamul authors and of Books which were formerly composed by celebrated Gyananool (or sages), Dravida authors or kavisars' (Walter Elliot Papers, British Library). It contains eleven sections in which a detailed list of Tamil literary and grammatical works has been presented, along with a short description of each work. The texts referred to in the catalogue range from the ancient Tamil grammar, the *Tholkappiyam*, the eighteen minor works or *Patinenkilkanakku*, the *Thirukkural*, to medieval grammatical and literary works.[8] It is true that *Ettuthogai* (Eight Anthologies) and *Pathuppattu* (Ten Songs), which have been understood as the earliest strata of Tamil literature, are absent in the list, but the mere fact that such catalogues were collected by surveyors during the early nineteenth century holds potential for further investigation into this archive.

In the Walter Elliot papers at the British Library, we found a few other catalogues and works collected by Mackenzie, like the 'Rough Copy of an account of Tamil Literature with list of various works', 'The Birth and History of Auvaiyar: The Legend of Poetess's Birth', which await investigation along with Mackenzie's papers at the Government Oriental Manuscript Library in Madras. Mackenzie's collection from the Jain monastery at Sittamur, titled 'A Catalogue of Jain Books in possession of the head of Jaina Mutt of Sittamur', has detailed the literary works that were preserved in the Jain institution. Collected by one J. N. Appavoo, from whom Mackenzie seems to have obtained a copy of the catalogue, it provides the list of Tamil literary and grammatical works. Literary works like *Sivakacintamani*, *Thirukkural*, *Naladiyar*, *Kalinkattupparani*, *Nilakesi*, *Sudamani*, *Udayana Kumara Kaviyam*, and *Yosatara Kaviyam* were included in the list. In another catalogue of Mackenzie's collection, titled 'List of ancient poets and their works of Dravida Country', found at Government Oriental Manuscript Library, works like *Nannul*, *Thirukkural*, *Sivakacintamani*, *Naladiyar*, and *Kalinkattupparani* were included.[9]

These catalogues referred to above do not provide any further information except a descriptive list of literary and grammatical works. The authors, chronology, and provenance of these catalogues and the manuscripts listed in them have been difficult to reconstruct. The fact that Mackenzie collected and compiled these catalogues indicates that the literary and grammatical works mentioned in them were in circulation and preservation by the late eighteenth and early nineteenth century. The catalogues invoke a variety of Tamil literary and grammatical works. It is true that we do not find any explicit reference to the earliest strata of Tamil literature, but the legend of the Sangam was not totally absent.

There are many such catalogues in the early colonial archive that await investigation by scholars.

The proliferation of indigenous printing during the first half of the nineteenth century in south India created conditions for the reproduction of ancient and medieval Tamil literature. Interestingly, many of the printing presses were owned by Tamil scholars. Among them, Visakaperumal and Saravanaperumal played a significant role in the publication of pre-modern literary and grammatical works in Tamil. Blackburn argues that together, the Perumal brothers wrote or edited some twenty-four books till 1847, including works like the medieval Tamil grammar *Nannul* and ancient literary works like *Thirukkural* (Blackburn 2003: 104–105). Except for the *Tirumurugarruppadai*, none of the Sangam works were published by them. Even here, this particular text was understood by them to be a part of the Saiva literary canon and not published as one of the *Pathuppattu* or Ten Songs. Even though they did not print any of the Sangam works, the Perumal brothers seemed to have possessed manuscript copies of literary works like the *Kalithogai* and the *Purananuru*, as testified by Damodaram Pillai and Swaminatha Iyer when they edited and published these works in the later part of the nineteenth century (Iyer 1894; Pillai 1887). In the middle of the nineteenth century, Arumuga Navalar, who spearheaded the revival of Saivism in Jaffna in response to the missionary activities there, published a number of Tamil literary and grammatical works of the pre-modern period. His printed editions of pre-modern literary works in Tamil have earned him a distinction among students of Tamil literature as *Navalar Pathippu* (Navalar Editions). It is interesting to note that for Navalar, Tamil literary consciousness was not merely confined to Saivism. This is evident from the list of books that he advertised for publishing in the *Thirukkovaiyar* edition in 1860. It only indicates that Navalar had at his disposal a large collection of palm-leaf manuscripts, including Sangam works like the *Kalithogai* and the *Purananuru* (Navalar 1860). Apart from these well-known Tamil scholars, a number of kavirayars (poets) in different parts of Tamil Nadu seemed to have preserved the palm-leaf manuscripts of Sangam texts throughout the nineteenth century. In the Preface to the first printed editions of Sangam literary works, editors like Swaminatha Iyer noted down the names of these poets who gave him the palm-leaf manuscripts (Iyer 1894). Consider the following information on the collection of palm-leaf manuscripts of one such poet from the autobiography of Swaminatha Iyer:

> There was a private library at the house of Iswaramurthy Pillai. It was their ancestral home. They opened the door of their private library for me. I was taken by surprise when I saw it. 'Did the Tamil Sangam in those days keep the manuscripts in this fashion?' I wondered. The manuscripts were arranged and maintained in order. Even the individual manuscripts were tied properly. There was no dust. No insect. Manuscripts never stuck with each other. The library appeared like a temple for Tamil goddess (Iyer 2008: 637).

As far as literary histories of nineteenth-century Tamil Nadu are concerned, we do not get any information or references to the life histories of these kavirayars, who seemed to have had a distinctive literary culture beyond the orbit of the formal sectarian monasteries.

Conclusion

To sum up, the historiography of the nineteenth-century reproduction of Sangam literature has largely tilted in favour of the 'rediscovery' argument, with a lack of convincing demonstration on the part of those who emphasised the continuities in the literary tradition. However, with the 'manuscript turn' in literary history, greater attention was paid to these manuscripts to explain the cultural history of texts. Diversifying the sources of study might enable historians to approach this transmission and reproduction of texts in a challenging manner. Similarly, moving away from binaries, historians need to pose alternate questions that might provoke newer ways of finding answers. While the first editorial ventures of Tamil scholars during the nineteenth and early twentieth century enabled the reproduction of classical Tamil literature, recounting such episodes in literary history must go beyond their perceptions. Such a history must examine the role of manuscripts in the Tamil literary tradition, the literary cultures of poets, teachers, and scholars not necessarily affiliated with the Hindu sectarian monasteries. In a penetrating set of lectures, Sri Lankan Tamil scholar Sivathamby had argued that we need to move beyond the pro-establishment versions of literary history, which required the bringing in of all available sources (Sivathamby 1986). The historiographical position on the 'rediscovery' of classical Tamil literature can be further questioned by highlighting the oral sources, especially folk narratives and popular stories from various parts of Tamil Nadu. Such narratives and stories need not be an oral telling of Sangam literature, but the recounting of legends, information around poets and events remembered and retold in popular traditions. It is our submission, then, that by examining multiple sources, our understanding of Tamil literary history will undergo radical transformation.

Notes

1. Central Institute of Classical Tamil (CICT), an autonomous institute under the Ministry of Education (MoE), Government of India has declared forty-one Tamil texts as representing classical literature in the Tamil language, and started to publish critical definitive editions of them. These include *Ettuthogai* (Eight Anthologies), *Pathuppattu* (Ten Songs), *Patinenkilkanakku* (Eighteen Minor Works), *Tholkappiyam*, *Iraiyanar Agapporul*, *Silappatikaram*, *Manimegalai*, and *Muttollayiram*.
2. One of the exhaustive and influential histories of Tamil literature written in the Tamil language during the twentieth century is by M. Arunachalam. Despite the magisterial effort, his multi-volume century-wise history of Tamil literature is noted for a Saivite bias. See P. Velsamy (2006).
3. Commenting on the years between 1812 and 1819,Trautmann observed,

   > I believe in that brief period the most interesting interactions between Indian and English scholars about languages and nations were taking place in Madras resulting in a distinctive school of Orientalism that stood in some degree of dissension with the pronouncements of the Calcutta Orientalists. I call this formation the Madras School of Orientalism (Trautmann 2006: xxi).

4. However, in another place, Wilden writes, 'Oblivion, however, cannot have been complete. In the grammatical tradition at least, fragments and quotations of individual poems had survived' (Wilden 2014: 30). Further, she writes elsewhere in the book,

   > The sheer number of witnesses that have survived up to our days and the even higher numbers that are testified to by descriptions in the early editions clearly show that tradition, if dormant, cannot have been all dead, although the protagonists of the revival movement give a vivid picture of the hazards involved (Wilden 2014: 26).

5. In particular, Tieken criticises the writings of A. K. Ramanujan and Kamil Zvelebil for importing the ideology and politics of Non-Brahmanism in their literary histories.
6. The important contribution of Eva Wilden's study on manuscript, print, and memory of Sangam relics, and the emerging works of Jonas Buchholz, Giovanni Ciotti, and the team of researchers firmly anchored in studying palm-leaf manuscript traditions of classical Tamil texts must be noted here (Buchholz 2018; Buchholz and Ciotti 2017; Wilden 2014).
7. Francis Whyte Ellis, *On Virtue* (This volume is a translation of the first twelve chapters of the section on *Aram* by Ellis, without the title page and the year of publication, and can be found in the Indian Institute Collection of the Bodleian Library, Oxford University with shelf number 18 D 25).
8. 'List of Eminent Tamul authors and of Books which were formerly composed by celebrated Gyananool (or sages), Dravida authors or kavisars', Walter Elliot Mss Eur F 48, Local History (Mackenzie Manuscripts) III: 159–169, British Library, London.
9. 'A particular list of the Jain Books which are in the possession of Jain Monastery collected by J. N. Appavoo', Mackenzie's collection, M 65, D. No. 3125, Government Oriental Manuscript Library, Madras; 'List of ancient poets and their works in Dravida Country', Mackenzie's collection, D 3127, Government Oriental Manuscript Library, Madras.

References

Arooran, Nambi K. 1980. *Tamil Renaissance and Dravidian Nationalism 1905–1944*. Madurai: Koodal.

Bergunder, Michael, Heiko Frese, and Ulrike Schroder (eds). 2010. *Ritual, Caste, and Religion in Colonial South India*. Halle: Franckesche Stiftungenzu Halle.

Blackburn, Stuart. 2003. *Print, Nationalism and Folklore in Colonial South India*. New Delhi: Permanent Black.

Buchholz, Jonas. 2018. 'Mayilai Annacami: A 19th Century Tamil Scribe and His Manuscript Collection', Unpublished Paper presented at 10th NE Tamil Workshop, EFEO Pondicherry.

Buchholz, Jonas and Giovanni Ciotti. 2017. 'What a Multiple-text Manuscript Can Tell Us about the Tamil Scholarly Tradition: The Case of UVSL 589'. *Manuscript Cultures* 10: 129–144.

Cutler, Norman. 2003. 'Three Moments in the Genealogy of Tamil Literary Culture'. In Sheldon Pollock (ed.), *Literary Cultures in History: Reconstructions from South Asia,* 271–322. Berkeley: University of California Press.

Francis, Emmanuel. 2017. 'The Other Way Round: From Print to Manuscript'. In Vincenzo Vergiani, Daniele Cuneo, and Camillo Alessio Formigatti (eds), *Indic Manuscript Cultures through the Ages: Material, Textual, and Historical Investigations,*319–351. Berlin: Walter de Gruyter GmbH & Co KG.

Irschick, Eugene F. 1969. *Politics and Social Conflict in South India: The Non-Brahmin Movement and Tamil Separatism.* Berkeley: University of California Press.

Iyer, U. V. Swaminatha. 1894. *Purananuru Mulamum Uraiyum.* Madras: V.N. Jubilee Press.

———. 2008. *En Charitram.* Madras: U. V. Swaminatha Iyer Library, seventh reprint.

Nardini, Giulia. 2017. 'Roberto Nobili's Vivaha Dharma: A Case of Cultural Translation'. In Antje Fluchter and RouvenWirbser (eds), *Translating Catechisms, Translating Cultures: The Expansion of Catholicism in the Early Modern World,* 223–251. Leiden: E. J. Brill.

Navalar, Arumuga. 1860. *Tirukkovayar Mulamum Naccinarkinniyar Uraiyum.* Madras: Muttamilvilakka Accukoodam.

Pandian, M.S.S. 1994. 'Notes on the Transformation of "Dravidian" Ideology: Tamilnadu, *c.* 1900–1940'. *Social Scientist* 22(5/6): 84–104.

Pillai, C.W. Damodaram. 1887. *Nallantuvanar Kalittokai.* Madras: Scottish Press.

Rajesh, V. 2014. *Manuscripts, Memory and History: Classical Tamil Literature in Colonial India.* New Delhi: Foundation Books.

Ramanujan, A. K. 1999. 'Classics Lost and Found'. In Vinay Dharwadker (ed.), *The Collected Essays of A. K. Ramanujan,* 184–196. New Delhi: Oxford University Press.

Ramaswamy, Sumathi. 1997. *Passions of the Tongue: Language Devotion in Tamil India, 1891–1970.* Berkeley: University of California Press.

Shulman, David. 2016. *Tamil: A Biography.* Cambridge: Harvard University Press.

Sivathamby, Karthigesu. 1986. *Literary History in Tamil: A Historiographical Analysis*. Tanjore: Tamil University.

Stokes, H. 1830. *The Nitinerivilakkam of Cumara Gurupara Tambiran: A Hundred and Two Stanzas on Moral Subjects with an English Translation, Vocabulary and Notes, Illustrative and Explanatory*. Madras: Vepery Mission Press.

Sweetman, Will. 2012. *Bibliotheca Malabarica: Bartholomaus Ziegenbalg's Tamil Library: An Annotated Edition*. Pondicherry: EFEO.

Taylor, Rev. William. 1857. *A Catalogue Raisonnee of Oriental Manuscripts in the Library of the (Late) College, Fort Saint George*, Vol. 1. Madras: Fort St. George Gazette Press.

Tieken, Herman. 2010. 'Blaming the Brahmins: Texts Lost and Found in Tamil Literary History'. *Studies in History* 26(2): 227–243.

Trautmann, Thomas R. 2006. *Languages and Nations: The Dravidian Proof in Colonial Madras*. New Delhi: Yoda Press.

Umamaheshwari, R. 2017. *Reading History with the Tamil Jainas: A Study on Identity, Memory and Marginalisation*. New Delhi: Springer.

Vaithees, V. Ravi. 2015. *Religion, Caste, and Nation in South India: Maraimalai Adigal, the Neo-Saivite Movement, and Tamil Nationalism, 1876–1950*. New Delhi: Oxford University Press.

Velsamy, P. 2006. 'Ilakkiya Kalattil Uyarcatik Kuttani: Mu Arunacalat in Tamil Ilakkiya Varalarru Nulkal—Oru Virivana Parvai'. *Kalachuvadu* 80(August).

Venkatachalapathy, A. R. 1995. 'Dravidian Movement and Saivites: 1927–1944'. *Economic and Political Weekly* 30(14), 8 April: 761–768.

———. 2005. '"Enna Prayocanam?" Constructing the Canon in Colonial Tamilnadu'. *Indian Economic and Social History Review* 42(4): 535–553.

Wilden, Eva Maria. 2014 *Manuscript, Print and Memory: Relics of the Cankam in Tamilnadu*. Berlin: Walter de Gruyter GmbH & Co KG.

Zvelebil, Kamil. 1972. *The Smile of Murugan: On Tamil Literature of South India*. Leiden: E. J. Brill.

2

Virtual Hegemonies and Literary Imaginings

Reading the *Jātakas* 'Against the Grain'

Sagnik Saha

> *... the nature of this sadness becomes clearer if we ask: with whom does historicism actually sympathize? The answer is inevitable: with the Victor...Hence, empathizing with the victor invariably benefits the current rulers...There is no document of culture which is not at the same time a document of barbarism, so barbarism taints the manner in which it was transmitted from one hand to another. Historical materialist therefore dissociates himself from this process of transmission as far as possible. He regards it as his task* ***to brush history against the grain***
> (Benjamin et al. 2007: 256–257; emphasis mine)

Against the Grain

In his zealous crusade against fascism, Walter Benjamin recognised its germination in the prevailing historical accounts as the manifestation of an all-pervasive polemological field, enshrined by the constant victories of the dominant established power. An imagined past, which has been conceived as a hegemonic space of ubiquitous and systematic injustice, was judiciously organised both by the victors and their history as an inescapable everyday reality. Yet, notwithstanding this ostensible impossibility, his agenda has been to intervene in this dominant discourse 'against the grain' in pursuit of the 'tradition of the oppressed' (Benjamin et al. 2007: 257). In a 'fascinating presence of absence' in the prevalent historiographical discourse, this tradition was engraved by scattered traces of 'the marks of active hands and laboring bodies' (de Certeau 1984: 21). Embracing a similar teleological trope, the dominant imaginings of the early Indian past have envisaged either an apocalyptic event such as conquest, or the immutable 'substantialized agents'[1] such as caste, religions, and idyllic villages serving as an impetus to the encoded civilisational destiny (Inden 2000a: 17–33; 2000b: 25). Consequently, the acts of the people were perceived as a mere resonance of the absolute civilisational essences[2] that augmented the dominant impression of history. Bolstering this historiographical tradition, the early Indian historiography has manifested an 'archival impulse', that is, a disposition toward the predominant strategy of inquiry, which primarily extracts principal legal, political, and socio-economic apparatuses/institutions of power out of the heterogeneous ensemble of voices and procedures available in the existing textual traditions. The socio-economic sphere of the early Indian past has hitherto been recognised as a standard space organised by the authority, where the voices and acts of the dominated section have been silenced, and remained dormant as a mere instrument to the dominant force of the major 'substantial agents'.

Yet, in the domain of production, control, and redistribution of resources, beneath a superficial acquiescence to the dominant regulatory norms, endures a relentless adaptation and contestation of authority in a prosaic and quotidian fashion that can be designated as 'everyday politics' (Kerkvliet 2009: 227). Consequently, routine existence appears to be an 'entanglement of power and resistance',[3] where the domain of power is incessantly ruptured and vampirised by the unrelenting, infinitesimal subversive 'tactics'[4] of the subordinates to assert their claims. Moreover, corresponding to and yet distinct from this authoritarian space, a phantasmagoric utopia of dissent has been materialised by the anonymous 'poets of their own acts' to encounter this immutable relation of force ethically, and proclaim the moral unacceptability of the prevailing condition that has been naturalised by its apparent factuality (de Certeau 1984: 16). Beyond this dominant trope of an inexorable reality, a pursuit of the 'tradition of the oppressed' in the early Indian context therefore requires an interrogation of the ordinary practices in opposition to the normative. An endeavour in retrieving the fragmentary traces of recalcitrant 'tactics' from obscurity and to probe the inherent operational logic of these manoeuvres have eventually led to an examination of narratives and tales, infused with the transformative capacity of human acts that quintessentially give rise to a utopian zone of fantastic retributions.[5]

In the early Indian historiographical tradition, the transgressive landscapes in the tales are rarely perceptible beyond the domain of 'scriptural economy', which has mediated and altered them through a protracted archival process, rendering any pursuit of unadulterated 'voices-off'[6] as untenable.[7] The *Jātaka* tales, which form the fulcrum of this chapter and are cursorily regarded as stories of the innumerable former lives of the Buddha, belong to the *Jātakattavannana*, a commentary compilation of *Jātakapali*, a primary canonical set of verses and their auxiliary set of 550 tales.[8] Amidst a plethora of morphological narrative divisions (*Paccuppannavatthu*, *Atitavatthu*, and *Sambodhanam*) in the unified literary structure of this commentary, the 'stories of the past' will be scrutinised to locate the quotidian subterfuges of the 'weak'.[9]

The innate fluidity of these fantastic 'stories of the past' divulges their preceding autonomy in genesis as well as in their transmission, both prior to and parallel with the process of their crystallisation as a literary genre.[10] In a complex multi-phasic, 'interlacing' process of appropriation and transmission, at one level, these tales function as a quintessential supplement to a number of moral verses, without an inherently Buddhist disposition, which were consolidated as *Jātakapali*, in the tenth section of the *Khuddaka Nikaya*.[11] The presence of the scenes from these tales on the sculptures of the *stūpas* also substantiates the crystallisation of these narratives. However, an absence of any canonical composition of these tales till the fifth century CE reveals a simultaneous existence of their enduring orality and autonomous fluidity, at another level (Appleton 2012: 41–64). The agents of this appropriation and mediation, the Buddhist *bhikkhus*, with their access to the domain of ordinary subaltern expressions and cultural forms, understood that the vitality of a tale was contingent primarily on its storytelling, an 'intersubjective' process of dialogic transmission that sustains its relevance. Therefore, in anchoring and altering the meanings of these tales to serve as a vehicle for Buddhist principles, a number of literary apparatuses were employed in the *Jātakattavannana* to manufacture a genre out of the unruly narratives, situating them within a Buddhist framework (Chakravarti 2007: 238).[12] However, despite the functioning of this archival mechanism, the human and animal tales not only communicate, through penetrating visualisations, the experiential conflict and domination in succinct and economical prose, but their pursuit of an apparatus to transform this environment of domination in their process of resolution also leads to the developing of a sense of solidarity among the common subjects, humans and non-humans/animals alike (Roy 1996: 25; Zipes 2012: 2–8). Hence, in the shadow of an apparent epistemological stalemate, the insinuation of orality into the network, as 'one of the threads…in the tapestry of the scriptural economy', appears to be an escape to retrieve the hidden transcript beyond the 'official version' (de Certeau 1984: 131).

However, the fictionality or the counter-factuality of these tales has, along with the complex temporal architectonics of the *Jātakattavannana*, been regarded as an expression of its failure to represent reality. Consequently, with a few exceptions, in most standard philological/historical explanations, these stories have been employed fragmentarily to reinforce the arguments of the dominant historiographical inquiry, or have been relegated to the obscurity of footnotes beyond the surface of the dominant historiographical operation (Chakravarti 2007: 211). This, however, demonstrates their capacity to imbue subjects with an agency and ways to reconstitute and subvert the events and relations, and determine their meanings symbolically, where a moral truth prevails in an otherwise predominantly disempowering environment (Jackson 2013: 34–35). It is the construction of a 'hidden transcript',[13] composed in a language of hope and belief 'beyond the official story' that reinvigorates the counter-factuality of these fantastic tales (de Certeau 1984: 17; Jackson 2013: 36–43).

A few noteworthy studies of these tales, which have interrogated the vividly illustrated oppressive power relations and their subversion, remain mired in essential tropes such as caste, gender, and class in the broader framework of Buddhist–Brāhmaṇical relations.[14] Yet, amidst this remarkable scholarship, this chapter takes as its point of departure, an exploration of the operative schematics of these varied subterfuges and performances in different encounters, accessible in the 'counter-archives'[15] of these tales. Therefore, this indulgence in the *Jātaka* tales can be perceived as a process of excavating the site of 'readable space' of historiography, in an attempt to elevate the heterogeneous ensemble of subversive procedures and residual voices buried in the 'subsoil' under the 'blasted tree of dominant scholarly polemic' (Grafton 1997: 13).

Strike the Iron While....

Everyday politics has several modes of manifestation, whether it is of support and compliance, of modifications and evasions, or of course that of resistance (Kerkvliet 2009: 233). However, the public performance of veneration on the part of subordinates may occur out of fear, prudence, or a desire to attain advantages at the expense of this performance (Scott 1990: 2). The prospect of acquiring the necessary goods and services by appeasing the dominant authority, or remitting the oppressive taxation and other similar favours only encouraged the peasants living a marginal life of subsistence to defer to the ruling elites (ibid.: 33). Therefore, an investigation of this performance of deference must largely follow the external motives behind these acts (ibid.: 24). In the tale of the *Kāma Jātaka* (no. 467),[16] the elder prince who had retired in a frontier village was treated with the courtesy appropriate to a monarch by the villagers. However, as revenue officials arrived in this village to assess the revenue, the rural populace cajoled him to seek a tax remission by exercising his royal power. Recognising the political potential of the prince, the villagers manipulated him to realise their political goal of revenue remission in exchange for their compliance and devotion. The villagers' eagerness to pay him the tax also inspired him to usurp the throne, which not only underlines the political potency of these acts of veneration, but also manifests their profound perception of the political scenario and the vigour with which the villagers used such political tactics. A princely contender to the throne, who was expected to restore order and lower taxes, had been championed by the disgruntled villagers, who as potent political agents, influenced the decisions taken in the royal court from the lowest rung of the hierarchy. Again, in the *Mahāassāroha Jātaka* (no. 302), the villagers were astute enough to assign the task of negotiation with the king for the diminution of heavy taxes to one who was not only connected to a member of the elite group, but was also an apt representative on account of his expertise in performing deference at the royal court. Here, his previous obedience and loyalty endowed him with an added advantage in persuading the king to consider their demands. Hence, it will be proper to suggest that, while negotiating with authority, as F. G. Bailey has argued, the peasants employ the connections of personal relationships to diminish the unpleasantness of an official relationship (Bailey 1987: 286).

These tales manifest the state authority's deliberate disregard of even the most minimal requirement of subsistence of the peasants through their expropriation of arbitrary taxes (Adas 1980: 532). An elaborate inventory of land revenues in the *Arthaśāstra*, of which the majority were of coercive disposition, reinvigorated the claim that the state authority had been coercive in their taxation. The centralising bureaucratic mechanisms had concomitantly given rise to a centrifugal force, which transformed the executives into active political agents appropriating the sovereignty of the suzerain (Claessen and Skalnik 1978: 19, 602).[17] This signified little diminution in the onerous taxation, extracted coercively from the peasants, as the revenue officers were known for their persistent exploitation (Basham 1993: 110; Mehta 1985: 146). Their arrogant attitudes signalled their intention to accumulate the maximum resources with no concern for abstract ethical principles, as they also anticipated a covert, yet determined resistance from the peasants (Adas 1980: 532). With respect to the elite exploitation inflicted on peasants, the opportunities for collaboration between peasants and officials could occasionally furnish the peasants, through personalised relations, with a considerable cushion against these incessant arbitrary exactions, as these tales narrated above had demonstrated (Adas 1980: 537; Ghoshal 1930: 7).

These tales are undeniably fine examples of the manipulative nature of the rituals of so-called 'conformity'. James Scott has rightly postulated that the ritualised disposition of these etiquettes of subordination is proportionate to the level of the arbitrariness of power, and the gap between the privileged and the subordinate. In a highly stratified social setting, such as that of early India, the subordinates were customarily socialised into the art of compliance to avoid any elite retaliation. Nevertheless, by concealing one's feelings and restraining reflexive responses, the act of compliance and humility through proper gestures and speech has always been a demanding task (Scott 1990: 37). Some of the stories discussed below bring out this complexity.

The tale of the *Somadatta Jātaka* (no. 211) illustrates the complexity of mastering the art of persuasion, as a simple poor peasant Brahmin failed to present his demands to the king, despite a diligent, year-long practice of the public performance of humility, obedience, and reverence. The relationship between the elite and the subalterns in public spaces (therefore, 'public transcript'), which consists of eulogising speeches and humble gestures from the latter, mirrors the self-gratifying image of the dominant group (Scott 1990: 18). On the one hand, this tale reflects the prevalent court culture etiquettes and the lofty dialect used for court business, which was quite distinct from the coarse, prosaic language of the common peasantry (Guha 1986: 43-44; Scott 1990: 31), which made acclimatisation to the culture of the court quite challenging for a poor peasant. On the other hand, devious manipulation of the lofty court culture and the ideological baggage accompanying this public performance of the ruler also furnished the peasants with ample opportunities to affirm their right to subsistence and procure the wealth they required. In spite of the vain attempt to present his demands, the incredible performance of humility by the poor peasant, together with the firm assertion of devotion to the monarch by his son, the *Bodhisatta*, who was well-equipped with the tactical art of obedience, finally resulted in the attainment of greater wealth than had been demanded. It can be assumed that members of peasant society who had acquired a place in the elite circle and yet ascribed to peasant values were expected to take on the responsibilities and obligation of a kinsman. The actions stigmatised as nepotism and corruption, as Bailey understands them, are quintessentially a response to obligations in the traditional world (Bailey 1987: 286). A similar performance of allegiance and devotion to the king in the tale of *Nana Cchanda Jātaka* (no. 289) eventually satisfied the desire for assets of the Brahmin and his family. The ubiquitous presence of the gift in these processes of negotiation and persuasion, albeit as a symbolic gesture or token, referred to the appropriate etiquette of these encounters. Despite the apparent voluntary nature of these donations, the authority was obligated to reciprocate generously in these cases.

The public performance and observance of acts of acquiescence and allegiance by subordinate groups like the peasants undoubtedly perpetuated the political system by buttressing the hierarchical structure, and the simultaneous subjection and humiliation inflicted upon them. Yet, these observances of acquiescence bestowed upon the peasants the necessary political and cultural raw materials to ambush the dominant group in their own domain of highly choreographed public performance that legitimised their claim to power, and by the shrewd manipulation of their self-gratification, the subalterns obtained the resources vital to their subsistence, and more. In the *Mahāassaroha Jātaka* (no. 302), the king, who had a reputation for generosity, bequeathed half his kingdom to his villager friend to return the favour of sincere loyalty, and the prince and courtiers grudgingly consented to this impractical administrative decision and grave loss of resource base, as any alteration of the royal decision would breach the royal code and lead to defamation and loss of legitimacy. The peasants, who believed that famines were a consequence of the malevolence of the monarch, again a plausible byproduct of percolation of elite perceptions of just rule into the peasant psyche, in the story of

Kuru Dhamma Jātaka (no. 276), forced the Kalinga monarch to perform the necessary rituals and penances to augment rainfall, along with necessary relief activities. The *Arthaśāstra* (4.3.17–20)[18] had also illustrated pragmatic understandings of famine and its momentous consequences since it recommended famine relief to the distressed while also creating provisions to exploit the labour force in return for food.[19] Hence, the enduring idea that submissive early Indian subjects had voluntarily conformed to the oppressive hierarchical social structure and endorsed the inherent injustice must be considered a consequence of the misinterpretation of the subjects' behaviour (Scott 1990: 33). Like everyday resistance, which forms the major expression of peasant political consciousness, these negotiations and public performances of subordination, permeated with tactical manoeuvres, were intrinsically related to the mechanisms of production, redistribution, and utilisation of resources, which makes them irrefutably political in nature.

Verbal and corporeal abuse and violence, along with denigration, insult, and assaults upon the lower strata, comprising mainly the poor peasantry, labourers, and slaves, were systematically generated by the hierarchical social structure based on the dominant discourse of power. While these forms of violent oppression denied the subordinates what Scott has termed the 'ordinary luxury of negative reciprocity: trading a slap for a slap, an insult for an insult' (Scott 1990: 23), we submit that these heinous acts against human dignity never went unreciprocated. In the *Nandi Visala Jātaka* (no. 28), a story narrates that a Bull[20] declined to cooperate with his Brahmin master, who had inflicted ignominy upon it as a dominant performance in the regular public transcript to accomplish his objective. This norm of publicly condemning and compromising the slave's dignity was challenged by the Bull through an observance of non-cooperation, which subsequently led to great misfortune for the master. When encountered, the Bull asked for a justification of this vilification inflicted upon him as he had performed, on his part, the ritual of subordination and observed all the etiquettes of the slave diligently thus far.

Interestingly, such an explicit complaint from a slave animal about its maligned dignity, an expression which is usually resorted to only outside the gaze of authority among fellow slaves or family, had been treated with sincere commiseration by the master. The Brahmin reciprocated this challenge by addressing him publicly as his associate, thus restoring the dignity of the Bull. Hence, this story betrays the potency of an act of non-cooperation in the transfiguration of the dominant discourse by situating the slave on the same hierarchy, and consequently rupturing the pattern of a master-slave power equation. The *Sarambha Jātaka* (no. 88) portrays an analogous narrative of a similar power equation between an Ox and its Brahmin master, which was contested in an identical fashion. Practically, however, similar articulations of these challenges directly to an oppressor were not easy for the subordinates, as there always loomed a constant threat of strong retaliation from the former.

As an alternative to forthright verbal complaint, non-cooperation empowered the disgruntled subalterns to convey their discontent to the authority without provoking any open act of defiance that would otherwise trigger repressive repercussions from the elite. The *Kanha Jātaka* (no. 29) demonstrates the delaying tactics or foot-dragging of a labourer who obstructed the way of his patron, a rich merchant, as the latter had denied him the complete payment for his labour, as previously agreed upon. Similar instances of deceit on the part of the patrons vis-à-vis hired labour can be seen in the agricultural sector as well. In obstructing the way of the cart as a symbolic mode of remonstration, he had communicated and demonstrated his dissent and grievances without infringing upon the public custom of deference. This manner of resistance, however, had rarely led to any grand rupture in existing power relations, but only satisfied specific demands (Adas 1986: 69). Yet there are multifarious instances of similar demonstration by groups and individuals in the early South Asian context, which subsequently led to the patron submitting to the demands of the aggrieved clients (Haynes and Prakash 1991: 5).

Eye for an Eye

In contradiction to the prevalent notion about their passivity, the early Indian peasant made a claim to the virtue of prudent political perception, which entails a critical examination of the 'offstage'[21] behaviours of these subalterns, conducted beyond the gaze of the authority. This sequestered zone of existence had empowered them with an uninhibited expression of 'reciprocal aggression' and anger, concealed so far by amiable conformity (Scott 1990: 38). The elite vocabulary of exploitation, often cloaked under exaggerated euphemisms, seldom expressed peasant anguish and strenuous experiences appropriately (Scott 1985: 197). This acute disparity in dialect, sort of a diglossia, made the subaltern expressions, both verbal and non-verbal, opaque to the dominant group (Guha 1986: 43). Deployment of elementary terminologies by the subaltern, such as 'weighing down', 'squeezing like sugarcanes in a mill', 'pressing', 'slaughtering of the poor', etc., and their irrefutable disposition to physical distress betrayed the strenuous nature of the cultivation and concomitant labour, and the resultant physical anguish and pain. This orientation towards physical metaphors, permeated with their everyday experiences can be inferred from their choice of phrases, while formulating their exposition of the oppression and injustice inflicted upon them (Mandal 2007: 41).

In the *Mahāpingala Jātaka* (no. 240), set in an urban milieu, ignominious metaphors describe tyrannical oppression, such as 'speck of dust that falls in the eye' (*akkhimhipatitarajam*), 'gravel in the broth' (*bhattapindesakkharā*), 'like a thorn sticking in the heel' (*panhimvijjhitvapaviṭṭhakantako*), which are among the mundane, yet recurring problems of regular peasant life that impede, however briefly, the daily course of routine labour. The most intriguing deployment of these prosaic metaphors was in encapsulating the most exasperating subaltern experience under a depraved tyrant who had gravely degenerated living conditions, jeopardising the steady course of production, albeit the ephemeral nature of this distressing experience. The semantic ranges of these metaphors denoting annoyance and impediment, which essentially connote an irksome, yet inherently transient experience, were enlarged to accommodate their similar political experiences under a malevolent ruler (Guha 1986: 238). Apparently, an astute application of similar metaphors in a power-laden public, or political situations would hardly alarm the authority, owing to their inability to grasp the latent acrimonious message within. The demise of a tyrant, which presented as the realisation of a fantasy, a transitory absence of authoritarian oppression, was celebrated with overtly joyous acts and laughter, which again betrays the tactical veneer of acquiescence in the public sphere.

The *Gandatindu Jātaka* (no. 520) demonstrates a host of disgruntled villagers uttering curses on the king Paňcāla for his repressive unrighteous rule. This episode was preceded by a compelling and graphic illustration of the atrocious rule of an evil monarch and his degenerate and corrupt bureaucratic apparatus. The reasons behind the severe indignation and repugnance can be easily understood from the striking imagery of deserted villages and the mass exodus of the peasantry into the bandit-infested forest, along with the frequent visits of vile state officials. The act of invoking the demise of the king symbolised a convoluted yet unequivocal vision of vengeance, since all the variant details surrounding the king's termination mirrored the anguishes of the peasants, whether of a corporeal nature or indicative of the loss of kin and beloved. Curses like 'struck by an arrow in the fray', 'may the king die', 'fall to earth by spear thrust of his foe', 'by the stroke of sword Paňcāla's lord shall fall' were called upon to inflict physical anguish on the king, whereas curses like 'pine away and childless weep in vain', and 'killed in fight and be eaten sons and all' inflicted on him bereavement or the threat of complete obliteration. Besides, the innate violence of these curses, the invocation of the saga of oppression infused in them, all imbued them with the symbolism of justified retribution (Scott 1990: 43). Despite the artistry, ingenuity, and spontaneity involved in summoning the curse, which had inverted the power domination, the content of all these curses was rehearsed rather than innovative. Situated in almost similar or familiar strata in the hierarchical structure and thus having experienced familiar systematic exploitation and repression, the subaltern, through social interaction and exchanges, had collectively manufactured a discourse that incorporated all such similar experiences of extortion and atrocities, which provided the oppressed and disgruntled villagers with a resolved code of distress and retribution (Scott 1990: 8–9).

An inquiry into the 'offstage' culture of peasant society is imperative to assess the potential of this aligned discourse of oppression that emerged out of the collective experiences of systematic subjugation, expressed as rumours.

> *arakkhitājānapadāadhammabalinā hatā. Rattimhi corā khādanti, diva khādanti tuṇdiyā, raṭṭhasmiṁkuḍḍarājassabahuadhammikojano* (Fausbøll 2008: 102).
>
> .... defenceless folk are oft by their oppressors slain/by night to thieves a prey are we, to publicans by day/lewd folks abound within the realm, when evil kings bear sway (Cowell 1973: 94).

This message, as the common exposition of oppression, had been transmitted beyond the sequestered zone of the village, and contaminated even the villages on the way to the citadel, to the extent that even a distressed frog is said to have endorsed it. On the question of subjective renditions, one should consider that the collective nature of its initiation had endowed the rumour with anonymity, and consequently with an aperture (Guha 1986: 257–261). Owing to the presence of this aperture, this intrinsic structural freedom, along with a spontaneous and uninhibited process of transmission, made the simultaneous accretion and erosion of the rumour more than a random phenomenon within its standard gestalt of ideology. These rumours had incorporated diverse aspirations and the world views of varied transmitters, as well as eliminated the redundant portions accordingly to widen its sphere of dissemination and the range of its audience (Guha 1986: 262; Scott 1990: 145).

Most interestingly, however, an examination of the plot where a king was witnessing incognito the transmission of a rumour and a curse against himself is both poetic and illuminating (*Gandatindu*

Jātaka no. 520). On the one hand, at a methodological level, for both a ruler and a scholar, this plot referred to the acute necessity of considering the offstage behaviour of the peasants to critically grasp the complexity of the political milieu. On the other hand, this plot has engineered a poetic justice where a king is stripped of his authority to exercise swift retaliation against this subversion and defiance due to his disguise as a common Brahmin. Instead, albeit unknowingly, he was exploited from both ends, as a receiver and eventually as a transmitter of the curse against his own self. It is worth considering that the constant alteration of the king's identity and anonymous authorship of the curse would have troubled the authority enough to locate the original perpetrator, a legible inciter, of whom an example of prompt justice could be made. This episode might be observed as a process of symbolic penance, where a king was deprived of his royal authority and humiliated by public cursing. Thus, subalternity was imposed on him momentarily, analogous to the denigration of an evil king who was compelled to attain the status of untouchables.

A more resolute example of the power of rumour can be found in the tale of the *Padakusalamāṇava Jātaka* (no. 432), where the Bodhisatta, in his attempt to admonish an iniquitous king, persistently applied the central expression of the rumour, as it appears, 'my refuge proved my bane', which underlined the injustice and consequent angst in diverse settings and situations. After a relentless but wasted admonition, by repeating the same core message, the protagonist Bodhisatta urged the subjects from the city and villages, mainly peasants, to execute that depraved ruler who denied justice to his subjects. This message, devoid of any discernible authorship yet imbued with the potent ingredients of insurgency, caused a mass uprising and the violent execution of the ruler. All the distresses mentioned in these tales, which led the subjects to reiterate these messages, would, if evaluated with standard rationale, reflect their isolated and somewhat private nature, but the spontaneous association with the code of vendetta reflected not only the cognitive orientation of the peasants to the 'images of limited good',[22] but also the amplification of an insurgent psyche within this given society. The wide circulation of these last two expressions that went beyond a single settlement, along with their intriguing adaptability to divergent situations, a capacity to encompass multiple social tensions and to generate insurgency, certainly lead one to conclude their social existence as a core expression of rumours. Evidently, these metaphors were epistemologically indebted to the rival dominant discourse, yet were implemented to engineer a just rule, any violation of which would generate vehement criticism and resistance. These *gāthas*, as rightly observed, were imbued with the potential to develop into a slogan that could spread beyond the restraints of the narrative (Roy 1996: 25).

Apart from rumour, a principal transmitter of the insurgent consciousness, the prevalence of gossip as a medium of articulation of popular indignation, can be regarded as a *modus operandi* for assailing the reputation of an identifiable person. Character assassination in a milieu of 'politics of reputation' was administered as a routine social weapon by subject peasants to sanction any transgression of standard ethics and public conduct (Scott 1985: 184–197; 1990: 142). The formulation of a standard corpus of ethics and conduct, permeated with shared popular perception, was imperative for the creation of an exclusive group with common shared values and perception, consequential to the custom of gossip (Wickham 1998: 18). Without a parameter to evaluate the degree of transgression, the elements of social sanction would have been evaporated from the act of gossip. Restoration of the desecrated code of conduct in peasant society not only highlighted the intersection of normative high culture and the subaltern perception, but also the divergences between them. This protocol had elaborated on the virtues that had only nominal status in the dominant discourse, and possessed the potential to accentuate the shared values of peasant society that could be manipulated in favour of subaltern aspirations (Roy 1996: 29–30). Reciprocation, the embryonic principle of this subaltern code of conduct, in issues like patronage, support, consideration of demands, etc., was expected from the more affluent strata of the rural society and administrative body, through acts of charity, employment, tenancy, and generosity. Any non-observance or apathy on the part of the latter would result in the public maligning of their reputation. Governed tacitly through reprimands, retribution, or imposed isolation, offenders were often informed about their victimhood by gestures and insinuation, yet if challenged, the perpetrators could disavow any connection (Scott 1990: 142–143). Gossip, thus, also had the potential to engender a subversive discourse in the process, and subsequently became more opaque to the dominant groups (Wickham 1998: 18). Appreciating the potential of gossip as a social sanction against the dominant strata, the Kautiliyan state (3.18.7) had proposed a series of penalties against multifarious verbal assaults, especially against the Brahmins, which underscored the prevalence of verbal violence against the dominant section of society (Olivelle 2013: 218).

In the story of the *Illisa Jātaka* (no. 78), the scrooge treasurer, Illisa, who had abandoned his family tradition of charity and destroyed the almonry, summoned severe criticism upon himself as stingy, heretic, vile, etc. He was instantly recognisable by his physical deformities which, for the subalterns, accentuated his malevolence and also, somewhere down the line, were signs of symbolic retribution. Yet, while the Sakka, the karmic reincarnation of the treasurer's deceased father, resumed the tradition of charity in the guise of Illisa, the treasurer himself, to admonish his son (from his previous birth) Illisa, the maligned image of the latter was reversed almost spontaneously with the spread of the news of charity. The rural subjects associated oppressive rulers with the vices of malice, unrighteousness, malevolence, and corruption, along with the unscrupulous and degenerate bureaucratic officials and Brahmins, whose civic images were tarnished by deep criticism that was public knowledge. Thus, it is evident that the construction and reconstruction of public knowledge were under the constant influence of the practice of gossip, which caused most public acts conforming to the shared values of peasant society to be performed with 'ritualized formality' by the affluent section of society to influence the gossip network (Wickham 1998: 6). Offstage, groups with shared perceptions, generated by the act of gossip, could tyrannically impose these shared values onto the peasants, whose relation with his patron, if known to be close, that is, beyond a customary patron-client relationship, could infringe upon the plane of the subaltern code of conduct and inflict ignominy on the peasant since such a relationship maybe considered a breach of mutual trust by the rest of the dominated clients and therefore, might attract hostility from their own groups. Thus, it did endorse a mechanism of social control, over both the dominants and among the virtually equals (Scott 1990: 143). Later, when the real treasurer made an effort to restrain his subordinate employee from obtaining his wealth as charity, the treasurer was thrashed by his own clients, which signified the readiness, on the part of the subalterns, to transform a voluntary act of charity into a moral claim of the clients.

The *Gahapati Jātaka* (no. 199) demonstrates an arrangement between the common peasants and the village headman to procure help during famines, which would be reciprocated by a payment in kind after the harvest. A clear distinction between an act of charity and help is shown to be resolved. A promise of payment had liberated the peasants from succumbing to the humiliation of being dependent and subordinated to the patron, and secured a dignified social standing for poor peasants as intrinsic in such insurance was a mutual reciprocity (Scott 1985: 192–193). Instances of reciprocity are not rare, as another account (*Jātaka* no. 257) illustrates. For instance, the prevalent custom of seeking a loan for the means of production (livestock) from a friend eventually led to inviting trouble for the protagonist peasant.

However, any transgression or immoral endeavours to exploit the situation of peasants as clients were viewed with repugnance, as illustrated in the last account (*Gahapati Jātaka* no. 199), where the patron headman demanded a reimbursement before the agreed period, concealing his affair with the wife of the protagonist, only to generate a violent reaction on the part of the latter, who not only ridiculed him, but also thrashed him publicly. This episode of violence inflicted upon the headman is endowed with several layers of resistance. At one level, in this episode, the inclusion of an affair with a strong scandalous angle and a sentimental scope for sympathy and support was perhaps only to make a strong case for the public act of physical denigration against a superior in class and status who had just breached the arrangement. At another level, however, an extraordinary act of negative reciprocity and public defiance inverted the power structure, even if momentarily, by deviously legitimising the otherwise retaliatory act with a law of property, which he reiterated publicly while assaulting the headman. This sort of physical assault, especially if it inverted the caste hierarchy, could follow penalties or even mutilation, as suggested by the *Arthaśāstra* (3.19.8). Hence, through a devious application of property law that exposed the innate patriarchal disposition of peasant society, the peasant inverted a means of exploitation into a means of aggression by invoking the moral claim to secure his own property. Consequently, he demonstrated a clear understanding of the nature and operation of exploitative rules concerning resource management.

Leaving aside the issue of the romantic affair, a close examination of the account underscores the constant tension over the social arrangement of reciprocity. While the patron wished to exploit the discretionary feature of these services to acquire greater social control and much genuine conformity from the clients; the clients strove to transform these discretionary services into mandatory provisions by proclaiming their legitimate rights, which would solve the problem of subordination and consequent humiliation. However, this tension rarely indicated the peasants' ignorance of existing inequalities in the hierarchical socio-economic structure in which they were situated, but underlined their principal concern, reinforced through gossip and disparagement, to safeguard the mutuality and conceptual equality of and among the common peasantry (Scott 1985: 194–195). The veneer of dissimulation, the density and the specialised features of the prevailing common knowledge and practices of the given society, gathered generationally, entwined with the potency of rumours as a conductor of insurgency, had hardly been alluded to in the *Arthaśāstra*. Acknowledging the inadequacy of the existing state apparatus to penetrate these cloistered domains necessitated envisaging a rural space infested with informers and agent provocateurs, who were 'the eyes and arms of the sovereign' (Mabbett 1972: 48–49).[23]

Virtual Hegemonies and Ethical Epistemology

Through the trajectory of narrative sequentiality and diverse subterfuges, which incessantly encroached into the statist space of domination and control, the *Jātaka* tales formulate a comprehensive routine existence in a counter-hegemonic form. These nomadic infiltrations of tactical manoeuvres challenge the hegemonic claims of authority by inverting the meanings of the existing cultural system, both in the dominant socio-political and the discursive domains, informed by dogmatic legitimations. In this chapter, however, privileging the *Jātaka* narratives over the systematic thoughts of the Śāstric expositions on legal and everyday conduct and behaviours as 'theory of practice' themselves makes an epistemological point.

An investigation of the epistemological domination of doctrinal source-materials in the early Indian historiographical tradition reveals the violence inherent in manufacturing a monolithic unified system. Yet, the 'presence of the absence' of the stifled voices of the subaltern in this field of 'scriptural economy' does generate an ethical obligation to craft a space for these voices to speak. A grand depository of archival material, enriched with the dynamic plurality of the actual past, has been structured by the epistemological violence of hierarchising the doctrinal 'systematic thought' as an 'archival impulse',[24] and the dominant tradition of the early Indian historiographical operation. Therefore, prior to the interrogation of any doctrinal tradition (Śāstric or others, even in the case of the *Jātakas*), a probe into the archival framing is also imperative to comprehend how and to what degree the historical evidences underwent change in the process of subduing the heterogeneity of lived experiences (Highmore 2006: 83–90). This critical exercise of navigating the labyrinth of 'archival grain' creates an epistemological possibility of acquiring an 'against the grain' understanding of the innate erosion and incongruences of the institution of the archive, produced by a tension between a desire to collect the heterogeneous materials, and an arduous homogenising order. A counter-reading of the measures opted by Śāstric literatures in their negotiation with the legal-political or cultural transgressions of their natural organising principle would demonstrate this underlying inherent tension. Hence, a perception of the plurality, contingent on specific historical situations, in any existing cultural system beyond the archival scope is essential for constructing a liberating epistemological space that discards as redundant any broad teleological explanatory thesis of past societies.

However, this critical 'prose of counter-insurgency' approach would only provide us with a reflexive understanding of the subjugated voices; an excavation of the existing narratives and tales would offer a wider perspective on social reality through the quotidian lived experiences of the past. Although the *Jātaka* tales have constructed a parallel counter-factual, utopian space of conflict resolution, this place-making manifests a continuous dialogic encounter with the 'realist' authoritarian space of order. Drawing on hostile experiences from other spaces, these tales generate a space for rehearsing a range of tactical procedures contingent on different conditions as a survival mechanism beyond this utopian space. This 'meta-quotidian' aspect of these stories that approaches the everyday as a field of practice safeguards the 'weapons of the weak' against the reality of the established order (de Certeau 1984: 23). In the face of the absolute and hegemonic presence of the established authoritative order, the utopian spaces created by these tales were perceived as ethically real, and as the mausoleum of these rare subaltern voices and aspirations.

Notes

Acknowledgements: I would first like to convey my gratitude to Professor Aloka Parasher Sen for providing me with this opportunity to contribute to this book, and her constant guidance. I would also like to thank my parents, and my friends Aisarya, Ashesh, Shreyashi, Vaibhav, and Chitran for their insights into this chapter and their unceasing support.

1. A term derived from Collingwood that Inden uses to signify a hypostatised agent of history. Certain 'essences' (substantialised agents) of a culture have been considered as the primary stimulus for any historical action to become the driving force for the community, while remaining unaffected themselves by the historical processes. This eventually denies people of their own agency. For a detailed understanding, see Chapter 1 of *Imagining India* (Inden 2000a: 7-48; Inden 2000b: 3-28).
2. Absolute civilisational essences refer to the hypostatised features one associates with a certain culture/civilisation as its intrinsic values.
3. This term suggests the constant encounters between power and resistance that simultaneously transform each other, in which neither remains 'autonomous' (Haynes and Prakash 1991: 3).
4. A term used exactly in the way Michel de Certeau has introduced it, in contrast to 'strategy'. He argues that tactics is a ruse, an art of the weak; a calculated action determined by the 'absence of a proper locus'. Devoid of any base, it takes advantage of the provided opportunities, but cannot accumulate its spoils. For details, see Chapter 3, 'The Practice of Everyday Life' in de Certeau (1984: 29–42).
5. A zone where retribution can be sought without dangerous repercussions is utopian. This zone is also fantastic because the subjects often get support from the divine/semi-divine entities in their quest for justice/retribution, which is not possible in 'reality'.
6. 'Voices-off' refers to background voices, beyond the prevalent elite voices in the scriptures and the archives. The voices of the common get obscured as background noise in the archival process that seeks to establish and legitimise an elite historiography as the only voice of the past.
7. The inescapable chain of significance inherent in the archival impulse can be explained as a process of epistemological violence that has been inflicted upon the heterogeneous, dynamic actuality of life (Highmore 2006: 86).
8. The connection of the commentary with the *Jātakapali* verses that form the tenth section of the *Khuddaka Nikaya* of the Theravāda tradition can be derived from the division of tales in *Jātakattavannana* on the basis of the *Nipāta* system, which is the categorising index for the verses themselves (Appleton 2012).
9. Each *Jātaka* has a 'Story of the Present' (*Paccuppannavatthu*), which narrates the occasion that inspired the Buddha to preach the 'Story of the Past' (*Atitavatthu*). Canonically, the *Atitavatthu* narrates a tale that displays an innate secular disposition, where Bodhisattva, as an animal

or a human, resolves a conflict situation primarily through intelligence, wits and tricks, etc. Terms like '*Jātakas*' or '*Jātaka* tales' are employed in referring to the 'Stories of the Past', as they are the narratives of the former lives of the Buddha, as Bodhisattvas. They also carry traces of subaltern tactics against various forms of conflict and oppression.

10. The recent monograph by Naomi Appleton (2012) rekindled the debate of the popular vs. Buddhist dispositions of the *Jātaka*. While scholars like Chakravarti (2007) and Roy (1996) substantiated the popular nature of these tales, Appleton believes that even though some of the stories may have an earlier independent existence, these stories should not be considered anything but as existing within Buddhist frameworks. Chakravarti, whose study of the *Jātakas* remains a landmark contribution in the existing historiography on the subject, has considered this a literary device for Buddhist appropriation, which was able to transform any story into the *Jātakas*. She also believes that these tales were solely used for Buddhist preaching, which were transmitted by a community of specialised reciters of the established genre of the *Jātakas*, i.e., *Jātaka-bhanakas*.
11. However, a genealogy of this phase of crystallisation would possibly direct one to the 'embedded Jātakas' in Vinaya and Sutta materials, where these tales, accompanied by moral verses in the former, were appropriated to illustrate the juxtaposition between the Bodhisattva and the Buddha himself (Appleton 2012).
12. The formulaic trope of the 'Story of the Present' was introduced to institute Buddha as the storyteller of the core tales, accompanied by the identification of the story characters with other prominent Buddhist characters to reinvigorate the narrative control, and finally the deployment of *Nidānakathā* that incorporated a simple teleological tale within the grand temporal architecture of a large karmic cycle (Chakravarti 2007: 238).
13. A hidden transcript is, as Scott has reckoned, a complete record of the subversive speech and non-speech gestures of the subalterns, beyond the official observation (Scott 1990).
14. Scholars like Richard Fick, Ratilal Mehta, Atindra Bose, Uma Chakravarti, Kumkum Roy, and others have taken a serious look at these stories and have rightly recognised the subversive traits inherent in them. While the landmark contributions of Chakravarti and Roy investigated these subversive traits through the prism of caste, gender, and class, they obscured the tactical manoeuvres and their operational logic within the same institutionalised categories of the Buddhist critique.
15. For a detailed discussion of this concept, see Chapter 4, 'Zones of Silence: Orality, Archive and Resistance', in Highmore (2006: 81–115).

16. All *Jātaka* references cited are from the original edition of V. Fausbøll (2008). For the English translation, except the *Nidānakathā*, see E. B. Cowell (1973).
17. This mechanism of 'co-sharing' resources by rival elite factions (Heesterman 1985: 133), about which the *Arthaśāstra* was apprehensive, had severely circumscribed the authority of the central power and resulted in corrupt practices.
18. All the *Arthaśāstra* references are cited from the translation by Patrick Olivelle (2013).
19. This was with reference to a provision, recommended in this text to repair a lake or reservoir with the help of adequate means of sustenance from the royal storehouse and granaries (Olivelle 2013). Serious measures against this calamity were recommended since, devoid of subsistence, the simple producers had a proclivity to adapt to different modes of subsistence or migrate to other states, which would devastate the production base of any state. Therefore, equipped with diverse subsistence strategies, peasants were also furnished with diverse avenues to impose their demands on the authority.
20. Animals in these tales are imbued with the values of the given society. Though they articulate the hidden voices of the subalterns, they could never escape the hierarchy that directed them as well (Chakravarti 2007: 222). In this context, the Bull may represent a labourer who is as strong as a bull, and who has possibly experienced an 'animalistic' exploitation as well.
21. This idea of 'offstage' behaviours is derivative of James C. Scott's application of the said term which suggests the insurrectionary behaviour of the subalterns that escapes the vigilance of the authority. Here, 'offstage' doesn't always refer to a permanent sequestered space 'outside' the domain of authority, it can also be a momentary tactical opportunity or a zone of refuge within the authoritarian space.
22. This phrase 'the cognitive orientation of the peasants to the images of limited good' has been adopted here from an essay by anthropologist George M. Foster, based on his fieldwork on Mexican villages (Foster 1965). This phrase 'cognitive orientation' actually stands for a prevailing set of assumptions that underlies the majority of the behaviour of a community. 'Image of limited good' refers to a pattern of peasant behaviour that reflects that peasants believe the social, economic, or natural resources as well as desired objects, both abstract and concrete, are only finite or of limited quantity, like land. Therefore, there is a serious competition and contestation over the claims on fortune and resources, etc., as it is believed that someone's fortune must come only at the expense of the others, whether that is visible or not.

23. The markets, taverns, brothels and gambling houses, as the *Arthaśāstra* (4.4.4) has envisioned, were privileged sites of an anonymous crowd and anti-hegemonic discourses that fostered dissents and rumours. (These sites were considered 'privileged' because, unlike other offstage sites of subversions, these sites were in full public view in front of the authorities, who acknowledged their anonymous counter-hegemonic potential and yet did not try to eliminate them.) These places were swarmed with clandestine operatives who possessed the skill of maintaining an innocuous presence in the clamour of these sites and yet were able to acquire necessary information and restrain criminal activities (Olivelle 2013). The operatives were recruited from various subordinate strata of the larger society (Ghosal 1966: 135). The informers, masquerading as students, were to be instructed by the authorities to create an artificial collective disputation to proclaim the divine attributes of the monarchs. In this context, the *Arthaśāstra* endorsed the manipulation of the ingrained impulse to transmit oral information present in these sites, in order to channelise the concept of divinity of the royal authority in these counter-hegemonic sites. This process was designed to neutralise sedition, either by recreating a public knowledge of royal divinity or by inciting a seditious retort from subjects, which would then be eradicated furtively.
24. Steven Collins made this distinction. He argues that people can either acquire comprehension through storytelling (narrative thought) or by thinking logically or scientifically (systematic thought). While systematic thought is governed by logic and unifies a field by organising it into a system by means of categories, a narrative thought produces meaning through a sequentiality of its constitutive parts.

References

Adas, Michael. 1980. '"Moral Economy" or "Contest State"?: Elite Demands and the Origins of Peasant Protest in South East Asia'. *Journal of Social History* 13(4): 521–546.

———. 1981. 'From Avoidance to Confrontation: Peasant Protest in Precolonial and Colonial Southeast Asia'. *Comparative Studies in Society and History* 23(2): 217–247.

———. 1986. 'From Footdragging to Flight: The Evasive History of Peasant Avoidance Protest in South and South-East Asia'. *Journal of Peasant Studies* 13(2): 64–86.

Appleton, Naomi. 2012. *Jātaka Stories in Theravāda Buddhism: Narrating the Bodhisatta Path.* Ashgate: Routledge.

Bailey, Frederic G. 1987. 'The Peasant's View of Bad Life'. In Theodor Shanin (ed.), *Peasant and Peasant Societies*, 284–299. New York: Basil Blackwell.

Basham, Alfred L. 1993. *Wonder That Was India*. New Delhi: Rupa & Co.

Benjamin, Walter. 2007. *Illuminations: Essays and Reflections*, Hannah Arendt (ed.) and Harry Zohn (trans.). New York: Schocken Books.

Bose, Atindranath. 1970. *Social and Rural Economy of Northern India Cir. 600 B.C.–200 A.D.* Calcutta: Firma K. L. Mukhopadhyay.

Chakravarti, Uma. 2007. 'Women, Men, and Beasts: The Jatakas as Popular Tradition'. In Aloka Parasher Sen (ed.), *Subordinate and Marginal Groups in Early India*, 210–242. New Delhi: Oxford University Press.

Claessen, Henri J. and Peter Skalnik (eds). 1978. *The Early State*. The Hague: Mouton Publishers.

Collins, Steven. 1998. *Nirvana and Other Buddhist Felicities: Utopias of the Pali Imaginaire*. Cambridge: Cambridge University Press.

Cone, Margaret and Richard Gombrich. 1977. *The Perfect Generosity of Prince Vessantara*. Oxford: Clarendon Press.

Cowell, E. B. (ed.). 1973. *The Jātaka or Stories of the Buddha's Former Births*, 6 vols. London: The Pali Text Society.

de Certeau, Michel. 1984. *The Practice of Everyday Life*, Steven Rendall (trans). Berkeley: University of California Press.

Drekmeier, Charles. 1962. *Kingship and Community in Early India*. California: Stanford University Press.

Fausbøll, V. (ed.). 2008. *The Jātaka Together with Its Commentary Being Tales of the Anterior Births of Gotama Buddha*, 6 vols. Oxford: The Pali Text Society.

Foster, George M. 1965. 'Peasant Society and the Image of Limited Good'. *American Anthropologist* 67(2): 293–315.

Ghoshal, Upendra Nath. 1930. *The Agrarian System in Ancient India*. Calcutta: University of Calcutta.

———. 1966. *A History of Indian Public Life*, Vol. II. Bombay: Oxford University Press.

Grafton, Anthony. 1997. *The Footnote: A Curious History*. Cambridge: Harvard University Press.

Guha, Ranajit. 1986. *Elementary Aspects of Peasant Insurgency in Colonial India*. Delhi: Oxford University Press.

Haynes, Douglas and Gyan Prakash (eds). 1991. *Contesting Power*. New Delhi: Oxford University Press.

Heesterman, J. C. 1985. *The Inner Conflict of Tradition*. Chicago: University of Chicago Press.

Highmore, Ben. 2006. *Michel De Certeau: Analysing Culture*. London: Continuum.

Inden, Ronald. 2000a. *Imagining India*. Bloomington and Indianapolis: Indiana University Press.

———. 2000b. 'Introduction'. In Ronald Inden, Jonathan Walters, and Daud Ali (eds), *Querying the Medieval: Texts and the History of Practices in South Asia*, 3–28. New York: Oxford University Press.

Jackson, Michael. 2013. *The Politics of Storytelling: Variations on a Theme by Hannah Arendt*. University of Copenhagen: Museum Musculanum Press.

Kerkvliet, Benedict J. Tria. 2009. 'Everyday Politics in Peasant Societies (and Ours)'. *Journal of Peasant Society* 36(1): 227–243.

Kher, Narendra Nath. 1973. *Agrarian and Fiscal Economy in the Mauryan and Post-Mauryan Age (Cir. 324 B.C.–320 A.D.)*. Delhi and Varanasi: Motilal Banarsidass.

Mabbett, Ian W. 1972. *Truth, Myth and Politics in Ancient India*. New Delhi: Thomson Press (India) Ltd.

Mandal, Krishna Kumar. 2007. 'Note: Forms of Peasant Protest in the Jatakas'. *Social Scientist* 35 (5/6): 39–46.

Mehta, Ratilal L. 1985. *Pre-Buddhist India*. Delhi: Anmol Publications.

Olivelle, Patrick (ed.). 2013. *King, Governance, and Law in Ancient India: Kauṭilya's Arthaśāstra* (trans. from Sanskrit). New York: Oxford University Press.

Roy, Kumkum. 1996. 'Justice in the Jatakas'. *Social Scientist* 24(4/6): 23–40.

Scott, James C. 1976. *Moral Economy of the Peasants: Rebellion and Subsistence in Southeast Asia*. New Haven and London: Yale University Press.

———. 1985. *Weapons of the Weak: Everyday Forms of Peasant Resistance*. New Haven and London: Yale University Press.

———. 1990. *Domination and the Arts of Resistance*. New Haven and London: Yale University Press.

Spellman, John W. 1964. *Political Theory of Ancient India: A Study of Kingship from the Earliest Times to circa A.D. 300*. Oxford: Clarendon Press.

Wickham, Chris. 1998. 'Gossip and Resistance among the Medieval Peasantry'. *Past & Present* 160: 3–24.

Zipes, Jack. 2012. *The Irresistible Fairy Tale: The Cultural and Social History of a Genre*. Princeton and Oxford: Princeton University Press.

3

Perceptions of History in Images of Space and Power

The *Kāvya* Narratives

Mrinalini

Introduction

Literary texts have occupied an important place in the writing of Indian history, and their domain has ranged from the religious to the mundane in the form of epic and lyrical, dramatic and didactic, as well as narrative and scientific prose. *Kāvya* literature constitutes an important part of the Indian literary tradition, but its efficacy as a source in serious history writing started quite late, perhaps because of its nature. There are various forms of Kāvya like poetry (*sargabandha* or *mahākāvya*), drama (*nāṭya*), tales (*kathā*), and biography (*ākhyāyika*) (Warder 1989: 122). The earliest traces of Kāvya poetry can be found in the epic *Rāmāyaṇa* (Winternitz 1963: 3). The Kāvya texts qualify under the category of art because the chief characteristic of Kāvya was to produce *rasa* (aesthetic experience), which could be experienced by the audience (Warder 1974: 19). It is thus understood that Kāvya texts should primarily be considered imaginative because conventionally, they have been embellished and adorned with figurative speech like similes and metaphors. Poets of the Kāvya texts tend to imitate reality and refashion it according to their own needs. Hence, one can postulate that in 'imagination', hints of reality can be found. However, while dealing with the work of fiction, one has to be critical and sensitive. In order to read a literary text, one has to carefully understand the genre or the type of literature and, in the case of poetry or drama, one has to be sensitive to the connection of the given text with other literary texts of the time, and to the writer's style and imagination (Singh 2008: 15).

In the pre-Independence era, Orientalists/Indologists held the general perception and advertised the idea that India did not have a sense of history and Indian art and literature was degenerated, grotesque, and full of fiction, fables, and tales, and thus history could not be derived from them. For instance, James Mill severely criticised the corpus of Indian literature to propound that India was a degraded civilisation and its society had remained substantially unchanged (Thapar 1987: 4).The period from 1900 to 1950 was when historians, swept by nationalist fervour, strove to glorify India's ancient past. This period saw a surge in the use of literary texts on a large scale, but hardly any attention was paid to the corpus of Kāvya literature (Mrinalini 2015: 31–32). However, prominent historians like R. S. Sharma, Romila Thapar, B. D. Chattopadhyaya, A. K. Ramanujan, etc., writing in the 1970s, used a large variety of Indian literary texts to write about the society, economy, culture, and polity of ancient India. In fact, Romila Thapar argued at length that Indians had their own way of recording their past, and that it is very unfair to compare Indian literary texts with the ancient classical texts of Greece, Rome, or China (Thapar 2004: 268–269). She went on to discuss various Indian literary texts that were endowed with a historical consciousness, and this consciousness is said to be found embedded even in non-historical works (such as, literary texts containing anecdotes, legendary stories, and mythical references).

Although a strong case was made for the inclusion of literary texts on a large scale in history writing, Kāvya as a valid source in serious history writing remained at best marginal. As mentioned above, the main reason cited for not using Kāvya texts in history writing was their fictional nature as historians tended to look for the so-called 'real' facts of the past to generate historical narratives. Nevertheless, the earliest attempt to study Kāvya literature was made by A. K. Warder. He put together *Indian Kāvya Literature* in several volumes and thus traced the history of the Kāvya texts, starting from the second century BCE (Warder 1989, Vols. I–IV).

V. S. Pathak was another scholar who did seminal work by assessing the nature of several literary genres and their impact on the evolution of *Caritas* (historical biographies) (Pathak 1997: 1–21).

In recent times, Daud Ali in his *Courtly Culture and Political Life in Early Medieval India* has thrown light on the culture of royal courts and political life in early medieval India by using Kāvya texts like *Priyadarśika*, *Mālavikāgṇimitra*, etc., as well as inscriptions (Ali 2006: 1–262). Shonaleeka Kaul, in her *Imagining the Urban*, has written the history of urban cities and urbanism in ancient India based largely upon the Kāvya texts (Kaul 2010: 1–256). Another scholarly work has been done by Indira Peterson in her *Design and Rhetoric in a Sanskrit Court Epic*, which has taken up the study of a specific Kāvya text, namely the *Kirātārjunīyam*, to analyse it in terms of its linguistic styles (Peterson 2003: 1–188).[1] The use of Kāvya literature in serious academic writing is a current trend, and is being used to generate various images of the past.

This chapter makes a strong case for engaging with Kāvya texts in serious history writing by refuting the claim that history cannot be culled from fictional texts, and thereby promulgating the idea of the study of Kāvyas as a valid source for the following reasons. Kāvya literature produces some scintillating images of the past, in which historical consciousness can be found embedded; and we cannot agree more with the words of Daud Ali, who writes that 'literary texts corroborate many practices from prescriptive literature and thus if read critically, can serve as useful evidence. . . .' (Ali 2006: 18). We look closely at two near contemporaneous Kāvya texts, that is, the *Kirātārjunīyam* (fifth century CE) and *Harṣacarita* (seventh century CE),[2] with the aim to unravel the spatial, socio-economic, political, and ideological features from the perspective of the forest that defined the Himalayan and Vindhyan areas during the fifth–seventh centuries CE. The perception of the forest as a historical entity shall be analysed on multifarious levels, and a case shall be made for the use of Kāvya texts in academic history writing as they produce an alternative view of the past in opposition to one that merely uses literary sources to project them as definitive 'facts' on to the past.

UNDERSTANDING THE IDEA OF SPACE: *VANA* AND *AṬAVI*

The entity of space is complex and ever-changing, and this essence of complexity is aesthetically captured by the Kāvya texts. The forests constituted a major feature of the landscape and were found prominently described in the texts, as these were also the locales against which the narratives were often set. Thus, many of the geographical features of the forests have been described using ornate language. In our reading of the *Kirātārjunīyam* and the *Harṣacarita,* we find bountiful descriptions of the Himalayan and Vindhyan forests, respectively, that lay outside village boundaries. The English word 'forest' derives from the Latin word 'foris', which implies 'outside'. The term 'outside' alludes to being outside a village boundary or fence, which in turn would have included all the uninhabited and uncultivated land beyond the village (Sagreiya 1967: 1). In the *Kirātārjunīyam*,the Himalayan forest is described in a very picturesque way as being wild and untamed. The poet postulates that the jungles of the Himalayas were so dense that they could only be effectively fathomed and described by the divine, namely Lord Brahma. As quoted below, it is noted that its rear and middle parts were so full of trees that it was impossible for any human being, including the most learned Brahmin, to describe them (Misra 2012: 128).

> *ihdurdhigamaiḥ kinchidevagamaihḥ satatamsutaramvarṇyantaram* (I)
> *amumativipinimvcdadigyupinampuruṣmivaparampadmayoniḥ param* (II, v. 18).

The author of the *Kirātārjunīyam* has used '*vana*' (garden/forest) to describe the Himalayan forest as in the mention of the *kamalavana* (garden of lotuses). In a very poetic manner, it is described that the Himalaya was replete with river banks that were pure, and thus considered fit for *dharmic* (religious) purposes because of its kamalavana (Misra 2012: verse 7, 123). Another mention of the kamalavana in the text occurs when the author describes the grassy fields on the Himalayan mountain, Kailasa (ibid.: v. 37, 140). The author has also used the term *udyān* (garden) in the text to allude to the forest. In this case, the Himalayas have been visualised as an entire city established on earth, a city said to be decorated with gems, stones, etc., wherein lay a vana full of flowers. The term used here is *puṣpaudyān* (flower garden) (ibid.: v. 5, 122). Further, the text also offers a description, albeit limited, of trees like the Kadamba (ibid.: v. 9, 125), the Ashoka (ibid.: v. 6, 186), and the Chandana.

It is interesting to note that in the *Harṣacarita,* on the other hand, its author, has throughout the text used the term '*aṭavi*' (wild forest)to refer to the Vindhyan forests. For example, the *Harṣacarita* elaborates that when King Harṣa set out in search of his lost sister Rajyashri, he reached the Vindhya forest called *Vindhyaṭvi* (Cowell and Thomas 2004: Chapter vii, 878–880, 285). Further, the *Harṣacarita* gives an exhaustive account of a variety of trees, as narrated below:

> As he went on, there rose in his view all sorts of trees, some full of fruits, *karṇikāras* in blossom, *campaka* in abundance, large *phalegrahis*, *namerus* bowed down with fruits, palms and *naladas* with dark green leaves, *saralapines* and the yellow *nāgakesaras*, lines of *kuruvakas* bristling with their opening buds; every direction was painted with the beauty of the shoots of the red *aśoka*, while a beautiful grey hue was thrown over them by the pollen of the blossoming *kesara*. . . , betel nuts abounded on all sides, the *priyaṇgus* were brown with quantities of flowers. . . , while the *tamala* trees darker than midnight obscured the sunshine; the deodars were sprangled with their clusters of flowers, while the lines of rose-apples and *jambhīras* were studded with patches of flickering betel-vines; the air was kissed by *dhulikadamaba* trees white with the powder of their flowers. . . (Cowell and Thomas 2004: Chapter viii, 108–130, 295–296).

In this way, in a very poetic manner the author has given a vivid description of the trees and plants of the Vindhyan region. Most of the trees are identifiable though for some, modern equivalents are not available (Apte 1965: 339, 510, 684; Monier-Williams 1889: 113, 388, 530, 1182).

Traditionally, in Sanskrit literature, the terms '*araṇya*', 'vana', and 'aṭavi' have been used to denote the forest. However, it is to be noted that these terms alluded to different aspects of what we loosely refer to as the forest, and the different periods in which they were used conveyed varied meanings. The terms 'aṭavikā'/ 'aṭavi' were often used as a suffix in ancient India to denote the *mlecchas* or barbarians. For example, it has been pointed out that the term *mlecchāṭvikā* is found in the *Arthaśāstra* at several places, and that an Aśokan inscription uses the term aṭavi to denote regions specifically inhabited by 'wild' people, who had to be tamed according to the Dhamma policy (Parasher Sen 2012: 127–151).[3] Interestingly, an araṇya has been elaborated as virgin land which was neither cultivated nor grazed upon (Monier-Williams 1889: 86). The term 'araṇya' referred to something which was located opposite the village, and therefore, it could also be explicated as the village's 'Other' (Malamoud 1996: 77).

It is not plausible to simplistically suggest that during the fifth century CE, the terms 'vana' and 'araṇya' were used synonymously. The author of the *Kirātārjunīyam* used terms like 'vana' and 'udyān' to differentiate the forest from a garden of flowers, and did not use araṇya at all to designate the Himalayan forest. The poetic style enabled him to simultaneously produce various meanings in the use of 'vana' to denote both a cultivated forest and an untamed one, that is, the same word has been used to describe a forest which was wild as well as its gardens (Mrinalini 2015: 98). On the other hand, the *Harṣacarita* presents a description of the Vindhyan forest that is more realistic. Thus, the forest of the Vindhyan region has been depicted as containing different varieties of thick trees, each one of them given a name and a character. So we can surmise that the author of the *Harṣacarita* was referring more aptly to a full-fledged forest as 'aṭavi', a forest which was really dense and contained a large number and different varieties of trees.

Images of Economic Sustenance—Forest and Village

The forest and the village constituted two different entities, and one cannot study the locales of forest in isolation without taking into consideration its adjoining areas. In literary texts, the narratives on forests have often been contrasted to the theme of a settled society, specifically the village. In the Kāvya texts, terms such as 'vana', 'aṭavi', and 'araṇya' stood in stark contrast to the more settled/civilised spaces of the *grāma* (village), *kṣetra* (area), *janapada* (habitable territory), and so on. In fact, the binary of the forest and the so-called civilised spaces always existed (whether dichotomous or complimentary), but were sometimes diluted in the wake of the expansion of the larger state. In the words of B. D. Chattopadhyaya: '... as a historical process forest-scape could never remain constant; its boundaries would change, and particularly with the expansion of frontiers of the complex society, the forests themselves could be transformed into nuclei of local complex societies' (Chattopadhyaya 2017: 57–58). These historical processes of spatial transition have been captured to some extent in the Kāvya texts under study.

In the *Kirātārjunīyam,* the protagonist of the story, Arjuna, while proceeding towards the Himalaya from Dvaitvana, saw a village (Misra 2012: Chapter iv, verse 1). On the outskirts of the village settlement, the process of cultivation of *śāli* rice has been described (Misra 2012: Chapter iv, verse 2, 101–102). The rice fields were said to be guarded by the women of the forest community (Misra 2012: Chapter iv, verse 7, 103). Similarly, in the *Harṣacarita* when King Harṣa entered the Vindhya forest, he is described as having seen forest settlements which were separated and marked by woodland districts (Cowell and Thomas 2004: Chapter vii, verse 881–882, 285). It is specifically mentioned in the *Harṣacarita* that people from the neighbouring villages came to collect timber from the forest, and they were easily identified by the special kinds of torn and rugged clothes that they wore in order to avoid thieves from within or outside the forest, who could rob them (ibid.: Chapter vii, verse 924–932, 287).The text further details that people from the village localities collected various items from the forest, like *sīdhu* bark, *dhātaki* flowers, cotton plants, flax and hemp, honey, peacock's feathers, wax, *khadira* logs without the bark, bundles of *kuṣtha* and *rodhra,* and so on (ibid.: Chapter vii, verse 924–932, 288).

From the description given in the *Kirātārjunīyam*, it appears that there must have existed some level of interaction between the forest and the village as agricultural activity has been described as being carried out in the vicinity of the forest. In fact, the *Harṣacarita* clearly mentions the free movement of villagers in the precincts of the Vindhyan forest to collect materials from the forest. Thus, the forest not only fulfilled the need of the people living in the forest areas, but also played a pivotal role in the lives of the non-forest dwellers. The forest provided them with various economic products like *sīdhu* bark, which was used for making molasses or rum (Apte 1965: 1218), *dhātaki* flowers, which were used for making the yellow colour (ibid.: 889), cotton for various clothing purposes, and so on. The forest also provided medicinal plants and herbs like *kuṣtha* and *khadira*, which were used as remedies for specific diseases. Hence, the texts under consideration provide a glimpse of the forest as a potential space that is capable of generating resources of distinct kinds, and also talk about the relationship shared between the forest and non-forest dwellers.

In fact, the elaborate and vivid description of the economic activities mentioned in both texts produces different pictures of the forest areas in the *Kirātārjunīyam* as well as the *Harṣacarita*. Simultaneously, the Kāvya texts provide some glowing images of the lifestyle of forest-dwellers. In the *Kirātārjunīyam*, apart from cultivating rice, the people of the Himalayan forest are shown to be engaged in cow-herding and cattle-rearing. In this context, it is highlighted that Arjuna saw *gavām,* which refers to *gavendra* (cow-herders), according to Misra (2012: Chapter iv, 11, 105), who were depicted as powerful and mighty as they could defeat the bulls and metaphorically speaking, destroy the banks of the mighty rivers, which refers to their ability to cope with adverse conditions such as overflowing rivers. In another verse, cow herders were described as very simple people who had affectionate ties with their cattle (Misra 2012: Chapter iv, verse 13, 106). Apart from agriculture and cow-herding, hunting activities have also been highlighted. For example, it is explained that under Lord Śiva's command, his *gaṇa* (group) adopted the guise of a Kirāta (a generic term used for hunters; it also refers to an autochthonous tribe known to inhabit the Himalayan region) and prepared for hunting (ibid.: Chapter xii, verse 33–34, 354).

The *Harṣacarita* provides a vivid description of agricultural activity. From a reading of these sections in the text, it appears that forest dwellers of the Vindhyan forest region were primarily agriculturalists. The *Harṣacarita* states that the woodland enclosures were filled with smoke due to the burning of chaff of the *śāli* rice and granaries (*vanyadhānabījadhāninām*), and so agricultural products have also been mentioned (Cowell and Thomas 2004: Chapter vii, verse 881–885, 285). The farmers residing in the forest were said to own small areas of rice land with threshing grounds, and cultivation was mainly done on ploughed fields (tilth) with implements such as spades (*kudālaprayakṛsibhiḥ*). The land, it is narrated, was hard to plough as the soil was as hard as black iron (*kālāyasairivakṛṣṇmrittikākathinai*) (ibid.: Chapter vii, verse 891–892, 286). The text also provides a description of the kitchen gardens. The houses of the forest dwellers in this text had gardens where they cultivated a variety of fruits and vegetables, and a picture of these products is given thus:

> There were charcoal tied with *valvuja* grass, numerous heaps of cotton from the *semul* tree, fruits, stores of *nala* rice, waterlily roots, candied sugar, white lotus seed, bamboos, and threshed rice ready at hands; also collection of *tamala* seeds…, a wealth of withered *rajadana* and *madana* fruit, abundance of *madhūka* fruit decoctions, lists of safflower in excellent cupboards, no lack of *rajamṣa*, cucumber, *karkaṭika* and ground seeds…. (ibid.: Chapter vii, verse 985–993, 289–290)

At another place, cow pens were also mentioned (Cowell and Thomas 2004: Chapter vii, verse 886, 285).The hunters were depicted in the text as walking around the precincts of the forest, holding cages of falcons, partridges, and *kapiñjalas* (a small bird), while young hunters have been described as practising bird-catching in the forest (ibid.: vii, verse 944–945, 288).

Thus, the descriptions given in both these texts enable us to deduce that apart from hunting, other economic activities also played an important role in the lives of the forest dwellers. The *Harṣacarita* also provides a vivid description of the houses of the forest dwellers, and states that their houses were to be set wide apart at a distance from each other and were to be fenced (Cowell and Thomas 2004: Chapter vii, verse 970–972, 289). The walls of the houses were said to be made of bamboo leaves, stalks, and reeds, painted with *gorocana* (yellow pigment) and decorated with *kimcuka* (orange-red flowers) (ibid.: Chapter vii, verse 982–985, 289). These descriptions enable us to gather that the forest dwellers' houses were humble and simple, but aesthetically made. From the above descriptions, it is our submission that the space of the forest was not always seen as alien, wild, or mystifying. Due to the close proximity of the village and the forest, people of neighbouring villages often frequented the forest areas to further their needs, and there existed some sort of complementary relationship between them. From the images produced in the *Kirātārjunīyam* and the *Harṣacarita*, it can be stated that the realm of the forest was in itself a settled society with its own characteristics, which was very similar to the description of what we understand as a village settlement. The descriptions of the forest and the village are entangled when describing economic activities like cultivation, cow-herding, and hunting, which were practised within the Himalayan and Vindhyan forest zones. In fact, the mention of granaries in the *Harṣacarita* is a strong indication that some of the forest settlements may have been self-sufficient in food grains.

Hitherto, scholars have viewed the relationship between the forest and the village in contrasting terms. Thapar, in her overarching essay on this relationship, shows how the early marked distinction between the grāma and the araṇya changed over a period of time in later Sanskrit texts. Initially, the order and predictability of the grāma was considered the opposite of what the araṇya depicted, namely a disorderly, unknown, and unpredictable terrain. This image changed when certain areas of the forest came to be known and accommodated as areas where the heroes of the two epics sojourned during their respective exiles

(Thapar 2009: 34–35). How the state handled the resources of the forest as well as kept its wild areas at a distance has been vividly discussed by Parasher Sen (2012). The janapada settlement was contrasted with different kinds of forests. In fact, some of the janapadas were said to be guarded from forest dwellers as they were considered a dangerous threat to the state. This did not stop the state from exploiting the more accessible forests for their resources (ibid.: 133).

In this historical evolution of the change in the image of the forest in earlier texts, Thapar pertinently points to literary works like the writings of Kalidasa, dated around fourth century CE, to argue that in such texts, the forest came to be highly romanticised and seen as an imagined alternative which was often equated with paradise (Thapar 2009: 37). However, for the same period, when one turns to inscriptions as a source of information, she rightly points out that agriculture started spreading at the expense of the forest, as a result of the grant of lands by kings (ibid.: 38). Based on the above studies, it is safe to conclude that by this time, particularly after the fourth century CE, the forest and the village existed together, in some cases in complementary ways, while in others, the forest gradually became subordinated to the village. In extending the tenor of the arguments of earlier scholars, it can be pointed out that by the seventh century CE when the *Kirātārjunīyam* and the *Harṣacarita* alluded to the forest, there was continuity between the forest and the village that were depicted. As mentioned above, the forest was engaged with by the settled society in both texts. However, between the fifth to seventh century CE, land was being donated on a large scale in forest areas by the state, and this then resulted in the forest dwellers becoming subordinate and marginal to mainstream society. In fact, both texts under study allude to the blurring of the rigid binary between settled and non-settled spaces, that is, the village and the forest. These images produced in them thus pertinently reflect the times they were written in, wherein we get a distinct image of the forest as being a dynamic space, interacting with the areas around it.

Kings and Barbarians: State and Society of the Forest

From time immemorial, larger states have been created by subsuming the smaller and neighbouring areas, and incorporating them into well-established kingdoms. In the process of expansion, forest areas were often tamed and assimilated into mainstream society to cater to the demands of these large kingdoms. The complex historical processes of the state, which expanded its hold over the forested regions, are found embedded in the Kāvya texts, as the narratives of these texts are commonly woven around kings and their activities and attitudes. As pointed out earlier, in the *Kirātārjunīyam,* Arjuna was seen visiting the Himalayan forest to practice penance, and in the *Harṣacarita,* King Harṣa went into the Vindhyan forest in search of his lost sister. Here, both Arjuna and Harṣa represented a sort of central authority. However, it is interesting to note that at the same time, both texts refer to the presence of forest chieftains in the Himalayan and Vindhyan forest terrains. In the *Kirātārjunīyam,* we find a reference to the presence of the *Kirātapati* (chief of the *Kirātas*, a hunting tribe). The context in which they are mentioned is narrated thus: When Arjuna went to perform penance in the Himalayan forest, the residents of the forest, such as the *munis* (ascetics), became nervous and complained to Lord Śiva. After listening to them, Lord Śiva said that he would adopt the garb of a Kirātapati and resolve the problem of the munis (Misra 2012: Chapter xii, verse 16–17, 342). In the narration that follows, the Kirātapati is depicted as a mighty person who possessed an army of his own (ibid.: Chapter xii, verse 43, 354), controlled the reserve of gems and stones in the forest and owned elephants (ibid.: Chapter xii, verse 44, 387). Similarly, the *Harṣacarita* provides information about a person named Bhukampa, who has been described as the general of the Śabaras and lord of the forest settlements of the Vindhyan mountainous range (Cowell and Thomas 2004: Chapter viii, verse 65–70, 284).

The presence of forest chieftains in these texts, who possess armies and control the resources of the forest, shows that the forest was in reality under the control of these chiefs and not under the larger state. Perhaps the forest chieftains had, in some cases, a special relationship with the larger kingdom, or held an independent seat of power that could pose a threat to the larger state. In this regard, one would concur with B. D. Chattopadhyaya, who writes:

> [T]his however, offers only a partial view of the wide range of fundamental mutations which were likely to take place in the forest space and among forest-dwellers when the forest space emerged as the nucleus of a 'forest kingdom' which, however, would be a segment of larger political formation to which it could be either subservient or with which it would contest for relative autonomy (Chattopadhyaya 2017: 65).

The above is in contrast to the *Arthaśāstra's* views, which consciously referred to the presence of the forest chieftains who, without any intermediaries, singularly controlled the forest resources and could pose a threat to the state, and could even seize the throne from the ruler (Parasher Sen 2012: 133). By the Gupta period (fourth to seventh century CE), they had well-established kingdoms of their own. As is well-known, Samudragupta is said to have reduced *āṭavikarājas* (many forest kings) to the status of *paricārakī-kṛta* (servants) (Chattopadhyaya 2017: 64). Another inscription from the late Gupta period gives information about a forest king named Samkṣobha, who was governing the Ḍābhala-Rājya, which was constituted of eighteen forest kingdoms (*sāshṭā daśāṭavi rājyābhyantaram*) under the sovereignty of the Gupta kings (ibid.: 65).

However, as discussed above, fifth–seventh century CE was marked by agricultural expansion. The ancient state, being dependent largely on agrarian revenues, gradually accessed the forest land to increase their revenues, and thus established an economic relationship, which in turn enabled them to exert their political power over the forest tracts. D. N. Jha has pointed out that the practice of land grants became prolific in the subsequent centuries and led to an agrarian expansion in the primarily backward and peripheral areas (Jha 2005: 163). Most of the data

Plates

Plate I: Kanheri Caves—Cave 1, Borivali, Mumbai, Maharashtra (ASI monument no. N-MH-M7)

Source: Photograph by Bikashrd, 13 March 2004, licensed under the CC BY-SA 4.0. Available at https://commons.wikimedia.org/wiki/File:Kanheri_Caves_-_Cave_1_,_Borivali_,_Mumbai.jpg (accessed January 2022).

Plate II: A Brāhmī stone inscription in a veranda of the Great Chaitya, Kanheri, Maharashtra (ASI monument no. 8)

Source: Photograph by Kankana266, 9 July 2016, licensed under the CC BY-SA 4.0. Available at https://commons.m.wikimedia.org/wiki/File:INSCRIPTION-KANHERI-MUMBAI-MAHARASTRA-DSC_0008.jpg (accessed January 2022).

Plate III: Karla Caves, Maharashtra, Great Chaitya left pillar no. 9—label inscription

Source: Photograph of pillar by Udaykumar PR and of inscription by Sunitaburra, 27 September 2017, licensed under the CC BY-SA 3.0. Available at https://commons.wikimedia.org/wiki/File:Karla_Caves_Great_Chaitya_Left_pillar_No9.jpg (accessed January 2022).

Plate IV: A Brāhmī inscription script at Nanaghat, Maharashtra, second century BCE

Source: Photograph by Elroy Serrao, 17 October 2009, licensed under the CC BY-SA 2.0. Available at https://commons.wikimedia.org/wiki/File:2nd_century_BCE_Nanaghat_Hindu_Inscription_Brahmi_script_Maharashtra.jpg (accessed January 2022).

Plate V: Early historic caves 19 and 20 at Nasik, Maharashtra

Source: Photograph by Kaho, 28 September 2017, licensed under the CC BY-SA 2.0. Available at https://commons.wikimedia.org/wiki/File:Nasik_caves_19_and_20.jpg (accessed January 2022).

Plate VI: Earliest historic coins (I) discovered at Kotalingala, Telangana

Source: Courtesy of State Department of Archaeology and Museums, Government of Andhra Pradesh (before its bifurcation in 2014).

Plate VII: Earliest historic coins (II) discovered at Kotalingala, Telangana

Source: Courtesy of State Department of Archaeology and Museums, Government of Andhra Pradesh (before its bifurcation in 2014).

Plate VIIIa: Coins of Sātavāhana king, Sātakarṇi

Source: Photograph by Ancientcoinsofindia1, 2007, licensed under the CC BY-SA 3.0. Available at https://commons.wikimedia.org/wiki/File:Coin_of_Satkarni.jpg (accessed January 2022).

Plate VIIIb: Coins of Sātavāhana king, Sri Vasisthiputra Pulomavi

Source: Photograph by Classical Numismatic Group, Inc., http://www.cngcoins.com, 7 September 2019, licensed under the CC BY-SA 3.0. Available at https://commons.wikimedia.org/wiki/File:Satavahanas._Sri_Vasisthiputra_Pulumavi.jpg (accessed January 2022).

Plate IX: Aihole Inscription of Ravi Kirti at the Meguti Temple, Karnataka: A eulogy of the conquests of Pulakesi II

Source: Photograph by Dineshkannambadi, 1 August 2008, licensed under the CC BY-SA 3.0. Available at https://commons.wikimedia.org/wiki/File:Aihole_inscription_of_Ravi_Kirti.jpg (accessed January 2022).

Plate X: Indian ivory statuette (front and back) found at Pompeii, Italy, first century CE

Source: Photograph by Public.Resource.Org, 28 August 2017, public domain. Available at https://commons.wikimedia.org/wiki/File:Pompei_Indian_Statuette_front_and_back.jpg (accessed January 2022).

Plate XI: Purnaghata, or auspicious vase from Amaravati, Andhra Pradesh (now in Sculpture Gallery, Indian Museum, Kolkata), second century CE

Source: Photograph by SuvadipSanyal, 29 April 2018, licensed under the CC BY-SA 4.0. Available at https://commons.wikimedia.org/wiki/File:30._Vase_of_prosperity-_2nd_century_CE-Limestone-Amravati-Andhra_Pradesh-Sculpture_Gallery-Indian_Museum-Kolkata-NS3699-A25075.jpg (accessed January 2022).

Plate XII: Lord Narasimha wooing Chenchu Lakshmi at Ahobilam, Andhra Pradesh

Source: Courtesy of State Department of Archaeology and Museums, Government of Andhra Pradesh (before its bifurcation in 2014).

underlying these processes comes from inscriptional evidence. For instance, an inscriptional record of 517CE talks about a king named Hastin who granted a village named Navagrāma to *brāhmaṇas*, and this village was located in Pulindarājarāśtra, a region inhabited by the autochthonous tribe of the Pulindas (Chattopadhyaya 2003: 177).

The *Kirātārjunīyam* and the *Harṣacarita*, as described above, were familiar with the cultivation that took place in the border areas of the forest, or in the forest itself. For instance, the *Kirātārjunīyam* highlights that forest dwellers looked after the forest and mountains, and when they became agitated with Arjuna's penance, they went to Lord Indra to complain. Here, Arjuna is a metaphoric representation of some sort of external authority. A similar incident is mentioned in the *Harṣacarita*, wherein it is significantly highlighted that the forest was fiercely guarded by *ayantrita vanapālas* (independent guards). They could have been representing the chiefs of the locality, protecting the community's resources. In this text, it is stated that 'zealous foresters seized the axes of trespassing woodcutters' (Cowell and Thomas 2004: Chapter vii, verse 888–889, 286). The above instances invoke the image of the forest as being ferociously protected. We postulate that the forest dwellers were probably aware of the effects of encroachment on the forest's resources and land by the state, and the presence of independent forest guards is indicative of the fact that intrusion by outsiders in the forest vicinity was disliked and resisted by the forest communities (Mrinalini 2015: 82). Enough scholarly attention has been invested to show that the state appropriation of the land of the forest dwellers was a continuous process and most explicitly witnessed in colonial times and even in princely states, which then adversely affected the condition of the forest dwellers (Gadgil and Guha 1993: 148–149). Though during earlier (pre-modern) periods of forest occupation, these processes were more gradual yet they also ultimately led to 'The forced sedentarization and the loss of their habitat [which] induced a feeling of helplessness, as outsiders made greater and greater inroads into what was once their undisputed domain' (ibid.: 149).

The *Kirātārjunīyam* and the *Harṣacarita* refer to the Kīrātas and Śabaras inhabiting the Himalayan and Vindhyan forests, respectively, as the original inhabitants of these areas. Each of these terms has a long history of usage that ultimately assigned them the status of autochthonous people of the subcontinent. The term Kīrāta is well-known as the name of a tribe of ancient India who inhabited the woods, and their main subsistence activity was hunting (Monier-Williams 1889: 283). The term '*Śabara*' has been literally translated as meaning barbaric and brindled. According to Monier-Williams, Kīrātas and Śabaras can be considered synonymous as both came to be associated with the hunting communities residing in the forests (ibid.: 1052). The pejorative view of the state and settled society vis-à-vis the forest dwellers was not a new phenomenon that began in the fifth–seventh century CE. In fact, if we check the early social history of the forest and forest-dwellers, then the classical Sanskrit texts in general also presented the forest as a space that was considered impure, dangerous, and unrefined, and with the inhabitants of the forest being viewed as atrocious and wild. These texts traditionally designated the land of the Himalayan and Vindhyan regions as the land of the mlecchas, or *mlecchadeśa* (Thapar 2004: 246). The kings adopted these social attitudes while broadly formulating their policies. On occasion, pragmatic considerations were kept in mind while dealing with the forest peoples. Parasher Sen has extensively discussed those tribes that were excluded, like the Kirātas, Śabaras, Pulindas, etc., based on references in early Indian texts to argue that 'the forest tribes are marked by exclusion rather than by subordination' (Parasher Sen 2004: 20). In the eyes of the settled society, they were considered outside the mainstream order of the *varṇa*-oriented society, and hence designated as mleccha (ibid.: 21).

A concomitant effect of state policies in the forest resulted in attempts to assimilate the forest population into mainstream society, but within the orbit of the so-called outsiders who considered themselves superior to the indigenous peoples. In the *Kirātārjunīyam,* it is stated that Arjuna tried to explain to the followers of Lord Śiva (Kirātapati) that he was the protector of the varṇa and *āśrama* system, and that there was no match between the kings and the forest dwellers (Misra 2012: Chapter xiv, 22, 408). Similarly, King Harṣa in the *Harṣacarita* alludes to the Vindhya forest being full of wicked foresters (Cowell and Thomas 2004: Chapter viii, 335–339, 304). However, under changed historical circumstances during the middle of the first millennium CE, the *Purāṇas* recognised the rising power of the mlecchas. In fact, in their descriptions of the Kaliyuga, the power and influence of the mlecchas is said to have increased. This has been explained as one of the characteristics of this age because many kings who rose to prominence during the early centuries of the Common Era were from a tribal background (Thapar 2004: 247). Parasher Sen has analysed that whenever forest dwellers assimilated into mainstream society, they were considered at one level as *vrātya* (degraded kṣatriyas), but more commonly as *anatyas*, *anatyayonis*, or *anatyāvasāyins* (other different kinds of 'impure' jātis) when the new forms of social hierarchy were established (Parasher Sen 2004: 298, 2019: 126). It has been pointed out that when we consider poetic texts of around the same period (fifth to seventh century CE) like the *Śakuntala* of Kalidasa, we get a picture of greater familiarity and less fear towards the forest and forest dwellers as compared to the earlier period (Thapar 2009: 37). This is partly due to the fact that the *Dharmaśāstra* were prescriptive texts that spoke primarily of a norm, while the Kāvya literature, though fictional in nature, reflected on the reality in society and actual social behaviour. Thus, based on historical contingencies, the tribal groups did not remain permanently excluded. It is our submission that Kāvya literature shows an inherent flexibility in the definitions, designations, and descriptions of the space called vana, araṇya, or aṭavi.

Conceptualising the Image of *Āśrama* in Forest

Another aspect of life in the forest described in Kāvya texts was the habitation of ascetics and renouncers. As noted above, the forest was the natural habitation of the indigenous forest dwellers, but over historical time, select locales of forest came to be legitimised as spaces for the people who had renounced worldly affairs. These were people who have moved into the stage of *sanyāsi*s (renouncers) in the four-fold *āśrama* system described in the *Dharmaśāstra*, or were those who had left home and hearth in an early stage of their lives and wanted to settle down in the vicinity of the forest to perform austerities or penance.[4] In both cases, there was a desire to move away from the settled society of the village, bounded by social norms. In fact, if we go by the prescriptions put forth in the theory of *varṇāśrama dharma* then a brāhmana was expected to spend the last two stages of his life, namely *vānaprastha* and *saṁyāsin*, in the vicinity of the forest. Given these rules, Romila Thapar pertinently points out that for the ascetics, forests were not strange or unusual places; rather, they provided them with an opportunity to discard the rules of civilisation and helped them attain their desired goals of solitude and spiritual emancipation (Thapar 2009: 143). Later, the forest was also appropriated by various other sects like the Buddhists, Jains, etc., to carry out their monastic and spiritual activities. It can be argued that due to this intense and frequent human association, some entities and components of the forest began to look different and were defined by the terms *tapovana*, *upavana*, *puṣpavana*, and so on (Parasher Sen 2019: 130). So essential had these habitations become that the *Arthaśāstra* enunciates conditions under which the demarcation of the special forest areas had to be done for the settlement of ascetics and respected brāhmaṇas devoted to the study of the Vedas. In this text, these specially demarcated areas were called tapovana and *braḥma-samāraṇya,* respectively (ibid.). Hence, it is in this context that B. D. Chattopadhyaya says that the forest should be viewed as a part of the complex system of society (Chattopadhyaya 2017: 59).

Both the texts under discussion provide references to the āśramas built in the forest. In the *Kirātārjunīyam,* the Himalayan forest was described as the abode of *rṣis* (sages). It is mentioned that when Arjuna was performing penance in the forest, the rṣis living in the forest were impressed by his severe austerities

(Misra 2012: Chapter vi, verse 32, 165). The *Harṣacarita* also describes the forest as a habitation site for monks and people who had renounced worldly affairs. The *Harṣacarita* highlights that Buddhists, along with Jains, Kapilas, Lokāyatikas, followers of the Kanada sect, followers of the *Upanishads*, etc., resided in mutual respect in the forest and enthusiastically raised doubts, studied, disputed, and explained issues around their respective doctrines and philosophies (Cowell and Thomas 2004: Chapter viii, verse 193–203, 298–299). With such references, especially to the Śramanic sects, we notice a shift in the view about the forest. Earlier, in Buddhist and Jain circles in particular, the monks and nuns were asked to avoid the forest areas while travelling. Now, especially after fourth century CE, the forest began to be perceived as a space where civilised people could easily go as well as use as a habitation site (Parasher Sen 2012: 131).

The spiritual essence that these religious enclaves became imbued with meant that they were also associated with some much-sought after moral and sacred essences. Thus, the *Kirātārjunīyam* highlights that after Arjuna set up an āśrama in the forest to perform penance, the forest became peaceful and violence-free. It is further narrated that due to Arjuna's penance, animals residing near and around the forest had renounced their violence (Misra 2012: Chapter xiii, verse 4, 361). The text is replete with such exaggerations that further tell us that due to the apparent effect of Arjuna's penance, the deer had let go of their hatred towards each other and the trees around also humbly bowed down when their flowers were plucked (ibid.: Chapter vi, verse 34, 166). Thus, the image generated is that Arjuna's penance led to the Himalayan forest becoming free of violence and fear (ibid.: Chapter x, verse 14, 269). The *Harṣacarita* similarly describes that due to the penance performed in the āśrama of the Buddhist monk Divakaramitra, hens became his disciples, monkeys performed the rituals in the *chaityas* (Buddhist prayer hall), *maināś* (a songbird) unfailingly performed the duties of monastic life, and owls listened attentively to the sayings of the Bodhisatta in order to attain spiritual insights. Hence, the metaphoric analogy of the power of penance and meditation suggests that even violent and fierce animals like tigers had left their meat-eating habits (Cowell and Thomas 2004: Chapter viii, 203–218, 299). These notions concerning the sacred space in the forest were part of a larger understanding of the metaphysical essences being sought in seclusion in various traditions of early Indian religious thought. In this context, Charles Malamoud has put forth the view that the entire construction of the idea of āśramas being established around a particular exalted spiritual leader, inspired seers, and rṣis was nothing but a utopian vision (Malamoud 1996: 88). We concur with Malamoud that clearly, these projections of an ideal, nonviolent world was not a reality, but a construction of literature in order to create an imaginary world of the unknown, namely the forest, through the power of the ideology of the āśrama.

The forest was also viewed as a place from where aspects of the *sādhārana dharma* in the form of *ahiṃsa* (nonviolence), *dama* (self control), *daya* (compassion), *satya* (truth), *akrodha* (to be without anger), *ārajavam* (to speak your mind and act accordingly) emanated. These ideas are said to have emerged from the āśramas of the forest and then later received by the settled society. Sontheimer suggests that ahiṃsa originated among the ascetics and saints, who came to be seen as the protectors of the animals who lived in harmony with them in the precincts of the forest. Due to the propagation of ahiṃsa, even the fierce animals of the forest were said to be against ecocide (Sontheimer 1994: 146). From the descriptions given in the *Kirātārjunīyam* and the *Harṣacarita*, it appears that both texts reflect these ideas, expressed through exaggerations such as accounts of inhabitants of the āśrama living in harmony with even violent animals,whom they had tamed by their prowess. Given the fact that the tradition of having āśramas in the forest had existed for several centuries, unhampered by natural and man-made hindrances, it is generally said that āśramas held a sympathetic view towards forest dwellers, whether they be animals or humans. It can also be suggested that the āśramas most likely acted as a threshold between the settled and a more nomadic society. The former frequented these locales of the forest as an escape from the so-called civilised outside world that had once defined the forest as a world of fear, the unknown, and the barbaric. It is not surprising, then, that most Kāvya narratives in general eulogise the forest, and in their story plots critically locate the meeting of the civilised and the wild in the āśramas.

Recapitulation and Conclusion

In this chapter, we focused on two texts of the same genre to study their views about the forests in two different geographical locations, that is, the Himalayan and the Vindhyan forest regions, described in them. The *Kirātārjunīyam* had defined the space of the forest as vana in a very picturesque manner, interspersed with the idea of gardens, which however were beyond human reach. However, from a careful reading of the text we concluded that the author was basically reflecting on the ecology of the lower tracts of the Himalayan forest. On the other hand, we also observed that the space of the Vindhyan forest described by the author of the *Harṣacarita* was more realistic and was referred to by the term 'aṭavi', which was used to denote the wilder and thicker forest usually inhabited by mleccha or barbaric groups in a variety of ancient texts. Clearly, of the two texts, the latter showed a greater knowledge of the ecology of the deep forest, as is indicated by its listing of the various trees that abounded in these forests.

Both texts, as we pointed out, reflect a close proximity between the forest and the village, due to which some sort of interdependence developed between these two zones of human activity. They have provided us with references to the presence of villages on the outskirts of the Himalayan and the Vindhyan forests. At times, a harmonious relationship has been depicted, while on occasion, contestation and conflict emerged between them. Due to the close proximity of the forest and the village, contact and communication between the forest and non-forest dwelling societies developed. Both texts point to the presence of non-forest dwellers in the precincts of forests for the collection of various forest produce.

This phenomenon can be termed the economic encroachment of the forest by people of the settled society.

We have argued in this chapter that from the fifth–seventh centuries CE, the space of the forest started changing drastically, as reflected in these Kāvya texts. The forest dwellers were shown to be engaged in various economic activities, especially agriculture. Based on the economic activities mentioned in the *Kirātārjunīyam* and the *Harṣacarita,* it can be inferred that the subsistence activity of the Himalayan region was most probably based on hunting, pastoralism, and agriculture, whereas the Vindhyan forest dwellers practised agriculture on a comparatively larger scale. These forested regions were not described as isolated, untamed, or mysterious for the people. Their habitations were in fact shown to be more like orderly, civilised grāmas. In fact, the *Kirātārjunīyam* and the *Harṣacarita* capture the major historical process of transformation of forest land into civilised space by the larger forces of state expansion into these parts.

From other literary sources and inscriptional evidence, we have seen that from the fifth–seventh century CE, agrarian expansion became prolific. The state initiated socio-economic processes by granting lands to officials and religious beneficiaries in the vicinities of the forest. These texts offer implicit evidence showing that the forest dwellers resisted these intrusions. This expansion is reflected especially in the *Harṣacarita,* whose author has vividly described agricultural activities. Another image that emerges from descriptions in these texts is the presence of forest chieftains as powerful persons in their respective localities, who wielded control over their space and had a grip over the rich resources of the forest. As mighty people, they are shown to control their armies, which further suggests the important role they played in defending their respective forest regions without the assistance of any central authority. Gupta inscriptions of around the same period alluded to them as having their own kingdoms or *rājyas*, which had to be conquered and merged into the larger state.

The *Kirātārjunīyam* and *Harṣacarita* provided references to social groups like Kirātās and the Śabaras as the entrenched forest population. They are shown as powerful and capable people, who had a lifestyle much respected by these texts, as is revealed from their descriptions in the same. These images that we dwelt upon above were found to be contrary to those reflected in other sources. At a conceptual and theoretical level, there was a contemptuous view held of the forest and forest dwellers. The state and the social elite in general, while exerting control over its resources, simultaneously held negative attitudes towards the forest communities. The processes of historical reorientation of forest-dwelling communities meant inducting them into mainstream society, but this was almost always done at a low ritual level so that opprobrious attitudes towards them continued even after their areas of habitation demographically became part of larger kingdoms. In the last part of the chapter, we focused on ascetics and renouncers who made the forest sojourn an integral part of their lives, which were devoted to spiritual and meditative activities. Like in other Kāvya texts, the texts we studied are replete with references to the āśramas, which were an important part of the unfolding of events in their narratives. These āśramas, built in the precincts of the forest, provide an interesting meeting place where the binary of the civilised and the barbaric collapse. Hence, it can assuredly be said that the forest, by the fifth–seventh century CE, were no longer mysterious places that were wild and untamed.

The use of Kāvya texts for history writing has been a debatable issue for scholars looking to them for direct information on historical events and facts. While analysing the historical sense embedded in Kāvya texts, especially the Carita literature, Romila Thapar stated, 'it is recording the present but with the knowledge that it will be read in the future' (Thapar 2013: 472), thus suggesting that this type of literature does represent some aspects of the reality of their 'present'. Furthermore, the authors of these texts had a clear perspective behind writing them, and this perspective was necessarily 'historical', rooted in the context of their times. It can be said that if used carefully, the Kāvya texts can prove an efficient source in producing information about the past that is not available in other sources, and thus can act as a valid source for writing history beyond conventional political history.

Overall it can be surmised that the Kāvya genre of the Indian literary traditions to which the *Kirātārjunīyam* and the *Harṣacarita* belong is quite different and unique in terms of the way historical consciousness was baroquely embedded in these texts. It is our further submission that one needs to go beyond the ornate and embellished language of these texts, which otherwise defines them as fictional and overtly exaggerated, to procure the hidden underlying meanings in their narratives. Therefore, it can assuredly be said that when read skillfully, the Kāvya texts are very proficient and adequate in producing wholesome alternate histories, which can mirror the realities of the past.

Notes

Acknowledgements: This chapter has evolved from my M.Phil dissertation, which I completed at the University of Hyderabad in 2014 under the supervision of Professor Aloka Parasher Sen. I owe my sincere gratitude to her and to my other teachers—Professor Bhangya Bhukya, Dr M. N. Rajesh, and Dr V. J. Verghese—who gave me valuable suggestions.

1. For the complete historiography on the use of literary texts, specifically Kāvya texts in history writing, see unpublished M.Phil dissertation submitted by Mrinalini to the University of Hyderabad (Mrinalini 2015: 5–26).
2. Although the dating of the *Kirātārjunīyam* is a much-contested topic, scholars have agreed to a common time period and believe that this text was written most likely during the fifth century CE. However, for the *Harṣacarita*, scholars unanimously agreed to seventh century CE as sound references have been found to support the theory that the text was written by a poet named Banabhatta, who was also the court poet of King Harsha of Kannauj. For the full discussion about the dating of the *Kirātārjunīyam* and *Harṣacarita,* see Mrinalini (2015: 28–36)
3. For a recent full-fledged discussion over terms like *vana*, *araṇya*, and *aṭavi,* see Parasher Sen (2019: 127–132).
4. G. D. Sontheimer is of the opinion that the forests were considered safe by all the different sects of the Buddhists, the Brahmins, the Saṃyāsins, the Saivites, the Lingāyats, and so on for attaining spiritual vision and revelation, which ultimately impelled them to compose principles of universal application (Sontheimer 1994: 146).

References

Ali, Daud, 2006. *Courtly Culture and Political Life in Early Medieval India*. London: Cambridge University Press.

Apte, V. S. 1965. *The Practical Sanskrit English Dictionary*. Delhi: Motilal Banarsidass.

Chattopadhyaya, Brajadulal. 2003. *Studying Early India: Archaeology, Texts, and Historical Issues*. New Delhi: Permanent Black.

———. 2017. *The Concept of Bharatvarsha and Other Essays*. Ranikhet: Permanent Black.

Cowell, E. P. and P. W. Thomas (trans.). 2004. *Harṣacarita by Bāṇabhaṭṭa*. New Delhi: Global Vision Publishing House.

Gadgil, Madhav and Romila Thapar. 1990. 'Human Ecology in India: Some Historical Perspectives'. *Interdisciplinary Science Reviews* 15(3): 209–223.

Gadgil, Madhav and Ramachandra Guha. 1993. *This Fissured Land*. Delhi: Oxford University Press.

Jha, D. N. 2005. *Early India: A Concise History*. New Delhi: Manohar.

Kaul, Shonaleeka. 2010. *Imagining the Urban: Sanskrit and the City in Early India*. Ranikhet: Permanent Black.

Malamoud, Charles. 1996. *Cooking the World: Ritual and Thought in Early India*. New Delhi: Oxford University Press.

Misra Narayan, Badri (trans.). 2012. *Kirātārjunīyam*. Varanasi: Chaukhambha Surbharati Prakashan.

Monier-Williams, Monier. 1889. *A Sanskrit-English Dictionary*. New Delhi: Motilal Banarsidass Pvt. Ltd.

Mrinalini. 2015. 'Depiction of Forest in Ancient Kāvya Literature: The Harṣacarita and Kirātārjunīyam', M.Phil dissertation (Unpublished). University of Hyderabad.

Parasher Sen, Aloka (ed.). 2004. *Subordinate and Marginal Groups in Early India*. New Delhi: Oxford University Press.

Parasher Sen, Aloka. 2012. 'Of Tribes, Hunters, and Barbarians: Forest Dwellers in the Mauryan Period'. In Mahesh Rangarajan (ed.), *India's Environmental History: From Ancient Times to the Colonial Period*, 127–151. New Delhi: Permanent Black.

———. 2019. 'Habitations, Woods and the Wild: Differentiating "Forests" in Early India'. In Kumkum Roy and Naina Dayal (eds), *Questioning Paradigms, Constructing History: A Festschrift for Romila Thapar*, 124–141. New Delhi: Aleph Book Company.

Pathak, V. S. 1997. *Ancient Historians of India: A Study in Historical Biographies*. Lucknow: Hindustani Book Depot.

Pathak, Jagganatha (trans.). 2012. *Harṣacaritam*. Varanasi: Chowkhmaba Vidyabhawan.

Peterson, Indira. 2003. *Design and Rhetoric in a Sanskrit Court Epic: The Kirātārjunīya of Bhāravi*. New York: State University of New York Press.

Sagreiya, K. P. 1967. *Forests and Forestry*. New Delhi: National Book Trust of India.

Sahu, Bhairabi P. (ed.). 2004. *Land System and Rural Society in Early India*. New Delhi: Manohar.

Sharma, Ram Sharan. 2005. *Aspects of Political Ideas and Institutions in Ancient India*. Delhi: Motilal Banarsidass.

Singh, Upinder. 2008. *A History of Ancient and Early Medieval India: From the Stone Age to the 12th Century*. New Delhi: Pearson Longman.

Sinha, Kanad. 2014. 'Mahābhārata's Spatial Politics and the Khanḍvadahana'. *Coldnoon Travel Poetics* 3(2): 79–105.

Soanes, Catherine, 2011. *Oxford English Mini Dictionary*. Delhi: Oxford University Press.

Sontheimer, Gunther D. 1994. 'The Vana and the Kṣetra: The Tribal background to some famous Cults in Eastern India'. In G. C. Tripathi and Hermann Kulke (eds), *Religion and Society in Eastern India: The Eschmann Memorial Lecture, The Eschmann Memorial Fund*, 117–164. New Delhi: Manohar Publishers & Distributors.

Thapar, Romila. 1987. *Ancient Indian Social History: Some Interpretations*. Delhi: Orient BlackSwan.

———. 2004. *Cultural Pasts: Essays in Early Indian history*. New Delhi: Oxford University Press.

———. 2009. 'Forests and Settlements'. In Mahesh Rangarajan(ed.), *Environmental Issues in India*, 33–42. New Delhi: Pearson Longman.

———. 2013. *The Past before Us: Historical Traditions of Early North India*. London: Harvard University Press.

Warder, A. K. 1974. *Indian Kāvya Literature*, Vol. II. Delhi: Motilal Banarsidass.

———. 1989. *Indian Kāvya Literature*, Vols I–IV. Delhi: Motilal Banarsidass.

Winternitz, Maurice. 1963. *A History of Indian Literature*, Vol. III. Delhi: Motilal Banarsidass.

———. 1977. *A History of Indian Literature*, Vols. I–IV. Delhi: Motilal Banarsidass.

4

The Idea of Water

A Reading of the *Cankam* Poems

Sreekala M. V.

> *When poetry is best, most healthy, most herself, she mingles together human nature and Nature and the love of each.*
>
> (Stopford A. Brooke 1920: 27)

Introduction

The Cankam age denotes an epoch in early Tamil history that is reflected in the collection of poems called the *Cankam* poems. The Cankam corpus is one of the important sources for understanding early Tamilakam.[1] The poems present the economy, society, and polity of the Cankam age, entwined in ecological imagery. Though not written as a record of events, the poems can be used to understand the historical sensibilities of early Tamilakam. Historians have attributed different dates to this age. K. A. Nilakanta Sastri places it in the first three or four centuries of the Common Era (Sastri 1958: 110), while Upinder Singh suggests that these were composed between the third century BCE and third century CE (Singh 2016: 27). The Tamil grammar text *Tolkkāppiyam* describes the form and content of the Cankam poems in the form of prescriptive rules in the third section, *Porulatikaram*. Vaiyapuri Pillai places *Tolkkāppiyam* in the latter half of the fifth century CE (Vaiyapuri Pillai 1957: 65). Classified into two themes, *akam* or the interior, consisting of love poems, and *puram* or the exterior, consisting of war poems, the Cankam poems draw a picture of early Tamil society. The *tinai* concept or the division of early Tamilakam into five ecological zones helps the readers to understand the different types of subsistence and living patterns. *Kurinci* (mountains), *mullai* (forests), *palai* (arid regions), *marutam* (wetlands), and *neytal* (coastal regions) were the five divisions. K. Sivathamby has used the tinai concept to understand society and economy. He opines that the contemporary existence of five types of subsistence patterns does not agree with the idea of unilinear evolution, and illustrates the law of uneven development. Further, he observes that in each of these areas, people were living in different stages of civilisation (Sivathamby 1974: 26).

Poetry is a product of the imagination, a work of fiction. However, events, people, and places are diffused in it, making it a carrier of history. A clear distinction between history and fiction cannot be located here. As Northrop Frye has opined, 'every work of literature has both a fictional and a thematic aspect, and the question of which is more important is often simply a matter of opinion or emphasis in interpretation' (Frye 1957: 53).While considering poetry and other works of imagination as sources of history, one needs to understand what history can be, besides being a mere record of events. As Hayden White observes, 'historical narratives are not only models of past events and processes, but also metaphorical statements which suggest a relation of similitude between such events and processes' (White 1978: 88). Insights offered by Frye and White provide us with the rationale to proceed with using ancient Tamil poems as ways of understanding human sensibilities around water in the Cankam age.

A close connection between man and nature, within the tropes of love and longing, forms the major essence of the poems. It has been aptly stated: 'The Tamil poets made man their greatest study, not man of one class or society, but ideal man and universal man. They were expected to be both psychologists and naturalists, and nature was important to them only in relation to man' (Adigal 1966: 43). This chapter is an attempt to understand the interaction between man and water in early Tamil society. The earliest extant Tamil work, the *Tolkkāppiyam*, has a metaphorical reference to water regulation: 'Like the Grand Anicut which stops water gushing with great force, a warrior blocks his enemy forces.'[2] A blending of eco-landscapes and mindscapes makes Cankam poems a source for understanding the lives of the people. One can find tropes that invoke economy, ecology, and a literary romantic mood in these poems, which have to be unravelled while we delve into the intimate relationship that human beings had with water. In some of the poems, the techniques to control water have been explained directly while in some others, the presence of reservoirs and embankments have been merely mentioned, entwined with the emotions of love and longing, thus giving us varied imagery of water.

The relationship between water and society in these texts has been primarily shaped by the patterns of usage of water resources. In fact, one concurs with Strang that 'Water is a metaphor for social, economic and political relationships—a barometer to the extent to which identity, power and resources are shared' (Strang 2004: 21). In early Tamilakam, different social groups made attempts to gain control over water resources. Agrarian activities required the systematic usage of water, which led to the implementation of various irrigation techniques. Channels and reservoirs were used to tame irregular flows of water. The references to accessibility of water, water rights, ownership of tanks, and so on enable us to draw a picture of the socio-economic position of the people, the attitude of the state towards water issues, and the pattern of the economy that existed. This chapter shall take a deeper look at the various ways in which water as an entity was conceived and used by early Tamil society. It is to be emphasised that 'The role of irrigation in society has to be studied in the light of man-environment relationship' (Sankaran 2001: 19). There are manifestations of the human–nature relationship, but the interaction with water resources is one of the most significant among them. Further, 'If nature cannot be understood apart from the social making of it, social life itself cannot be removed from nature' (Mosse 2003: 3). Channelising water and building techniques of irrigation were results of the system of water flow in each region. This, in turn, led to the development of agriculture, and also concomitantly contributed to the creation of the social and political structure of the region. In an explication of this phenomenon, David Mosse writes:

> The impounding of water in reservoirs creates a shared resource requiring cooperation within and between villages. As a common pool resource whose joint use is subtractive, irrigation water requires social arrangements for distribution and rationing in times of shortage, as well as for higher order regulation of water rights and dispute arbitration (ibid.: 4).

Water resources were directly linked to the means of livelihood adopted by the inhabitants of an area, which, in concurrence with Mosse, we argue, directly led to the formation of various social categories. He writes: 'The physical constraints of irrigation technology have influenced social organization in various ways' (Mosse 2003: 4). The management of water bodies and tank systems was not uniform across regions. These methods have to be studied and analysed differently, according to the eco-type of that region. As Mosse has said in his study on the rule of water, irrigation can be studied in different ways. Irrigation can be seen as an engineered paradigm which conceives of itself as a mathematically modelled system, which can be engineered to maximise water control. This view conceives of irrigation as bounded and knowable. The other perspective focuses on human behaviour. Here, technology is not seen as a fixed arrangement of science, but as what people do. Water, as an entity, is important for different strata of society. It becomes the basis of livelihood for one, while it can be a sphere of display of power for the other. We have analysed the different roles played by the same ecological resource, and the various perspectives towards procuring and managing it have been studied in this chapter.

It has been well-researched by scholars that irrigation was significant in south India for various reasons. On its necessity and character, Rajan writes:

> A series of networks of channels and reservoirs are used to control unruly water flowing over dry plains. A well-built irrigation system

> can bring more rent to the landowner and give better employment to the landless. It can also bring better returns to the cultivator of the land. In short, it can be said that a sound irrigation system can make the rural economy stable by enhancing the income of different sections (Rajan 2008: 2).

Since mountains are not high enough to provide rainfall throughout the year and the rivers are not perennial, artificial reservoirs or canals become important for the same reason throughout its history.

Tracing the origins of artificial irrigation, one needs to first look at the Megalithic Age.[3] The Megalithic monuments were mostly found on rocky high grounds as the availability of stones was ensured there. Another important factor to be noted is that most of these sites were located in proximity to large reservoirs or rivers. Evidence from sites such as Porkalam in Kerala, Maski and Brahmagiri in Karnataka, and Kunrattur and Amirtamangalam in Tamil Nadu show that the manufacture and use of iron implements as well as the first large-scale agricultural communities belong to the Megalithic Age. It can also be inferred from this that rice cultivation simultaneously with the use of iron implements began in this age. This culture, however, did not originate in the preceding Neolithic culture. The absence of a transitional culture, or a Chalcolithic Age (that is, the transitional period between the Neolithic and the Bronze Age in most parts of India) in south India and the presence of advanced technology lead us to the inference that this culture of iron implements was of local origin. The origins of the artificial tank irrigation system can, in all probability, be traced to the Megalithic tradition (Srinivasan 1991: 4) in south India. Peasant families, with inter-family cooperation, had to partake of dryland cultivation,which was essential in south India since irrigated land was scarce. If the water supply was regular and adequate, the value of the land certainly increased (Ludden 1978: 1). Therefore, water management becomes an indispensable component of society. As the poet Avvaiyyār had said: '*niragam porundiya uragattiru*',[4] that is, 'reside in a place where there is plenty of water'.

Interlinking Ecology and Polity: State and Water Resources

The nexus between the resource and the polity is complex. Resource appropriation and utilisation is a source of constant conflict, even to this day. Water is an important and scarce resource that rulers always tried to acquire. The interlinking of ecology and polity found in the Cankam poems gives new meaning to the resources of the country. Rulers tried to take over the water resources of the territories they invaded, and destroyed the reservoirs and tanks of rival rulers. Special measures were taken to ensure that these were guarded against attack. Reclamation of land, which included forest lands, barren lands, wastelands, inundated lands, and silted lands, was a task taken up by rulers. Land reclamation was a costly procedure, especially the reclamation of silted land, and therefore taking the help of the apex authority was necessary for farmers and village bodies. Bringing uncultivated land under cultivation was an act of valour and respect, praised by bards and subjects alike. The Cheras, Cholas, and the Pandyas took great steps to bring land under cultivation and increase production so as to make their respective territories prosperous. The building of tanks, canals, sluices, and so on, and facilitating irrigation was considered the duty of the king. Sometimes, these works were taken up by villages and private individuals.

The efficient management of resources was necessary for an economy to prosper. In early Tamilakam, the general understanding was that it was the duty of the king to protect and manage water resources, and protect agriculture. Scholars have understood the role of the king in water resource management in different ways. Karl A. Wittfogel, in his work *Oriental Despotism*, has stated that civilisations whose agriculture was dependent upon large-scale waterworks for irrigation and flood control were 'hydraulic civilizations'. However, there is a clear distinction between hydraulic and hydroagricultural systems, with the latter referring to small-scale irrigated agriculture, either owned by an individual or a small community. According to Wittfogel:

> If irrigation farming depends on the effective handling of a major supply of water, the distinctive quality of water—its tendency to gather in bulk—becomes institutionally decisive. A large quantity of water can be channelled and kept within bounds only by the use of mass labour; and this mass labour must be coordinated, disciplined, and led (Wittfogel 1957: 18).

This argument states that control over hydraulic resources decided political power and economic dominance. Irrigation technology in south India, according to David Mosse, was not developed simply out of the need for water, but through power relations, including the political choices of the administrative bodies, and cultural specificities of each society. Hydrology has been politically manipulated over the years. Changing the physical flow of water by building sluices and changing the height of weirs to satisfy the needs of the local elites was a common practice. Water flows shape social and political institutions and legitimise them as well. There is the story of a Maravar king who dropped flowers into the flowing water of a channel excavated by him. The passage of the flowers resolved an inter-village dispute over rights over the canal by revealing the natural flow of the water (Mosse 2003: 4). Thus, water was considered a lifeline for people in these parts. Boundary disputes and questions of accessibility were always present around a source of water. Water disputes were common all through history. It is in this context that the apex political authority of the territory comes in to focus. Hart thus writes: 'In ancient Tamil society, the king was the central embodiment of the sacred powers that had to be present and under control for the proper functioning of society' (Hart 1975: 13).

Land Reclamation

Rulers undertook the task of clearing forests and wastelands and making villages and agricultural lands out of them, references to which can be seen in the Cankam poems. Reclamation of forest land and wasteland was often taken up by political authorities in different time periods. Srinivasan has elaborately explained that reclamation of land was practised in different ways. Clearing forest lands and bringing them under cultivation for the first time and opening up irrigation facilities in these new settlements was one method of reclamation. Cultivable lands which had been left uncultivated for long were also brought back under cultivation. Reclamation of forest land was mainly due to the pressure of the increasing population. The state encouraged reclamation work by giving tax concessions. Three types of uncultivated lands were brought under cultivation—lands under cultivation for only a part of the year; fallow and wastelands; and finally, barren lands. Some lands were submerged under water during the rainy season, and were brought under cultivation during the dry season. Terms such as *āridupadugai* and *ēri-k-kōppu* denote the lands that go under floodwater (Srinivasan 1991: 47).

> When anger makes his red eyes blaze,
> The line of minor shepherd kings
> And Irungoval's race he wrecks.
> Where forests were, now hamlets rise
> He deepens tanks, makes rich the land
> Expands Uranthai where are seen
> High mansions. Makes secure its shrine
> And people....
> *Pattinappalai* 350–360 (Chelliah 1962: 47).

In the above lines, Uruthirankananar states that Karikala Chola made villages out of forests and deepened the tanks, which was indicative of his visionary water policies. The line '*kadu konru nadaki kulam tottu valam perukki*' indicates that the king cleared forests and expanded his territory. He shifted the Chola capital from Urunthai or Uraiyur to the port city of Kaveripoompattinam. The details of land reclamation are best illustrated in another poem below.

> In the *kurinchi* tract are mountains high where grow
> The short-stalked *thorai* rice on uplands sown
> From which the Akhil tree and the sandal wood
> Have been well cleared, the long-stalked pepper white,
> White rice and *aivanna* paddy mixed with it,
> Green pepper, ginger, turmeric, *tinai* these

And other plants do grow luxuriant there.
Maduraikanchi 294–300 (Chelliah 1962: 247).

Here, the poet Mankudimaruthanar is explaining the process of clearing trees on the mountains to cultivate pepper, paddy, and so on. Sandalwood and eagle wood (*akhil*) were cleared in the process. In the *Puranānūru*, Perumchithiranar describes the reclamation that took place on the Muthiram hill in the Palani mountain range. It is noted that this was carried out by the benevolent ruler Kumanan.[5] Besides the supreme political authority, there were several agencies like the village assembly, village communities, temples, and private individuals whose involvement in this direction was not only encouraging, but also substantial.

Water Policies in the Cankam Age

The raising of embankments, cutting canals, and digging of tanks were taken up by the rulers in the Cankam age. Literary and epigraphic evidence provide information on state initiatives for the development of irrigation facilities. A Tamil Brāhmī inscription, dated 200 BCE, from Mutalaikkulam village of Ramanathapuram district mentions the erection of a large tank by the *ūrār* of Vempirur[6] (Mahadevan 2003: 367).

You are the lord of the land
Watered by Kaveri and its branches. . . .
Listen to me and not gossips
If rains fail and harvests are bad
If something unusual affects people
This world will blame the king!
Take care of your farmers if you know this.
Puranānūru poem no. 35 (Parameswaran Pillai 1969: 61).[7]

This poem by Vellaikudi Nākanār is addressed to Chōlan Kulamutrathu Thunjiya Killivalavan. The poet expresses his concerns about farmers, agriculture, and rainfall. He requests the king to not listen to slanderers but bring about developments for the people. The poem goes on to narrate that the king should make efforts to protect farmers and other communities. Such policies would earn him the praise of even his enemies. It has also been pointed out that the poet was granted exemption from tax by singing this poem.[8]

The Cholas were pioneers in the construction of reservoirs and tanks. The state implemented a range of reforms, such as land grants, remission of taxes, and construction of embankments. The Grand Anicut, known popularly as Kallanai, built across the Kaveri in the Tanjavur district of Tamil Nadu, is one of the earliest state initiatives in water regulation. Its construction is attributed to Karikala Chola, who built an embankment across the river in the second century BCE.[9] The *Solamandalasatakam* mentions a construction on the banks of the Kaveri. The line '*Kaveri chiranda karai kallal anaikatta*' portrays that a *kallanai* or a water-regulator structure of stone was built across the Kaveri. He tamed the river Kaveri with this act of building flood tanks, cutting inundation channels, and strengthening the embankments. Karikala gained various epithets because of his policies such as *Karikal Peruvalathan* and *Kaverinathan*. *Pattinappalai* uses the latter title for him, which means 'Lord of Kaveri', for having successfully tamed the violent river, as discussed above. Since flood waters routinely breached the banks and silted cultivable lands, it was necessary to tame the river and cut inundation channels to use the water for irrigation.

Even prior to Karikala Chola and his water policies, the Kaveri was manifestly the source of fertility and prosperity. The abundance of water gave the land the name *Punal Nadu*, or land well-watered. This probably referred also to the frequent flooding of the Kaveri. The river was also called Ponni (Aravamuthan 1925: 8). In fact, the river changed its course frequently. There were several branches of the Kaveri—the Vennaru and the Arisilaru being the important ones.

> But I will not leave the girl
> with flowing, thick hair,
> ....pretty like the cool, rippled
> sands of Arisil River surrounding

Ampar town with tall flags tied to
.... ropes, belonging to King Killi.
Naṟṟinai 141.[10]

This poem in *Naṟṟinai* written by Salliyankumaranār describes the Arisil river surrounding the town of Ampar, which belonged to a king called Killi. The words *Paḷan Kaveri* and *Kollidam* appear frequently. The term 'Paḷan Kaveri' is proof of the fact that Kaveri changed its course. A new branch would be given a different name to distinguish it from the old one. For a later period, Appar and Tirunanasambandar had in their hymns also stressed on the importance of this river. Appar has the phrase *'paranthu paayum kavirinīr alaikindra karaiyil'*, which means 'against whose banks the water of Kaveri which flows spreading through many channels, dashes' (Thevaram, song no. 1820).[11] Tirunanasambandar describes it as *'kadal pol paranthu virintha kāveri'*, which means 'the Kaveri which is like the sea' (Thevaram, song no. 726).[12]

The interaction between the ruling class and the subjects regarding resource management was considered important. The rulers appointed guardians for reservoirs and tanks because the latter were targeted by enemies. Rulers often executed condemnable actions such as destroying the cultivable lands of their rival kings.

Your vast army proceeds for expedition
With its swift horses
....destroying fertile cultivable lands
And bathing elephants in their reservoirs.
Puranānūru, poem no. 16 (Parameswaran Pillai 1969: 23).

Here, Pandarankannnanar narrates the conquests of Cholan Irachachuyam Vetta Perunarkilli. This poem criticises the king for damaging the environmental resources as part of his expeditions. It indicates that the king is destroying productive lands and making the water sources of the rival lands unusable. The *Pattinappalai* also testifies that agricultural fields and tanks were made 'waterless' by the conquerors, as in the statement:*'Cheruvum vaviyum mayangu nirattru.'*

Her eyes attack without fail, those who
she sees, like the spears thrown at enemies
by Palaiyan, commander of the Chōla
king with victorious spears and elephants
with ornaments, lord of Pōōr with groves
and sluice gates with heavy floods, where
long bamboo poles cannot measure the
depth of the River Kāviri.
Akanānūru 326.[13]

In this poem, Paranar describes the brave Chola commander Palaiyan, and Pōōr, a place that had heavy floods and sluice gates. Kaveri was said to run deep here, so much so that even bamboo poles could not measure its depth. It is suggested that the town of Pōōr could be inundated with the Kaveri, and therefore, the presence of sluice gates is mentioned. This further suggests that the sluice gates could be the beginning of a canal or a reservoir to channel flood water, often for irrigation.

The Pandya rulers also initiated irrigation policies. It is quite clear that the later Pandyas had clear agrarian policies, as indicated in the poem below.

Those who bring together earth and water create life
You might want to conquer lands and gain heavenly pleasure
But O brave Ceḷiyan!
You should heed my advice and act quickly
Construct dams for water to collect…
For in this world, those who build none will not be praised.
Puranānūru 18 (Parameswaran Pillai 1969: 28).

Here, Kudapulaviyanar addresses the Pandiyan ruler Neduncheḷiyan. He recommends that the king initiate agrarian and irrigation policies. Rulers showed a keen interest in patronising poets and incorporating their creative suggestions in their administration. Peter Burke's understanding of patronage is relevant here. Burke observes that the three main motives for patronage were piety, prestige, and pleasure (Burke 2014: 103). Establishing a connection with the sacred was necessary for the legitimisation of power.

The king was an agent of the sacred and held a staff symbolising the connection between the sacred and the profane worlds. The staff of an unjust king would be broken, severing his connection with the sacred (*Cilappatikāram* 16.216) (Dikshitar 1978). The prestige of the state and the ruler had to be protected by implementing beneficial policies. The poets suggested some of these policies that would enhance the prosperity and pleasure of the subjects, which in turn would gauge the competence of a ruler.

The Pandyan territory, Pandiamandalam, was divided into several sub-regions or *nadus*, each of them being an agricultural unit. A decentralised agrarian administration catered to the needs of the subjects by providing facilities such as *vayakkāl* or a field channel, *nattukkāl* or district channel, and *ūrkuḷam* or village tanks. The Vaigai river was a major source of irrigation in this region. Rain-fed tanks were also extensively used. The Vaigai bed inscription by a Pandyan ruler, Sentan (also referred to as Jayantavarman, in Sinnamanur copper plate inscription [Sastri 1929: 23–24]) records the construction of a *mataku* or sluice, and the excavation of a *kāl* or channel. The inscription reads as follows: '*...cellanirkkavaigai [con] mataku ma...duttaarikesariyanenpeyarittukarodu... vittukanttaiodaiadaitt*' (*Epigraphia Indica* 1969: 27–32, 38). It can be inferred from the inscription that the construction of this sluice had been initiated by the king, and named after his son, Arikesari. It is an example of effective state involvement in water regulation.

This tendency of sluice constructions initiated by the state continued into later centuries as indicated by epigraphic evidences from the seventh and eighth centuries. In these examples, two types of technological advancements in irrigation are described. One was *nulitteruvitta* or the straight-line technique, and the other was *kartthumpu* or stone sluices that were used instead of Palmyra tree trunks. An advancement in techniques is noted, in that dressed stones were used instead of traditional rubble. The later Pandyas followed much the same technique. The poems clearly show that the rulers were prepared to spend huge amounts from their treasuries to build reservoirs, tanks, wells, etc., (Srinivasan 2016: 169). This shows that water management was considered a necessity. The masses nurtured a strong conviction that it was the responsibility of the king to protect this resource.

> .... bright bangles,
> beautiful like Sirukudi village of Vānan,
> where king Ceḷiyan owning fast chariots
> and elephants built a fine, huge reservoir,
> and when the sluice gates are open,
> thick-finned *vālai* fish escape, swim
> through the canals, and reach the fields
> .... farmers with furrows beat them with sticks.
> *Naṟṟinai* 340.[14]

Nakkirar writes this with reference to Thalailanganattu Ceruventa Neduncheḷiyan. A metaphorical description of bangles slipping off the hand is used to indicate the huge reservoir built by Cheḷiyan. Sirukudi village of Vānan had a huge reservoir, again built by the king. Here, the term used for sluice gate is *maḍai*. The terms *nadumaḍai* (*maḍai* at the centre) and *kadaimaḍai* (*maḍai* at the end), which occur in later inscriptions, show that sluices were installed at different places. The term *perumkuḷam* also appears in the poem, indicating the presence of a large pond. The reservoir here is described as huge, with a sluice gate and a channel flowing into it. K. Rajan opines that this irrigation device called the sluice or *kumuli* should be considered one of the greatest inventions of mankind (Rajan 2008: 42). These technological advancements brought large tracts of semi-arid land in these parts under cultivation. *Maduraikanchi* also elucidates the diverse irrigation techniques and efficient agricultural activities in the Pandyan kingdom of Neduncheḷiyan.

> In thy domain is heard the sound of those
> Who stand in rows and irrigate their fields
> From tanks with basket-pails to well-sweeps tied
> And buckets strongly made and softly bound....
> *Maduraikanchi*, line nos 89–94 (Chelliah 1962: 237).

The above poem describes various irrigation techniques, such as *ambi* and *kiḻar* (baskets, pails, and buckets), and the paraphernalia involved in it. *Cilappatikāram* also provides an account of the equipment used for lifting water:

> By finding her (Kaveri) movement arrested by the barrier—the anicut with its doorway—she noisily leaps beyond it in the sportive mood natural to her first freshes.[15] No sound other than this can be heard. We can hear there neither the sound of the bucket nor of the water-lift; neither the usually loud picotah[16] nor the palm-leaf bucket used in irrigation.
> *Cilappatikāram*, Nadukankadai, Canto X, line nos 107–119 (Dikshitar 1978: 161).

> Their streets were damaged by your chariots
> You ploughed their lands with donkeys
> And made them wastelands!
> Driving your chariot across rival lands
> And bathing elephants in their reservoirs…
> *Puranānūru*, poem no. 15 (Parameswaran Pillai 1969: 21).

This poem by Nettimaiyar about Palyakasalai Mutukutumi Peruvaluti is an account of the destruction of cultivable lands. The valour of the king is heightened by his action of destroying enemy lands, and the poet praises the act. The title '*Palyakasalai*' indicates that he had conducted a *yajňa* or a Vedic sacrifice. His expeditions and ritual achievements are equally praised.

> Oh man from the prosperous town, where
> a male stork with short wing span, and
> back wet like the plastered area above
> house eaves, stalks very slowly silvery
> carp that are white like flower petals,
> in the water that flows rapidly through
> a strong sluice gate of a curved dam
> created with effort by farmers drunk
> happily with liquor….
> *Akanānūru*, poem no. 346.[17]

Nakkirar, the author of the *Nedunalvadai* and the *Tirumurugarrupadai*, has been considered a contemporary of Neduncheḷiyan. J. V. Chelliah opines that the chieftain described in *Nedunalvadai* is probably Nedunchelịyan, based on the graphic description of his solicitude for his soldiers (Chelliah 1962: 222). This poem by Nakkirar, which refers to a strong sluice gate (of a curved dam) built by farmers, can therefore be located during the reign of Nedunchelịyan. This poem gives the idea that the Pandya territory had a system whereby farmers would build sluices for irrigation. State-funded irrigation could thus be carried out in this decentralised manner.

From the above, one can discern that state initiatives and the collective management of water resources solved several issues. Problems such as floods or seasonal droughts were brought under control with the far-seeing policies of the rulers. Reclamation of wastelands and the subsequent expansion in cultivated area brought in revenue to the state exchequer. Efficient state interference ensured that water resources were regulated and made available for the subjects. The Cankam age witnessed man's struggle with nature, his efforts to regulate the resources, and eventually use them productively. Technological advancements were applied to channelise water resources for improving agriculture, and consequently the lives of the people.

Ocean: Imagery and Livelihood

The ocean was a powerful imagery in the Cankam poems. A source of water and means of livelihood, it could shape as well as take lives. Often described in poems as a mysterious water body, understanding the ocean has always been a difficult task. Cankam poems speak of this powerful water body as one that provided livelihoods to many. It stood for adventure, toil, memories, love, and so on. Coastal land poignantly became a symbol of separation. Within these tropes of love and longing, one can read about the lives and ways of the people of coastal areas, the neytal, and the experiences of people from other ecological zones visiting the region. Descriptions of travels along the coastal tract are graphically etched out in later texts as follows:

....Thou may'st go with a heart of confidence
....to the place
Whose name implies a town that's fortified,
Which thou wilt reach by road that passes through
The sea-coast tract. There hamlets thou wilt find
Surrounded by the emerald sea, and ponds
Of waters cool. The screw-pines washed by waves
Have flowers as white as swans....
Sirupanarrupadai, line nos 190–200 (Chelliah 1962: 155).

This description, sung by Natthatthanar around the sixth century CE, speaks about the land ruled by Nalliakodan, a minor king who ruled one part of the Chola kingdom after the fall of the dynasty. According to the poem, he was the ruler of Mavilangai. The names Lanka or Ilankai were used to refer to several different places. The place named Mavilangai mentioned here could be placed in North Arcot of present-day Tamil Nadu. The mention of Velur, also a part of North Arcot, in the poem adds strength to this idea. The poem describes a fortified town which, according to scholars, is a reference to Eyilpattinam on the seacoast (Chelliah 1962: 142). A description of the surroundings and the flora adds to the visual impact of the lines. Different occupations were carried out in the neytal or the coastal tract by different communities. While the *Umanar* were involved in salt production, the *Paratavar* were engaged in fishing.

As mentioned above, poems also speak in detail about the occupations dependent on the ocean. There is a description of the Umanar in Korkai, located in Pandya country, in the following words:

The king too is the lord of Korkai's port
Whose boundaries are set by leaping waves...
....Follow orderly
Salt traders' row of carts by strong bulls drawn.
Sirupanarrupadai 78–86 (Chelliah 1962: 149–151).

Rows of carts full of salt have been described as being drawn by strong bulls on the streets. Despite being a busy trade centre and a natural port, Korkai (Colchi) also engaged in salt production. Ptolemy has referred to this place as Kolkhai, that is, an emporium or market. The *Periplus of the Erythraean Sea* also refers to this place and says that the Pandyan kingdom extended north from Comari, including Korkai. The *Periplus* has mentioned this as a pearl fishing centre as well (Malekandathil 2015: 339–368).

> Rest there O Suppliant....
> ....thou'lt meet some noisy carts....
> The men that trade in salts adorned with wreaths
> Of woven leaves....
> They take with them spare bulls
> And go through the hamlets reached by lengthy roads
> Announcing the sale of salt. Bold strangers sell
> To those who rest from the journey of a day
> Rare, useful things obtained from hills and seas.
> *Perumpanatrupadai*, line nos 50–75 (Chelliah 1962: 109).

The Umanar's carts are described as those with perfectly placed spokes, which have roofs made of woven grass. In this example, the salt merchant's wife is shown as sitting in the front with her child. The men are described as having adorned themselves with garlands made of Neem leaves. They are shown walking in front of the cart, holding the long rope tied to the oxen, and are depicted as calling out the price of the salt. This indicated that they were travelling to different towns to sell their product. It is suggested that the merchants took a long route. Along the same route, merchants were found selling other things like rice and buttermilk on the way to help travellers on this long route.

Apart from the Umanar, the Paratavar also depended on the ocean for their livelihood. The term 'Paratavar' has been understood as people of the sea. The word *para* meant 'vast expanse' and *paravai* or *parappu* is said to mean 'the sea'. *Para* could also mean 'breadth'. *Paratu* is said to mean 'to spread' (Burrow and Emeneau 1984: 352). Various theories have been put forth about the origin of the Paratavars. According to V. Kanakasabhai Pillai, they had a Naga origin. He argued that they knew the charm to ward off dangers from that part of the sea where they dived (Kanakasabhai 1956: 45).

Fishermen and their lives also formed a major subject of many poems. A poem by Ammuvanar (*Naṟṟinai* 4) (Ramanujan 1985: 46) dwells on these aspects. This poem describes their livelihood and subsistence. They are described as moving from a small town to the sea, and are then said to wait to gauge when they could enter the waters. The poem narrates that they waited under the shade of the Laurel tree. While they did so, they are described as using this time to dry their nets. The poem goes on to tell us that the heroine here is asking whether the hero would take her to his place, where the carts of the salt merchants trading in white rock salt moved on the sands. The houses there were surrounded by salt pans. The poet depicts her as being worried about her mother's reaction to her affair, and she therefore hopes that the hero would take her away to his land, which is on the coast.

> O lion! Thou dost contend with Paratava chiefs
> That live in southern noisy villages.
> Who eat rice boiled with meat and *kuvai* roots
> Who love to swear and who attack their foes
> With bowls that smell of fish.
> *Maduraikanchi,* line nos 130–40 (Chelliah 1962: 239).

The above poem by Mankudi Maruthanar offers vivid descriptions of the lifestyles of Paratavars. It describes their staple diet and other consumptions. They ate boiled rice with meat. *Kuvai* roots were also consumed. They were depicted as possibly aggressive people because they swore a lot and attacked their enemies with their utensils, and as the poet has told us, their bowls smelt of fish. They were also called Mukkuvar. This is derived from the word *mung* or *muk*, which means 'to dive' or 'to immerse' (Burrow and Emeneau 1984: 449), and they were thus also called *Mutthukkulippar*. This term evidently denoted their means of livelihood, that is, those who dived for pearls. Pearl-fishing, as is well known, was an important economic activity that boosted trade. Pearls from the Pandya country were popular, and those pearls obtained by the Paratavar who dived for them in the ocean at Korkai travelled across the world after being taken to Muziris, well-known as a port in present-day Kerala. Therefore, the Mukkuvar or Paratavar of the Pandya country were the first communities in south India who initiated and significantly boosted international trade across the oceans. Pearls and gems from India were in high demand in the Yavanadeśa, a term that occurs in texts to describe either Greece or Rome.

The imagery of water is present in the stories that legitimise the identity and power of social groups. Ilanthiraiyan, who ruled from Kanchi and is mentioned in the *Perumpanatrupadai*, is an example. The name Ilanthiraiyan can be translated as 'young wave-man'. There are two legends regarding this name. The first is alluded to by Nachchinarkkiniar,who speaks of a Chola king who had descended to the lower world and married a Naga woman. The child born to them was cast adrift on the sea with a creeper (*tondai*) around the neck for identification. This child, the narrative goes on to tell us, was washed onto the shores of Chola country, and the king granted a portion of his kingdom to the child. Another explanation states that Ilanthiraiyan was the chief of Thirayer, a maritime tribe. Thirayer can be translated as sea-men. They were a sea-faring race, said to be originally from Bengal. Some of them settled in south India and adopted the tondai as their emblem (Chelliah 1962: 97–98).

Ocean as a Force of Destruction

The ocean was perceived as a tool of nature that could give as well as take life. *Katalkol* is an important concept that one needs to understand while studying the close connection of Tamil culture with water, especially the ocean. Land seized by the ocean is an image seen in several Cankam poems. The term 'Katalkol' has been translated in several ways. It is often equated with 'the Deluge', a Judeo-Christian concept. References to Katalkol can be found in various texts. It is believed that the works of the first two Cankams, the first in Tenmaturai and the second in Kapatapuram, were seized by the ocean.[18] Reference to this can be found in Nakkirar's *Iraiyanar Akapporul*. Though there is no direct reference to the loss of land and the loss of these works, scholars have studied this in connection with Lemuria or *Kumarikantam*. In the nineteenth century, Lemuria was imagined as a land that bridged India and Africa, which later disappeared into the ocean. Katalkol is thus an idea that was considered dreadful because of the destruction that it caused—of history and of the ancestral homeland.

Rather than being considered an actual geological event, different perceptions have created the idea that Katalkol was an explanatory device to establish the connection of Tamils to a land of fortune that has since been lost. It was also an attempt to trace the history of Tamil speakers as a single community. The catastrophe is tragic in two ways. First, it was an uncontrollable force of nature that caused the loss of lives and property. Second, it was also a force that led to the loss of a homeland for a large community. And perhaps for this reason *kumarinatu* or *kumarikkantam*,[19] which is the fabled continent seized by the sea, is today very much a part of the symbolic paraphernalia of late Tamil modernity (Ramaswamy 2005: 142, 229).

'Taming' the Ocean—Ship-building and Types of Boats

Conquering or taming the ocean, for livelihood and for adventure, has been a common phenomenon across cultures. Cankam poems present vivid descriptions of ships and the ship-building industry in ancient Tamilakam. Ships were built to suit the oceanic conditions. From rafts for shallow fishing to ships for long-distance trade, they were all built in ancient Tamilakam, and references to different types of boats and ships can be found in the Cankam poems. They can be analysed to understand the importance of the ship-building industry of the time. A poem describes a set of boats thus:

> O man from a town,
> where tightly tied boats look
> like stout-horned buffaloes
> playing in the stream!
> Will your father and mother
> scold you more than this

> naive young woman wearing
> bright bangles on her arms.
> *Ainkurunuru*, poem no. 98 (Iyer 1949: 47).

The above poem explains the structure of boats that bear a similarity to buffaloes. The word *ampi* means 'raft or float' (Burrow and Emeneau 1984: 17). In the Cankam poems, ampi was compared to a buffalo, or an elephant, or a bullock. There are poems that compare a bullock and a boat, and a poem from the *Kalithokai* suggests this as follows:

> Look here my friend! Look at this man! Being the son of cow herders, he sits on a bull with spots, and rides, appearing like a boat that moves in shallow water.[20]

These descriptions help us to get an idea about the shape of the boat and its protruding parts, which must refer to the planks and ribs of the boat. Another term used while referring to ships was *timil*. This has been noted in a poem in the *Puranānūru* thus:

> In the sky above us, with the Red Mars flickering there
> like a lantern on a boat in the middle of the ocean, we saw
> the full moon. . . .
> *Puranānūru* 60 (Parameswaran Pillai 1969: 96).

This poem, by Uraiyur Maruttuvan Thamotharanar, is about Cholan Kurappalithunjiya Perunthirumavalavan. The boat is described in the words '*munneerppattatimirchutar pol*', which means 'like timil in the middle of the ocean'. In general usage, 'timil' actually referred to the hump of a bull. This gives us an understanding of the shape and movement of the ship or catamaran mentioned here. Timil was used for pearl fishing as well as long voyages. A neytal poem in which the heroine's friend is talking to the hero has described pearl-fishing in Korkai and the boats those fishermen used in words such as '*valampurimulkiya van timil Paratavar*' (*Ainkurunuru* 350 by Chēnthan Kannanār) (Iyer 1949: 152). Here, the friend is describing Korkai, where she lived. The poem also speaks of fishermen who dived into the ocean to avoid shark attacks, and who were then welcomed with the sound of conches when they returned successfully.

Further, poems speak of pearls from the sea, bright bangles, and other wares that the merchants sold on the sea shore.

> In the *neytal* tract are found sparkling pearls
> Which the shining sea doth yield, bright bangles cut...
> And other wares merchants sell.
> Sea captains that sail o'er
> The ocean high in showy ships that come
> From large and distant countries take away
> The salt that's formed........
> *Maduraikanchi*, line nos 330–340 (Chelliah 1962: 247).

One can also get a visual description of the ship's appearance. '*Vilumiya navai perunir occunar*' is the reference for captains who sailed on ships. The word *navai* referred to a ship or a vessel that had masts and flags. Excavations at Alagankulam provide an insight into maritime activities through pot sherds on which hand drawings of the navai have been found.

> And therefore we are like boats in the western ocean that belong to some lord other than Ceran who commands his raging armies and runs his ships that carry gold so that no other vessels dare to travel those waters.
> *Puranānūru* 126 (Parameswaran Pillai 1969: 176).

Marokkathu Nappachalaiyar wrote this for his patron king Malaiyaman Thirumudikkari. The poet is saying that Kapilar, a most esteemed poet of the Sangam era, had praised the king so perfectly that he had left no space for others to perform better. Thus, he was feeling like a boat that was trying to challenge the ship of Kadal Pirakottiya Cenkuttuvan. The term used for the ship of Cenkuttuvan here is also 'navai'. The term *kalam* is also used to denote a small boat. The poems that refer to the gold and pepper trade use this term to denote their vessels. Made of wood, these were called *marakalams*. One such poem can be seen in the *Kuruntokai*:

> O Friend, look at this!
> The northerly wind is here

> *avarai* beans have grown and spread
> with their red flowers like
> beaks of parrots
> and jasmine like the teeth of wild cats
> His home, the gem yielding
> tall mountain has disappeared from view
> Like a ship disappearing in the ocean waves.
> *Kuruntokai*, poem no. 240 (Ezhuthachan 1999: 159).[21]

This poem, sung by Kollan Alisiyār, gives us an idea about the size of a kalam. Here, the heroine is distressed and is telling her friend that she is losing sight of the tall mountain where the hero lives as evening approaches. This is then compared to a ship in the ocean that was disappearing into the waves. Marakalams were used for sea-faring trade. Ships and boats were made of teakwood and coconut wood. These poems show that ship-building was thus an important activity. The variety of ships and boats is evident from the use of different terms to describe them. Vessels were designed according to their requirement. This shows the skill of artisans in making small rafts for fishing as well as huge ships that could carry tons of cargo.

Conclusion

The imagery of water in the Cankam poems is boundless. These poems of love and war contain a plethora of information on early Tamil society and the various exigencies of life around it. This chapter attempted to understand the role of water in Cankam literature and its various manifestations. The significance of such an understanding lies in mining the poems for the critical role that water played in everyday life and in the sustenance of the people. Thus, technological advancements in irrigation ensured that cultivation was possible in the arid and semi-arid areas of early Tamilakam. Equipment such as palm-leaf buckets, described in the poems, were economic and effective for daily use. Techniques of lifting water in the Cankam age paved the way for intensive cultivation, apart from the annual cropping system that was dependent on rain. Over time, water became a commercial resource and thus a concern for the state, which drew revenue on it for further conservation, development, and protection of this resource. The poems dwell vividly on how rulers ensured that their subjects had access to adequate hydraulic resources.

The impact of power on ecological resources is well-reflected in the poems. The nature of the environment was a major factor in deciding the model of the state. Water was not just a commercial or common pool resource, but a collective responsibility and an idea. In early Tamilakam, much as in the later periods, too, collective action was given importance. The poems discussed by us above describe instances wherein the villagers (ūrār) constructed a tank for themselves. This must have been funded by the *vendan* or chief, but the construction process was in all probability decentralised. Wittfogel's idea of hydraulic despotism is not relevant for early Tamilakam. Rulers initiated and financed the construction of major irrigation projects, such as the embankment project of Karikala Chola. However, direct state control did not exist in reorganising production.

The idea of the lost portions of the Cankam begins with the concept of the lost land of Lemuria. The popular imagination is that the sea had taken away the original homeland of the Tamils. The fear of the ocean and the equally alluring fantasy of the mysterious water body in the Cankam poems portray a land and people remembering the labours of loss, and at the same time, attempting to tame and conquer it. Water in the early Tamil imagination was a source of income, a channel for trade, destroyer of lands, and a mystery that hid their homeland and textual treasures. The various manifestations of how an important life-giving resource like water was visualised, used, and imagined by the poets of this early period is a valuable way to remember that humankind has always been intrinsically related to the vagaries or plentitude of water or the lack of it, its fear and its mystery, and most importantly, the impossibility of life without it. These perceptions of the past remain relevant for understanding and acting on the troubled present of our water resources and their fragile future.

Notes

Acknowledgements: I wish to express my gratitude to Professor Aloka Parasher Sen for helping and guiding me in writing this chapter. I would also like to thank the Centre for Historical Studies, Jawaharlal Nehru University for providing all the facilities for my research. I also wish to thank Professor Vijaya Ramaswamy for guiding me through my M. Phil research.

1. Tamilakam refers to the geographical region that includes the present day regions of Tamil Nadu, Puducherry, Kerala, Lakshadweep, and parts of Andhra Pradesh and Karnataka. The earliest use of this term can be found in the Cankam anthology *Puranānūru,* which can be dated back approximately to the second century BCE.
2. *Porulatikaram of Tolkkāppiyam*, Verse 63.
3. Mortimer Wheeler (1948) observes that the Megalithic Age in south India can be placed between 200 BCE and 50 CE.
4. *Konṛaivendan* of Avvaiyyār, Verse 51
5. The poet describes the benevolence and the policies of Kumanan in verses 158–163 of the *Puranānūru* (Parameswaran Pillai 1969: 218–227).
6. The inscription reads: '*vempirurperayamcetavar*'. The term *ūrār* refers to villagers (Burrow and Emeneau 1984: 73).
7. I have translated all the poems from *Puranānūru* from Malayalam. Tamil to Malayalam translations were carried out by V. R. Parameswaran Pillai.
8. V. R. Parameswaran Pillai mentions this in his translation (Parameswaran Pillai 1969: 61).
9. Karikala Chola built an embankment to save the surrounding areas from river floods. This was later rebuilt by colonial administrators. Captain Coldwell repaired it in 1804, and Major Sim worked on it again and added undersluices in 1829. Available at https://www.thehindu.com/news/cities/Tiruchirapalli/a-rock-solid-project-that-has-survived-2000-years/article4491152.ece (accessed November 2021).
10. *Naṛṛinai* 141 in Vaidehi Herbert, Ettuthokai—Natrinai 1–200, *Cankam Poems Translated by Vaidehi.* Available at https://sangamtranslationsbyvaidehi.com/ettuthokai-natrinai-1-200/ (accessed November 2021).
11. Srinivasan 1991: 47, also available at http://www.thevaaram.org/thirumurai_1/songview.php?thiru=5&Song_idField=50750&padhi=075&startLimit=1&limitPerPage=1&sortBy=&ampsortOrder=DESC (accessed November 2021).
12. Srinivasan 1991: 47, also available at http://thevaaram.org/thirumurai_1/songview.php?thiru=1&Song_idField=10670&padhi=067&startLimit=5

&limitPerPage=1&sortBy=&ampsortOrder=DESC (accessed November 2021).

13. *Akanāṉūru* 326 in Vaidehi Herbert, Ettuthokai—Akananuru 301–400, *Cankam Poems Translated by Vaidehi.* Available at https://sangamtranslationsbyvaidehi.com/ettuthokai-akananuru-301-400/ (accessed November 2021).
14. *Naṟṟinai* 340 in Vaidehi Herbert. Ettuthokai—Natrinai 201–400. *Cankam Poems Translated by Vaidehi.* Available at https://sangamtranslationsbyvaidehi.com/ettuthokai-natrinai-2-2/(accessed November 2021).
15. The word in the poem is *putunīr*, which would mean new water. Dikshitar has translated it as 'freshes'(Dikshitar 1978:161).
16. Picotah or Pecottah was a commonly used water-lifting tool. It has a bucket/basket and a heavy weight attached on either side of a log balanced on a fulcrum. The stone is lowered to lift the filled bucket.
17. *Akanāṉūru* 346 in Vaidehi Herbert, Ettuthokai—Akananuru 301–400, *Cankam Poems Translated by Vaidehi.*Available at https://Sangamtranslationsbyvaidehi.com/ettuthokai-akananuru-301-400/ (accessed November 2021).
18. The first Cankam or the mutarcankam held in Tenmaturai is believed to have lasted 4400 years. The legend says that some gods, including Siva, Muruga and Kubera were members of this Cankam. The second Cankam or itaicankam, convened in Kapatapuram is believed to have lasted for 3700 years. Both these places were submerged by the sea and all the works produced in these gatherings were never retrieved (Iyengar 2001[1929]: 230).
19. Legends describe kumarinatu or kumarikkantam as the cradle of Tamil culture. Further, some legends say that the first two Cankams took place on this lost continent.
20. *Kalithokai* 103 in Vaidehi Herbert, Ettuthokai—Kalithokai 101–117, *Cankam Poems Translated by Vaidehi.* Available at https://sangamtranslationsbyvaidehi.com/ettuthokai-kalithokai-101-117-mullai/ (accessed November 2021).
21. Translated from Malayalam by me. Tamil to Malayalam translation was done by K. N. Ezhuthachan.

References

Adigal, Thani Nayagam X. S. 1966. *Landscape and Poetry*. Bombay: Asia Publication House.

Aravamuthan, T. G. 1925. *The Kaveri, the Maukharis and the Sangam Age*. Madras: University of Madras.

Brooke, Stopford A. 1920. *Naturalism in English Poetry*. London and Toronto: J. M. Dent and Sons Ltd.

Burke, Peter. 2014. *The Italian Renaissance: Culture and Society in Italy*. Princeton and Oxford: Princeton University Press, 3e.

Burrow, T. and M. B. Emeneau. 1984. *A Dravidian Etymological Dictionary*. Oxford (Oxfordshire): Clarendon Press, 2e.

Chelliah, J. V. (trans.). 1962. *The Pattupattu—The Ten Tamil Idylls*. Thanjavur: Tamil University.

Dikshitar, V. R. Ramachandra. 1978. *The Cilappatikāram*. Tirunelveli: The South India Saiva Siddhanta Publishing Society.

Epigraphia Indica.1969, Vol. 38. New Delhi: Archaeological Survey of India.

Ezhuthachan, K. N. (trans.).1999. *Kuruntokai*. Thrissur: Kerala Sahitya Akademi.

Frye, Northrop. 1957. *Anatomy of Criticism*. New Jersey: Princeton University Press

Hart, George L. 1975. *The Poems of Ancient Tamil: Their Milieu and Their Sanskrit Counterparts*. London: University of California Press.

Herbert, Vaidehi (trans.) n. d. *Sangam Poems*. Available at https://sangam translationsbyvaidehi.com/ (accessed November 2021).

Iyengar, P. T. Srinivasa. 2001 [1929]. *History of the Tamils: From the Earliest Times to 600 AD*. New Delhi: Asian Educational Services.

Iyer, U. V. Swaminatha (ed.). 1949. *Ainkurunuru*. Chennai: Kalyanasundaranar.

Kanakasabhai, V. 1956. *The Tamils Eighteen Hundred Years Ago*. Tirunelveli: The South India Saiva Siddhanta Publishing Society.

Ludden, D. 1978. 'Ecological Zones and the Cultural Economy of Irrigation in Southern Tamil Nadu'. *Journal of South Asian Studies* 1(1): 1–13.

Mahadevan, Iravatham. 2003. *Early Tamil Epigraphy: From the Earliest Times to the Sixth Century A.D.* Chennai: Cre A.

Malekandathil, Pius. 2015. 'Muziris and the Trajectories of Maritime Trade in the Indian Ocean in the First Millennium CE'. In K. S. Mathew (ed.), *Imperial Rome, Indian Ocean and Muziris: New Perspectives on Maritime Trade*, 339–368. New Delhi: Manohar.

Manavalan A. A. 2007. *Porulatikaram of Tolkappiyam*. Chennai: International Institute of Tamil Studies.

Mosse, David. 2003. *The Rule of Water: Statecraft, Ecology and Collective Action in South India*. New Delhi: Oxford University Press.

Parameswaran Pillai, V. R. (trans.). 1969. *Puranānūru Pāttukalum Bhāshāntaravum*. Thrissur: Kerala Sahitya Akademi.

Rajan, K. 2008. *Ancient Irrigation Technology Sluice Technology in Tamil Nadu*. Thanjavur: Heritage India Trust.

Ramanujan, A. K. 1985. *Poems of Love and War: From the Eight Anthologies and the Ten Long Poems of Classical Tamil.* New York: Columbia University Press

Ramaswamy, Sumathi. 2005. *The Lost Land of Lemuria: Fabulous Geographies, Catastrophic Histories.* New Delhi: Permanent Black.

Sankaran, K. R. 2001. *Studies in the History of Tamil Nadu: Irrigation, Society, Temple, Literacy.* Thanjavur: Anandam Veliyiidu.

Sastri, K. A. N. 1929. *The Pāṇḍyan Kingdom from the Earliest Times to the Sixteenth Century.* London: Luzac.

———. 1958. *A History of South India from Prehistoric Times to the Fall of Vijayanagar.* Madras: Oxford University Press.

Singh, Upinder. 2016. *A History of Ancient and Early Medieval India: From the Stone Age to the 12th Century.* New Delhi: Pearson.

Sivathamby, K. 1974. 'Early South Indian Society and Economy: The Tinai Concept'. *Social Scientist* 3(5): 20–37.

———. 1998. *Studies in Ancient Tamil Society: Economy, Society, and State Formation.* Tamil Nadu: New Century Book House.

Srinivasan, T. M. 1991. *Irrigation and Water Supply South India 200 BC–1600 AD.* Madras: New Era Publications.

———. 2016. 'Agricultural Practices as Gleaned from the Tamil Literature of the Sangam Age'. *Indian Journal of History of Science* 51(1): 167–189.

Strang, Veronica. 2004. *The Meaning of Water.* London: Berg Publishers.

Vaiyapuri Pillai, S. 1957. *A History of Tamil Language and Literature.* Madras: New Century Book House.

Wheeler, R. M. 1948. 'Brahmagiri and Chandravalli 1947: Megalithic and Other Cultures in the Chitaldurg District Mysore State'. *Ancient India* (4): 202.

White, Hayden. 1978. *Tropics of Discourse: Essays in Cultural Criticism.* Baltimore and London: The John Hopkins University Press.

Wittfogel, Karl A. 1957. *Oriental Despotism.*New Haven, Conn.: Yale University Press.

PART II

Producing the Past

5

Identities in Fragments

Early Deccan in Inscriptions

Nairita Ghosh

Introduction

It is often stated that inscriptions are one of the most valuable sources in understanding the early history of a place and its people. An eminent epigraphist, D. C. Sircar, has pointed out that 'there is no aspect of life, culture and activities of the Indians that is not reflected in the inscriptions' (Sircar 1965: 12). Therefore, it seems worthwhile to take a look at the social fabric of the Deccan region between the second century BCE and fourth century CE through the lenses of epigraphy. The 275 inscriptions, selected from Lüders' List (Lüders 1920: Vol. X, 98–179), depict the many identities of the men and women of the Deccan who made donations at various Buddhist sites. These inscriptions, in many cases, are damaged and found in fragments. In some cases, the inscriptions comprised single lines containing the donor's name and the object of donation. Thus, one inscription from Kanheri (no. 987)[1] contains information about the donation of a *chaitya* (prayer hall), where the name of the donors' father is missing due to damage, and the name of one of the donors, Gajami[ta], is found in a fragmented condition. Another inscription at Kanheri (no. 991) is in such damaged condition that the only information that could be gathered was about the beginning of Buddhism. In another inscription from Bhattiprolu (no. 1332), a portion of the name of a *gōṭhī* (assembly/committee) member is missing due to fragmentation. Nevertheless, they successfully paint a lively picture of the numerous social groups, namely the administrative officials, *gahapati* (householder, landowner), *seṭhin* (leader merchant), *vaṇija/vanijaka* or *vāṇiya* (traders), *nēgama* (trader), *sathavāha* (caravaneer), along with various artisans and professional groups such as the *sēṭi* or *śreṇī* (guild), goṭhī, and *āvēsani* (foreman of artisanal organisations), coming forward and asserting their many identities by mentioning their names, kinship status, and the places they hailed from. The groups make an authentic proclamation of the objects they donated, thereby establishing their financial standing. (See Plates I–V, this volume.)

In the past, scholars have made use of these inscriptions to undertake various aspects of study. James Fergusson studied these fragmentary inscriptions to understand the fascinating architectural aspects of the Buddhist edifices at Amaravati (Fergusson 2004[1873]: 167–179). This was a foundational study and one that has increasingly been used in scholarship on the history of the eastern Deccan. S. Nagaraju, while studying the architectural aspects of the Buddhist sites of western Deccan, analysed the palaeographic features of these inscriptions. His in-depth study of the cave temple sites there took into account all relevant sources, and laid bare the meaning and context in which these inscriptions were inscribed (Nagaraju 1970: 42–49). Amita Ray also studied the architectural merit of the Buddhist sites at Amaravati and Nagarjunakonda while analysing these fragmentary inscriptions, but pertinently, her scholarship attempts to understand for the first time the degrees of popular participation in patronising Buddhism in the social context of the eastern Deccan (Ray 1983: 19–37). It is refreshing to find that while discussing the social dimensions of the study of Buddhism, primarily from texts, Uma Chakravarti (1987) brought in data from these so-called fragmentary inscriptions in an appendix to corroborate and reflect upon the larger social forces defining the acceptance of Buddhism as an ideology. From the perspective of economic history, Himanshu Prabha Ray was the first scholar who employed the Lüders' List of inscriptions to analyse the various merchant and artisanal groups of the western Deccan, in order to elaborate on the ultimate quest of her research—the relationship between the monasteries and the guilds, which were both entangled in the conduct of commerce under the Sātavāhanas (Ray 1986: 172–199). In a similar vein, but with the broader intention of understanding the underlying forces that led to Sanchi becoming an urban centre, Basant (2012) has effectively used these inscriptions to highlight the relationship that these communities had with the larger countryside. Parasher Sen has used some of these inscriptions to reflect on how this data can be used to study the culture of travelling within the subcontinent (Parasher Sen 2007: 47–90).

However, apart from some of these recent studies, a large majority of scholars who have studied these inscriptions to shed light on the socio-economic aspects of early Deccan have either ignored their value, or referred to them only perfunctorily as a corroborating source. As mentioned above, this is primarily because these inscriptions offer limited information and rarely provide long sentences or paragraphs that would permit us to gain a complete idea of the context they are referring to. Therefore, this chapter attempts to use the totality of the data culled from these fragmentary inscriptions by analysing the pattern of donations that the people of the Deccan made, either as individuals, or in groups. While it is well-known that they belonged to numerous professions and organisations, it is significant that in most cases, they travelled from home in order to make donations, primarily to the Buddhist *saṅghas* (monasteries). For a keen assessment, in this chapter we compare the inscriptional data with relevant sections of the *Manusmṛti* (Sharma 2014: 32–477), in order to argue that the fragmentary nature of the inscriptions under study can be read in a variety of ways, rather than being dismissed as incomplete sources of information. Therefore, we submit that it is imperative to examine the merit of these inscriptions and use them to construct a parallel and new narrative of the social history of the Deccan, one that is completely different from the narrative supplied by normative texts such as the *Manusmṛti*.

Personal and Geographical Place Names as Markers of Identity

We have noted that upholding personal names was a consistent feature of these fragmentary inscriptions. This information has helped us to define the social profile of the region. The donors came from varied social backgrounds, though a majority of them bore names that spoke of a Buddhist affiliation. Unlike the inscriptions found along the Karakoram highway, where people just inscribed their names on rock shoals without proclaiming their caste identity, kinship relations, or residency, in the Deccan inscriptions personal names are inscribed along with other details that provide interesting clues to their social identities (Parasher Sen 2007: 75). The suffixes of the name endings provide the professional identity of some donors, and in some cases the erstwhile religious affiliation of the person concerned has also been indicated. Names like Sivasama/Sivasarman (no.117), Ayama/Aryaman (no. 1174), and Bhadasama/Bhadrasarman (nos 1101, 1102) end with '*sarman*' or '*sama*' (in Prakrit), which clearly point toward the donors being *brāhmaṇas* (priests). However, the majority of the donors (twenty-six of them) bear the name-ending '*data*', which indicates that they belonged to the trading community. Names like Sulasadata (nos 996, 1037, 1179), Sivadata (nos 1040, 1065, 1077), Simhadata (no. 1090), Idragnidata (no. 1140), Utaradata (no. 1037), Vishnudata (nos 1079, 1137, 1148), and Godata (no. 1067), bear testimony to a strong merchant presence among the donor community. Also indicating affiliation to the trading community are names ending with '*guta*'/'*gupta*', but they are found in only three instances, such as Dharmaguta (nos 990, 1185) and Bodhiguta (no. 1130).

Another important name-ending is that of '*mita*', which is mentioned in twenty cases. Some of them are Gajamita (no. 987), Vijayamita (no. 987), Rohanimita (no. 996), and Budhamita (no. 1169). Interestingly, '*mita*' name-ending donors came from varied professional backgrounds, such as *hēraṇika/hēraṇaka* (treasurer) (nos 996, 1033), *mahāraṭhi* (chief) (no. 1088), *bhāṇaka* (preacher) (nos 1094, 1095), sathavāha (nos 1065, 1066), and gahapati (no. 1277). Names ending with '*pāla*' are mentioned in four cases, '*sēna*' in three cases, and these point to those social groups that were in positions of power and had some ruling capacity. The professional affiliation indicated by these name-endings enables us to postulate that they belonged to a class that, in the conventional *varṇa* (caste) hierarchy, could be said to belong largely to the *vaiśya* (traders, merchants) varṇa, though this is not clearly indicated in these inscriptions. The strategic position of Buddhist shrines in the Western Ghats, along the routes and networks of communication and pilgrimage, facilitated trade and commerce in this region (Ray 1986: 24–29). In the western part of the Deccan, the monasteries seem to have engaged in activities of a commercial nature, one of which was to supply monetary loans and other provisions to the sārthavāhas/sathavāhas[2] (Kosambi 1965: 182; Sarkar 1987: 623).

Innumerable names found in these inscriptions betray a definite Buddhist affiliation. Names such as Dhamagiri, Dhammavatsa, Dharmapala, Samghamitra, Sagharakhita, Samghadasi, Siddhartha, Badha, Ananda, Rahula, Sramanadasa, Sujata, Tishya, and so on are found making donations at various Buddhist sites, both alone and in groups. Thus, the names of ninety-six male persons and thirty-nine female persons are found with Buddhist associations, both as donors and with kinship relations to donors. As opposed to the names of trading communities, these names do not dwell on the profession of these people except for four inscriptions, which bear the names of either the donor or people related to the donor, with the prefix Śākyōpāsikā or Śākyabhikshu (monks) added to their names (nos 1043, 1044, 1046, 1047). In other cases, there is no specific mention of religious affiliation. Though these popular names with religious affiliation do not necessarily allude to a certain religious background, they do indicate a personal choice being made by them, that of following the religion they wanted. Thus, Kanha or Kṛishna and Halaka (no. 1007) made a donation at a shrine in Kanheri. Here, though both names have a Vaishnava affiliation, that the donors made a gift to a Buddhist monastery is indicative of the fact that their familial religious alignment was very different from their personal adherence to the Buddhist faith.

The mention of 224 male and sixty-nine female persons with non-Buddhist sounding names and affiliations as either donors or kin of donors are found in these inscriptions. Four inscriptions (nos 1206, 1209, 1218, 1281) feature names with Buddhist affiliation, which are mentioned in the same donor list that includes names with strong Brahmaṇical associations, like Arjuna, Māriti, Samudra, etc. This further refers to the upholding of personal choice in matters of religious adherence. Three Jagayyapeṭa inscriptions (nos 1202, 1203, 1204) mention Kanika or Kṛishna among other family members who had names with strong Buddhist ties. A particular inscription (no. 1253) refers to a person named Koja or Kubja making a donation at an Amaravati site. The name of this donor was probably a reference to her/his physical appearance.[3] In two instances, it can be deduced that the donors had names which may originally be traced to a tribal background (nos 1014, 1243). One of these inscriptions records a gift made by a certain Damila at a Kanheri site, and the other mentions Damilakanha or Dravidakrisna, who made a donation at an Amaravati site (Ray 1986: 196). Both names carry regional association. The Deccan was well-known as a commercial hub from the first century CE. It has been pointed out that the *Arthaśāstra* referred to the huge mineral reserve along Dakshināpatha (ibid.: 2). During the post-Mauryan period, this region was bustling with commercial activities, which received further impetus from the spread of Buddhism in this area. The region thus attracted peoples from all parts of the subcontinent, as well as from the outside. Many people flocked to the early Buddhist monasteries from different parts of the Deccan itself. The inscriptions therefore throw light on the identity of the places these travellers came from, and that is where we turn our focus next.

In the western Deccan, donors came from Surparaka, that is, modern-day Sopara, to make donations at sites in Kanheri (nos 988, 995, 1005), Karle (nos 1094, 1095), and Nanaghat (no. 1119). Kanheri turned into a sprawling and popular Buddhist site along the west coast, and endorsement from the sea-farers fuelled its prominence, along with its proximity to the ports of Kalyan and

Surparaka. It is well-known that the Sātavāhanas continued to favour Buddhist sites along the west coast (Ray 1994a: 41) as the taxes procured from the sea traffic replenished the treasury. Though the Brāhmaṇical texts caution against sea voyages; in Buddhism, sea-faring merchants believed that they would be protected by the Bodhisattva (Ray 1994b: 153). The Bodhisattva Avalokiteśvara's image at three Kanheri caves bears testimony to this, and in one of the caves, the Bodhisattva is seen to be protecting against eight dangers, including shipwreck (Ray 1994a: 41).

Kalyan is mentioned in as many as eleven cases, and the donors from this region offered gifts at various sites of Junnar (nos 1177, 1179) and Kanheri (nos 986, 988, 998, 1000, 1001, 1013, 1014, 1024, 1032), among other places. Kalyan functioned as a crucial borough for major commercial activities, besides being a port town. This may explain the constant flow of popular traffic in this sub-region. Another place from which several donors have made gifts is Dhenukakata (Ray 1983: 20–21) or Dharanikota, the capital of the later Sātavāhana king, Vasisthiputra Pulomavi. Devotees from Dhenukakata travelled to Kanheri (no. 1020), Karle (nos 1090, 1092, 1093, 1096, 1097), and Sailarwadi (no. 1121) to make donations at all three places, which fall within the boundaries of the present-day state of Maharashtra. In another example, we have a seṭhin who hailed from Vijayanati, modern-day Banavasi in Karnataka, who made a donation to a Karle site (Habib and Habib 2012: 53). Two brothers from Bharukachha, Gujarat, are said to have made donations at a Junnar site (no. 1169), while two other inscriptions record Yavanas (ancient Greeks who came to India) making donations and declaring that they hailed from Gatas or Gartas (nos 1154, 1182), which has been identified as a part of Trigarta or the Kangra region (modern-day Himachal Pradesh) (Ray 1986: 195).

In the eastern Deccan, as many as ninety inscriptions state that donations were made to different sites in Amaravati. The abundant availability of the water supplied by several water bodies, and the alluvial soil made Amaravati a prosperous centre of agriculture and transportation (Shimada 2013: 37). Water reservoirs (*cheruvus*) catered to substantial agrarian activities, and scholars have suggested that these water saturation bodies had been maintained since prehistoric times (Sharma 1962: 309–311). Archaeological excavations at Dharanikota suggest the presence of a sprawling river port in this area (Archaeological Survey of India 1965: 1–2). Thus, Dharanikota, and its burgeoning suburb Amaravati, had both become pivotal centres of exchange (Shimada 2013: 122). The prosperity of Amaravati evidently nurtured a sizeable population, thus beckoning Buddhist monasteries to cluster around this area. Therefore, it is not surprising that Amaravati attracted many donors and, in twenty-six instances, the donors mention their original abodes. The places the donors hailed from, as mentioned in the inscriptions, are: Bhutayana (no. 1206), Sreshthivada and Turulura (no. 1209), Kevurura (nos 1213, 1240), Chandaka (no. 1220), Akhasavada (no. 1221), Valichaka (no. 1222), Virapura (no. 1224), Dhanyakata of Rajagiri (no. 1225), Mahavanasala (nos 1230, 1272), Mahemkhanaja (no. 1233), Mamdara (no. 1234), Narasala (no. 1239), Rajagiri (no. 1250), Hiralura (no. 1260), Chhadaka (no. 1261), Devaparavana (no. 1261), Odiparivenena (no. 1267), Dhanyakata (no. 1271), Rajasaila (no. 1280), Tompuki (no. 1281), Vijayapura (no. 1285), Kedura (no. 1295), Katakasola (no. 1303), Tulaka (no. 1205a). Three of the eleven inscriptions from Bhattiprolu mention place names, and two among these state that the donors hailed from *nigama/nēgama*[4] (town/city) (nos 1335, 1337).

Terms such as *gāma* (village/hamlet) (Monier-Williams 2005: 313) and nigama (ibid.: 545) have commanded multiple mentions. Eleven inscriptions record that the devotees came from a gāma (nos. 1000, 1077, 1133, 1153, 1163, 1166, 1167, 1202, 1203, 1204, 1261), and one specifies that the donor, a gahapati, belonged to a *dhaṁmanigāma* (pious hamlet). The citation of the unit of gāma can be understood in light of the fact that larger Buddhist sites like Kanheri commanded a hinterland comprising vast agricultural fields and multiple villages (Gokhale 1975: 21–25). The same was also true of Dharanikota, Amaravati, and Nagarjunakonda (Ray 1983: 22). An ironmonger, Mahika, hailing from Karahakada, is noted to have made a donation at a Kuda site (no. 1055). Karahakada has been identified with modern-day Kuda (Habib and Habib 2012: 51). Apart from this particular instance, of the twenty-nine inscriptions belonging to various Kuda sites, only one has mentioned the donor's habitation, Chemdina (no. 1047). It can be suggested here that all other donors were in this case probably locals, and hence the specification of their locational identity was not necessary (Parasher Sen 2007: 49). Similarly, of the nineteen inscriptions belonging to Nasik, only four record the donors' habitations (nos 1133, 1140, 1141, 1148), and a fifth has mentioned it as Nasik (no. 1144).[5] Nasik appears twice in two inscriptions as the donors' habitation (nos 985, 1109).[6] Along with the gahapatis, merchants and traders mentioned their original places of residence intermittently. Those that did perhaps needed to do so as the land they most likely possessed there had become a viable economic possession. Gahapatis in general, being major land-holders and agriculturalists, had to pay taxes, and therefore it was important for them to clearly demarcate their property limitations and emphasise the regions they hailed from (Basant 2012: 176–177). In the case of traders, merchants, and professional groups, belonging to a particular place probably offered them a form of identity. The invasive trading networks running through the Deccan replenished the mercantile communities. The spread and consolidation of Buddhism in this area further gave these communities a certain social merit and confidence to come forward and proclaim their social and habitation status. The recurring mention of their original places of residence can thus be explained as the donors asserting their identities within a spatially defined entity, which in turn could help them exert their economic might as well as politico-religious affiliations (Pirc 2015: 50).

Social Identity and Kinship Patterns

Another feature of these inscriptions is that they mention the kinship patterns of individuals who visited the various sites for religious and economic purposes. We identified two groups of donors. One group included those who mentioned kinship relations, and the other comprised those who did not affiliate themselves with anyone at all and only asserted their individual identity. In a singular case (no. 1127), while donating at a Nasik site, a gahapati mentioned his kinship relation in contravention to the common practice: in most cases, it is usually the people related to gahapatis who tended to proclaim their relationship with the latter. It is interesting to note that the majority of examples in the inscriptions mention male donors. In one instance (no. 1260), the grandsons of a woman called Kamma made a donation at an Amaravati site. However, even here, Kamma is described as the daughter of Bhagi and wife of the gahapati Rahula. It can be inferred that the gahapatis, being a prominent social class, did not need to assert their kinship ties to establish social status. Patriarchal values clearly existed, and explains why we find few examples of women from the gahapati group making donations in their own right. However, the nēgama (nos 998, 1000, 1001, 1024, 1172), the vāṇiya, a term found exclusively in the case of Amaravati (nos 1213, 1214, 1229, 1230, 1239, 1278, 1281, 1285, 1292), the vaṇija or vanijaka (nos 987, 1156), the sathavāha (nos 1062, 1065, 1066), the seṭhin (nos 1075, 1073, 1261), the hēraṇika (nos 1179, 993, 1247), the *suvanakara* (goldsmith) (no. 1177), the *manikara* (jeweller) (no. 1005) all enunciated their kinship status vigorously. Either they were the ones making donations as part of a larger kin group, or they were shown to be related to the donors.

The āvēsani are, however, quite explicit in the matter of proclaiming their kinship ties. Thus, one inscription (no. 1298) from Amaravati records a gift being made by the daughter of an āvēsani, and three inscriptions (nos 1202, 1203, 1204) from Jagayyapeṭa contain similar information whereby the donor, who was a foreman of artisans, declared that he was the son of a foreman while making the donation with his family members. The *Arthaśāstra*, as a prescriptive text, defines a limited access to father's property until the latter's death, and thus it is suggested that the sons and daughters did not have enough command over material resources to make independent donations, as found in the Sanchi inscriptions (Basant 2012: 181). In the case of the Deccan inscriptions, too, the sons and daughters made donations under parental supervision, and we have five Pitalkhora inscriptions (nos 1189, 1190, 1191, 1192, 1193) that bear testimony to this. In the first inscription, *rajavēja* (royal physician) Magila made the gift, and in the next two inscriptions, his daughter and son made the donation while citing their relationship with Magila.

The Dravidian system of marital alliances has a tradition of cross-cousin marriage that results in the perpetuation of kinship affinity. The Indo-Aryan marriage system strongly cautions against such marriage alliances, particularly those that would establish any kind of proximity among kinsmen (Trautmann 1995: 24–25). As pointed out by Trautmann, the Sātavāhanas of the Deccan practised cross-cousin marriages, as is evident from a number of examples that use the *gōtra* (lineage) matronymic. However, he also notes that this phenomenon can be discerned among the brāhmaṇas converted to Buddhism as well (ibid.: 336). This tendency also points towards identifying half-brothers who shared the same matrilineal descent (ibid.: 367; Ray 1986: 176–177). We infer that because of the prevalence of cross-cousin marriage, the Deccan witnessed a close proximity between maternal and paternal families. Thus, one inscription (no. 1018) mentions the inclusion of a nephew in its list of kin, and three Jagayyapeṭa inscriptions (nos 1202, 1203, 1204) included the brother of the donor, the brother's wife, and the brother's sons and daughter as close kin in the list. These inscriptions expand to tell us that the donor Sidhata was an āvēsani by profession, and his father Nakachamda practised the same craft. The fact this was a family business is probably why the brother of Sidhata was also included in the list of kin (Ghosh 2015: 39). In understanding kinship patterns as found in these inscriptions, we find a sharp contrast to what Kumkum Roy (2015: 43–44) and P. K. Basant (2012: 180) have discussed following Wagle's (1995) list of kin during Buddha's time, which consisted only of mother, father, son, wife of the son, brother, and sister, and excluded any reference to uncle, aunt, and cousins. However, the inscriptions under study bear testimony to donations being made alongside cousins and nephews.

Women constituted the largest group of donors in these inscriptions, and as many as seventy-two women made donations at various sites. It is also to be noted that, in forty-five cases, the women donors belonged to the more prosperous sections of society, and were either related through kinship to gahapatis or to administrative post-holders, and such families. In five inscriptions (nos 1111, 1021, 1045, 1052, 1054), women were related to mahāraṭhis and *mahābhōjas* (chiefs). In one instance (no. 1146), the donor Vasu, while donating at a Nasik site, identified herself as a *mahāsenāpatṇī* (wife of a great general). In two inscriptions (nos 1132, 1134) a person by the name of Dakhamitra is mentioned making donations at Nasik sites, who also indicates that she was the daughter of Khaharata Nahapana, the wife of Ushabhadata, and the daughter-in-law of Dinika, thus highlighting her kin affiliation to important personages of the region. The same is the case of Vishnudatā, who identified herself as a Śākanikā, daughter of Śāka Agnivarman, wife of Rēbhila, and mother of Viśvavarma, while donating at a Nasik site (no. 1137). These women, despite acquiring adequate social status through marriage or by birth, needed to mention their kinship ties with fathers, husbands, or sons. However, in a singular case, the donor has mentioned her father and mother as mahābhōja and *mahābhōjī* (wife of mahābhōja) while donating at a Kuda site (no. 1037). In another instance, Gōyaṁmā, the daughter of a *rājamācha* (royal minister), donated a cave at a Kuda site (no. 1053). A *baṁmaṇni* or *brāhmaṇī* (wife of a brāhmaṇa) donated a chaitya at Kuda (no. 1050). One interesting inscription (no. 1229) records the gift made at an Amaravati site by three women, Nakachampaka, Chadasiri, and Budhila, all of whom inform us that they were *vaṇiyinī* (wives of merchants).

A female ascetic (*tāpasinī)* made a donation of a cave at a Nasik site without mentioning her kin (no. 1128). Another inscription from Kuda (no. 111) mentions only the name of the donor as Śākyōpāsikā Vyāghrakā, and does not mention any other kin.

Similarly, an ascetic Sidhaṁthī or Siddhārthī donated at an Amaravati site without mentioning her kin (no. 1242). In two cases from Amaravati, women made donations to the Saṅgha and related themselves to female kin of the family. Thus, Sagharakhitā, mother of Haṁghā and grandmother of Jiyavā, donated upright slabs (no. 1262), and Rōhā, daughter of Sujātā, made a donation as well (no. 1264). On the basis of the above evidence, it can be said that irrespective of social status, women donors mentioned both male and female kin in these inscriptions. The ascetic women are the only exception, probably because they had joined the Saṅgha shunning their worldly relationships and lifestyle, and so did not have any kin to mention.

Identity of Groups with Administrative and Economic Status

Administrative rank-holders appear frequently in these inscriptions. They excavated rock surfaces and donated these caves to serve as residences of monks and nuns at many of these sites. Mahābhōja, Mahābhōjī, Mahāraṭhī, Mahāsēṇāpatṇī, and Mahāsēnāpati are titles that occur in thirteen cases (nos 1021, 1037, 1045, 1052, 1054, 1111, 1116, 1146). In five cases, caves were donated by these functionaries, and in one case a stone carving was donated. In one instance (no. 1266), there is mention of a Sēngōpa or general called Mudukutala, who made the gift of a pillar at an Amaravati site. It is well-known that the Sātavāhanas, who ruled over Deccan, married into the families of the Mahābhōjas and Mahāraṭhīs, and thus the latter were closely associated with them in the capacity of high-level officials. Though these titles have a military connotation, the political status conferred upon them probably became hereditary with time (Trautmann 1995: 369). Another notable administrative group that features in these inscriptions is the Āmatya/Amātya, deriving from rājamācha, which was the position of companion to the king, or minister (Monier-Williams 2005: 81). One inscription (no. 1174) records the gift of a *chaḍhi* (cane/ornamental stick gifted to great men [here, monks] in Marathi) and a hall, made by an Āmatya (in Sanskrit)/Amacha (Prakrit form) named Ayama at a Junnar site. Another inscription (no. 1341) cites one Amacha gifting an earth-dwelling at a Kondavolu site. It is explained that the duty of this particular rank-holder consisted of noting down the withdrawals of donations previously made, as well as their renewal (Ray 1986: 180). In one significant case (no. 1144), a Mahāmāta made a donation for the excavation of a cave at a Nasik site. Derived from the high ranking administrative post of Mahāmātra in Emperor Aśoka's regime assigned to spread the ideas of Dhamma, the duties of the office changed over time and the post of Mahāmāta (Prakrit form) came to refer to a high official or the Prime Minister in the post-Aśokan period, as Monier-Williams explains (2005: 789). All in all, the above set of donors were part of an administrative structure wherein these officials with high-sounding titles were prominent contributors to the Buddhist Saṅgha because they gave generous gifts like caves, pillars, and so on.

A collection of inscriptions refers to an amalgamation of disparate trading classes in the Deccan by the beginning of the first century CE as an outcome of the burgeoning commercial activities in this region. The opulence of the gahapatis, seṭhis, vanijakas, nēgamas, sāthavāhas, etc., can be gauged by reading the context and the kind of donation they made to Buddhist establishments in this region. The foremost mention among these commercial classes was of the gahapatis. In as many as twenty-nine cases, either the gahapatis themselves made donations, or people related to them did so. The economic might of the gahapatis, like that of the officials mentioned above, can be ascertained by the nature of their donations. Several inscriptions record major items of donation, such as the gift of a chaitya building (nos 987, 988, 1050, 1058, 1072, 1073, 1140, 1141, 1153, 1178, 1179, 1183, 1212, 1216), chaitya pillar (nos 1210, 1214, 1225, 1229, 1244), a parasol for the chaitya (no. 1276), a five-celled hall (no. 1157), the endowment of a certain field/fields situated below a cave (nos 1024, 1158, 1162, 1163, 1164, 1166, 1167), and wells (no. 1120). Other donations made by this class of donors included footprints or Buddhapadas (nos 1209, 1217,

1219, 1225, 1286), rail/rail bars/rail bars with sculptures/railbars with circular panels (nos 1089, 1102, 1104, 1143, 1241, 1247, 1254, 1261, 1263, 1269), coping-stones (nos 1221, 1225, 1231, 1251, 1256, 1281, 1283, 1285), the Wheel of Law (i.e., the Dharma Chakra)/ wheel (nos 1248, 1253), erection of a gate (no. 1255), lion pillar (no. 1088), and pillars (nos 1093, 1094, 1095, 1097, 1187, 1188, 1202, 1203, 1204, 1208, 1210, 1214, 1229, 1260, 1266, 1277, 1280, 1282, 1298, 1302). It has been pointed out that in the Deccan, the gahapatis were involved in the field of entrepreneurship as well (Jaiswal 2005: 278), riding the tide of prosperous trade in the period. A seṭhin (no. 1056), who was also a gahapati, made the gift of a bathing tank at a Kuda site, and the gahapatis probably took the initiative in providing a facility for the use of pilgrims and out-station donors who came to pay homage at Buddhist sites in the Deccan (Ghosh 2015: 78).

Scholars observe that as the economic prosperity of the gahapatis increased, they began investing in financing and, consequently, became śreṣṭhīns/seṭhin (Ray 1986: 197). The Pāli texts and the *Jātakas* abound with information that enables us to establish that a close alliance existed between the king and the seṭhins (Chakravarti, R. 2007: 102). This group was associated with financing and banking, and commandeered considerable economic might. Seven inscriptions studied mention the seṭhins as donors (nos 1063, 1064, 1073, 1075, 1087, 1109, 1261). Their donations were in the form of caves, a cistern, a chaitya hall, endowment of a field, and rail bars, referring to their prosperous conditions. In one case (no. 1075) the donor, a seṭhin, mentions that he was the son of a gahapati, and in another instance (no. 1073), the donor Vadasiri is mentioned as being the daughter of a gahapati and seṭhin, Samgharakhita.

The vanijakas would either be land traders or sea traders. One inscription (no. 1012) records the gift of a cave to a Kanheri site by the *sāgarapaloganas* (the traders of the sea) (Ray 2003: 195). The terms vaṇija/vanijaka/vāṇiyas have found mention in nine instances (nos 987, 1198, 1213, 1214, 1229, 1230, 1239, 1278, 1281), and on every occasion they offered expensive gifts. In one of them, Siridata made a donation (no. 1230) at an Amaravati site while identifying himself as a *gādhika* (perfumer) and also a vāṇiya. The objects donated by the vāniyas are a slab, a pillar for lamps, a chaitya pillar with a relic, a chief pavilion, a coping stone, and so on. The vāṇiyas differed from the seṭhins in the way they dealt with their business, as the latter were also bankers who indulged in money-lending activities as well. Numerically, however, the vāṇiyas formed the largest trading community. It is safe to surmise here that the seṭhins commanded a social position that was definitely superior to that of the vāṇiyas, as there are instances of the seṭhins being associated closely with the gahapati class, while the vāṇiyas were not.

The term nēgama probably alluded to general traders and as many as eight inscriptions (nos 987, 995, 998, 1000, 1001, 1024, 1127, 1172) record the nēgamas or nēkamas making donations at various Buddhist sites. The objects of donation were varied and substantial and indicate their economic prosperity. The sathavāha or sārthavāhas, as per the *Amarakośa*, was 'the leader of merchants who have invested an equal amount of capital and carried on trade with outside markets and are travelling in a caravan' (Ray 2003: 194). They feature thrice in the inscriptions (nos 1062, 1065, 1066) and on each occasion, they donated caves. In one inscription (no. 1084), Bādhā identifies herself as the wife of a *hālika* (ploughman). Going by the nature of the donation, namely a cave, the hālika could be understood as someone who probably owned the land that he tilled. In another instance (no. 1121), one Siagutanika makes the gift of a cave at a Sailarwadi site while stating that she was the wife of hālakiya and *kuḍubika* (a peasant family) Usabhanaka, and the mother of gahapati Namda. The conjunct of hālika-kuḍubika is understood to mean 'one who owns the land that he cultivates and is not merely a labourer' (Ray 1986: 197). Thus, the son of Siagutanika, a gahapati, must have climbed up the social ladder, despite being the son of an hālika-kuḍubika. This particular social group definitely enjoyed considerable economic prosperity. It is pertinent to point out that the *Manusmṛti* states that even though the vaiśya varṇa may follow the vocation of agriculture (Sharma 2014: 32), for a *kṣatriya* (ruling caste/class), taking up agriculture during a time of distress would rob him of his virtues (ibid.: 468).[7]

Gādhikas made donations on four occasions in the inscriptions studied (nos 1090, 1187, 1210, 1230). It is well-known that they retailed in perfumes and were regular traders (Ray 2003: 193). Their objects of donation were fairly simple, namely a cave door, a pillar, and a chaitya pillar. In the fourth case, a vāṇiya and gadhika, Siridata, donated a chief pavilion at an Amaravati site. The other notable professional group of similar economic standing was the *hēraṇikās/hairaṇyakas*. Six inscriptions (nos 993, 1033, 1179, 1239, 1247, 1297) feature these treasurers, who donated a chaitya building, a *stūpa,* a path, and a rail bar. In one case, the object of the donation is not mentioned. The suvaṇakāra/*suvaṇakō[kā]ra* (goldsmith) is mentioned twice (nos 986, 1177) and in both occasions, the donors gifted water cisterns.

Group Identity and the Guilds

Groups that feature frequently in these inscriptions include various minor professional organisations and artisans in the Deccan region, which indicate a society that witnessed active participation from these groups. Donations were made to a number of guilds in five inscriptions (nos 1133, 1137, 1162, 1165, 1180), where they have been referred to as sēṇi or śreṇī, which can be explained as an association of traders dealing with the same articles of trade or manufacture (Monier-Williams 2005: 1102).[8] Either the donation was made to the guilds or the guilds made the donation to the Buddhist Saṅgha. Thus, the guild of the *dhaṁñika* (corn dealers) (no. 1180) donated a seven-celled cave. Another guild (no. 1165) of *vasakara* (bamboo-workers) and another of *kāsākāra* (braziers) donated at the Junnar site. The *Jātakas* constantly mention the *senipamukha* (chief of the guilds) as a significant part of the king's council (Ray 2003: 193). Many texts have explained that these organisations were cooperative by nature, and every guild had its own set of regulations that determined the mode of its transactions (Chakravarti, R. 2007: 53). Another association of this sort is the gōṭhī or *goṣṭhī*. Mention of this organization is found in the Bhattiprolu inscriptions (nos 1332, 1333, 1335, 1338, 1339), featuring the names of persons belonging to each goṭhī. On two occasions, the objects of their donation were a casket and a crystal box. The goṭhīs were economically affluent, and hence, it was probably redundant to specify the objects of their donation on every occasion. Interestingly, one of these inscriptions (no. 1333) mentions Goṭhisamaṇa, or Goṭhiśramaṇa (ascetic of the committee), which can be interpreted as the Buddhist Saṅgha taking a rather direct interest in the affairs of this economic organisation. A third type of collective, headed by a leader, is discerned in inscriptions as the āvēsani. Āvēsani is also explained as a workshop or a manufacturing unit (Monier-Williams 2005: 155). Their mention is confined to four inscriptions (nos 1298, 1202, 1203, 1204). Three of them mention a single āvēsani who, along with his relatives, made a gift of five entrance pillars at a Jagayyapeṭa site, and on one occasion, the daughter of an āvēsani donated a pillar at an Amaravati site. Studying the objects of their donation, we can establish that these groups were economically well-endowed. As the erection of these edifices required professional expertise, the āvēsani groups were in great demand and were employed by the Saṅgha on many occasions (Ray 1986: 185).

The proliferation of crafts and expansion of trade fuelled the confidence in craftsmen, who came forward declaring their religious affiliation and commemorated their donations in these inscriptions. In one instance (no. 1005), a manikara named Nagapalita, along with his family, made a gift of a cave at a Kanheri site. The *sēla-vaḍhakī* (cave builders) (no. 987), *kamāra* (blacksmith) (no. 1032), *kulārika* (potters) (no. 1137), *kōlīkanikāya* (weavers) (no. 1133), *tilapiṣika* (oil-miller)(no. 1137), *lohavāṇiyiya* (ironmonger) (no. 1055), *dāsaka* (fisherman) (no. 1129), *pāniyagharika* (superintendent of water-houses) (no. 1279), and *pādamulika* (servant) (no. 1344) were groups of ordinary means who also recorded their humble donations in these inscriptions. Most of these artisans are known to us through their mention in the *Jātakas* and the *Periplus of the Erythraean Sea*[9] (Chakravarti, R. 2007: 52). The *Arthaśāstra* had prescribed that the *śūdras* (servant caste) should engage themselves in economic activities (Sharma 1980: 169). The *Manusmṛti* too points out that the śūdras should live by serving the three other varṇas, and in case there were no opportunities to serve the brāhmaṇas, during times of distress, they could take up the vocation of artisans and engage in painting, carpentry, and so on to sustain their families (Sharma 2014: 471). R. S. Sharma (1980: 170) opines that the artisans were often poorly paid and lived in penury.

However, the above views stand in sharp opposition to the inscriptional evidence noted earlier, wherein many of these groups designated as vaiśyas and śūdras in prescriptive literature such as the *Arthaśāstra* or the *Manusmṛti* had sufficient funds to make notable donations to the Buddhist Saṅgha. On one occasion, the profession stated is accompanied by a mention of the hereditary nature of a particular *jāti* (no. 1051)—a *mālākāra* (garland-maker) is spoken of and it is mentioned that he followed his father's craft. In another case where jāti is mentioned (no. 1273), just the opposite can be seen in the donation made by Vidhika, the *chaṁmakāra* (leather-worker), where he declares himself to be the son of an *upajhaya* (teacher). Therefore, it can be postulated that these inscriptions enable us to reflect on the fluidity of the jāti system in this region. Clearly, this was possible because the Buddhist community permitted members of all castes to join the Saṅgha, and were against following social hierarchy as formulated in the prescriptive Brāhmaṇical literature such as the *Arthaśāstra* and the *Dharmaśāstras* (Jha 1997: 23). What we see here is that instead of the practice of the caste system, these inscriptions reflected the class element of all major social groups, rarely mentioning their position in the caste hierarchy. In fact, except for a very few cases where brāhmaṇas are mentioned by their caste name and even fewer cases where the term 'jāti' is mentioned, all other information concerning social and economic identities can be gleaned from the personal names that individuals or groups left behind. The term 'varṇa' as a given marker of identity does not find mention in the inscriptions at all. Thus, we see how social reality and social changes can be distinguished more specifically from these inscriptions.

Inscriptions in Fragments and Their Significance

It is evident from the above inscriptions, often found in fragments, that the various communities making donations at different sites of the Deccan vigorously upheld their many individual identities as administrators, professional groups, women, and so on, and in the case of guilds, their collective economic identity as well. What is discernible here is how these communities lived, which reflects how kinship and business relations defined people's identities in this region. In some cases, while donating to various Buddhist sites, the administrators, gahapatis, numerous trading communities, and disparate professional groups also mentioned the places they hailed from. After the *parinirvāṇa* (passing away) of the Buddha, his disciples and followers started paying visits to worship his relics after building chaityas over them. At many other places, stūpas and chaityas were built to commemorate the teachings of the Buddha, which became the temporary residences for monks and nuns as well. This phenomenon is a marker of how, despite the existence of contesting ideological planes,[10] certain traditions gained popularity and became embedded in the fabric of popular culture, and thus survived the ravages of time in these small but critical inscriptions. These inscriptions were records left behind by many of the Buddha's followers during their visits to these places of veneration and pilgrimage.

Class differentiation existed within similar professional groups because some of them, namely the gahapatis, were a more dominant social entity than the vaṇijakas, nēgamas, vāniyas, and seṭhins, who were all involved in trade and commerce. However, in the *Dharmaśāstra* literature, these prosperous groups were classified together under the category of the vaiśya varṇa. Thus, for instance, the *Manusmṛti*, dated to around the same period as this inscriptional data (between second century BCE and second century CE), categorically prescribes the duties of the vaiśya varṇa as cattle rearing, trading in merchandise, money lending, and agriculture (Sharma 2014: 32, 451). It further warns traders against stealing from people and states that harsh punishments would be meted out to such offenders (ibid.: 440–441). Clearly, the hereditary specialisation of the so-called vaiśya groups has been recorded across the *Dharmaśāstra,* the *Manusmṛti* as well as these inscriptions. But the position of the vaiśya groups on the third rung in the caste hierarchy, as propounded in the two former texts, appears to be challenged in the inscriptional data in the way their identities are presented, as we have seen above.

It is important to point out that social hierarchy was brought to focus in ritual terms (i.e., this indicates the tradition in a caste hierarchy wherein only the upper varṇas were permitted certain rituals) as well, and it is in this regard that some of these professional groups were treated disparagingly. In another prescriptive statement, the *Manusmṛti* forbids the two upper varṇas from accepting food from a physician, a blacksmith, a goldsmith, and the manufacturer of bamboo articles (Sharma 2014: 203). It further elaborated that food given by a goldsmith to the upper varṇas impaired the latter's vitality, food given by a cobbler or leather-worker destroyed their reputation, food offered by an artisan killed their progeny, food offered by a physician resembled pus, and food given by an usurer or money lender resembled excreta (ibid.: 204). These statements, which banned the sharing of food with these well-to-do economic classes, degraded their social credibility. Such exclusionary rules based on certain rituals were meant to keep members of the third varṇa at a social distance, though it was well-recognised that at an economic level, they were dominating the socio-economic landscape of the times. The extent to which these rules were followed is difficult to gauge. In fact, on the contrary, data culled from the fragmentary inscriptions, discussed above comprehensively, paint an entirely different picture, indicating that physicians were well-placed in society, as evident from some inscriptions (nos 1189, 1190, 1191, 1192, 1193) wherein it is stated that they made donations at five

Pitalkhora sites, as well as at a Kuda site (no. 1048). Similarly, guilds of vasakara and kāsākāra (no. 1165), suvaṇakāra (nos 986, 1177), kamāra (no. 1032), chaṁmakāra (no. 1273), āvēsani (nos 1202, 1203, 1204 1298), and seṭhin (nos 1063, 1064, 1073, 1075, 1087, 1109, 1261) made donations while mentioning their professions. It is to be noted here that two inscriptions record that a baṁmaṇi or brāhmaṇī, wife of a brāhmaṇa, made a donation at a Kuda site (no. 1050), and another brāhmaṇa of Gōtama or Gautama gōtra donated at a Mahakal site (no. 1035).

What is clear in these above examples is that many among these professions had become ardent followers of Buddhism, and as such were not swayed by the vagaries of the rules that defined members of the Brāhmaṇical society. We have noted above that people from different class and caste backgrounds made donations at the Buddhist sites of the Deccan, and did not shy away from informing us of their various identities, including professional ones. Thus, the use of these fragmented inscriptions is significant in many ways. First, they highlight a very lively social scene without mentioning the ritual positioning and disparities in the underlying social structures, as opposed to the accounts found in the normative/prescriptive Brāhmaṇical literature of the time. Through the inscriptional data, we gain a more nuanced understanding of the differentiation that existed at the social and economic levels among a vast variety of groups, which had been clubbed together under the vaiśya varṇa in the *Manusmṛti*. Second, the absence of contemporaneous indigenous texts from this region hinders us from presenting a clear narrative of whether old identities were completely destroyed with the donning of new identities through which these groups preferred to remember themselves. In this vacuum, these inscriptions become a most critical and valuable source to construct the social history of the Deccan. Therefore, it can be postulated that though damaged and fragmented, these inscriptions enable us to present an alternative way in which people defined themselves. This does not concur with the static categories in which people were classified in the more didactic theoretical literature of the time. Finally, these descriptions have allowed us to highlight the particularity of the social landscape of the Deccan in the early historic period, and how people of this region contributed to religious, social, economic, and cultural well-being at a time when far-reaching changes were taking place in the subcontinent as a whole.

Notes

Acknowledgements: This chapter is based on my M.Phil dissertation, completed at the University of Hyderabad (2014–2015) under the supervision of Professor Aloka Parasher Sen, to whom I extend my sincere and heartfelt gratitude for her constant encouragement and guidance. I would also like to thank Professor K. M. Shrimali for his valuable advice, and Professor Anindita Mukhopadhyaya and Dr V. J. Varghese for lending me treasured books from their personal collections.

1. Henceforth, the inscription numbers cited in this chapter will follow the inscription numbers as found in Lüders' List (Lüders 1920: Vol. X, 98–179).
2. Throughout this chapter, two or more variations of certain terms will be found since many of these inscriptions are bilingual (Sanskrit and Prakrit), and using both forms will signify the plurality in contemporary society as different social classes/groups used different languages. Other reasons for variations in spellings and diacritical marks may also be due to the inscriber's error, or regional variations in dialects.
3. This is my view and I have not come across any scholar who mentioned this. Further, two *sūtras* from the Prakrit grammar of Hemachandra inform us that *kubja* in its Prakrit form is *koja*. The Sanskrit word, kubja, translates into English as 'hunch-backed'. It may also be mentioned that in Karnataka a small river-stream named Kubja runs through the Udupi district.
4. Prakrit word *nēgama* denotes both town and trader, and therefore the context in which the word is being used is important to decipher its meaning. Therefore, both these meanings are found in this chapter.
5. According to Shastri (1998), it is interesting to note that inscription no. 1133 mentions the donation of a coconut tree in the village of Chikhalapadra in the *āhāra* (district) (Monier-Williams 2005: 162–163) of Kāpura, made by Ushabhadāta, who was related to Kshaharāta Kshatrapa Nahapāna (in Sanskrit transcription; Kshatrapa is the political designation). The latter is also known as Khaharata Nahapana in the Prakrit form used in the inscriptions.

6. Inscription no. 1142 records a curious case of the donation of the village of Dhambhika at a Nasik site by Nāsikakas, or the people of Nasik. This is a unique case of the people of a place donating an entire village they had been living in to a Buddhist monastery.
7. While translating the *Manusmṛti*, R. N. Sharma states that any varṇa, during difficult times, may take up a profession worthy of a lower varṇa. Thus, the kṣatriyas may take up agriculture and sell wealth-accumulating articles of trade, and the vaiśyas may take up the work worthy of śūdras, even though such work is not regarded as respectable (Sharma 2014: 468–469, 471).
8. According to inscription no. 1137, Śakanikā Vishnudatā, who had identified herself as the daughter of Śaka Agnivarman, made a donation of money, which was invested in the guilds of kulārikas (potters), *odayaṁtrikas* (workers fabricating hydraulic engines), and tilapīṣakas (oil millers), at a site in Nasik.
9. The *Periplus of the Erythraean Sea* (or, *Periplus Maris Erythraei*) is a record of trade in the ancient world, which captures the first organised trading with nations of the East in vessels made and directed by countries of the West. It is an astonishing eyewitness account of ancient travel to Africa and India via the Red Sea written by an unknown Greek-speaking Egyptian author, in a mixture of classical and common Greek, in the first century CE. Schoff (2018) says that the book documents 'not only individual enterprise, but the awakening of a whole race toward new fields of geographical discovery and commercial achievement'. See *World History Encyclopedia*. n.d. 'Periplus of the Erythraean Sea'. Available at https://www.worldhistory.org/Periplus_of_the_Erythraean_Sea/ (accessed December 2021).
10. The contesting ideological planes refer to several sects of both the Brāhmaṇical and the Buddhist traditions as well as those of the Jaina. Further, popular local cults too existed in the Deccan prior to the onset of Buddhism. However, Buddhism became popular during the early historic period as is evident from the people who visited these sites of pilgrimage.

References

Archaeological Survey of India (GoI). 1965. *Indian Archaeology 1962–63—A Review*, reviews 1–4. Available at http://nmma.nic.in/nmma/nmma_doc/Indian%20Archaeology%20Review/Indian%20Archaeology%201962-63%20A%20Review.pdf (accessed January 2022).

Basant, P. K. 2012. *The City and the Country in Early India: A Study of Malwa*. New Delhi: Primus Books.

Chakravarti, Uma. 1987. *The Social Dimensions of Early Buddhism*. New Delhi: Oxford University Press.

———. 2007. *Everyday Lives, Everyday Histories: Beyond the Kings and Brahmanas of 'Ancient' India*. New Delhi: Tulika Books.

Chakravarti, Ranabir. 2007. *Trade and Traders in Early Indian Society*. New Delhi: Manohar Books.

Chattopadhyaya, B. D. 2005. *Studying Early India: Archaeology, Texts and Historical Issues*. New Delhi: Permanent Black.

Fergusson, James. 2004. *Tree and Serpent Worship, or Illustrations of Mythology and Art in India in the First and Fourth Centuries after Christ: From the Sculptures of the Buddhist Topes at Sanchi and Amravati*. New Delhi: Asian Educational Services.

Ghosh, Nairita. 2015. 'Social Groups in Early Brāhmī Inscriptions of the Deccan', M.Phil. dissertation (Unpublished). Hyderabad: University of Hyderabad.

Gokhale S. D. (ed.) 1975. *Social Welfare: Legend and Legacy*. Bombay: Popular Prakashan.

Habib, Irfan and Faiz Habib. 2012. *Atlas of Ancient Indian History*. New Delhi: Oxford University Press.

Jaiswal, Suvira. 2005. *Caste: Origin, Function and Dimensions of Change*. New Delhi: Manohar Books.

Jha, Vivekanand. 1997. 'Caste, Untouchability and Social Justice: Early North Indian Perspective'. *Social Scientist* 25(11/12): 19–30.

Kosambi, D. D. 1965. *Ancient India: A History of Its Culture and Civilization*. New York: Pantheon Books.

———. 1982. *Culture and Civilization of Ancient India in Historical Outline*. New Delhi: Vikas Publishing House Pvt. Ltd.

Lüders, H. 1920. 'A List of Brāmhī Inscriptions from the Earliest Times to about 400 AD, with the Exception of those of Aśoka', Appendix, II 'Southern Inscriptions', *Epigraphia Indica*, Vol. X, Sten Konow (ed.), 98–179. Calcutta: Archaeological Survey of India.

Monier-Williams, Monier. 2005. *A Sanskrit-English Dictionary: Etymologically and Philologically Arranged with Special Reference to Cognate Indo-European Languages*. New Delhi: Sharad Publishing House.

Nagaraju, S. 1970. *Buddhist Architecture of Western India, c. 250BC–AD300*. Andhra Pradesh: Agam Kala Prakashan.

Parasher Sen, Aloka. 2007. 'Names, Travellers and Inscriptions in Early Historic South India'. *Indian Historical Review* 34(1): 47–90. Available at https://journals.sagepub.com/doi/abs/10.1177/037698360703400103 (accessed November 2021).

Pirc, Tadej. 2015. 'Multilevel Identity Matrix and Necessity of Solidarity to Difference'. In Wojciech Owczarski and Maria Virginia Filomena Cremasco (eds), *Solidarity, Memory and Identity*, 48–63. UK: Cambridge Scholars Publishing.

Ray, Amita. 1983. *Life and Art of Early Andhradesa*. Delhi: Agam Kala Prakashan.

Ray, Himanshu Prabha. 1986. *Monastery and Guild: Commerce under the Sātavāhanas*. Delhi: Oxford University Press.

———. 1994a. 'Kanheri: The Archaeology of an Early Buddhist Pilgrimage Centre in Western India'. *World Archaeology* 26(1), Archaeology of Pilgrimage: 35–46.

———. 1994b. *The Winds of Change: Buddhism and the Maritime Links in Early South Asia*. New Delhi: Oxford University Press.

———. 2003. *The Archaeology of Seafaring in Ancient South Asia*. New Delhi: Cambridge University Press.

Roy, Kumkum. 2015 [2010]. *The Power of Gender and the Gender of Power: Explorations in Early Indian History*. New Delhi: Oxford University Press.

Sarkar, H. 1987. 'Emergence of Urban Centres in Early Historical Andhradesa'. In B. M. Pande and B. D. Chattopadhyaya (eds), *Archaeology and History*, 631–639. Delhi: Agam Kala Prakashan.

Schoff, Wilfred Harvey. 2018. *The Periplus of the Erythræan Sea (Classic Reprint): Travel and Trade in the Indian Ocean by a Merchant of the First Century*. Forgotten Books.

Sharma, I. K. 1962. 'Ancient Canal'. *Journal of Indian History* XL: 302–311.

Sharma, R. N. 2014. *Manusmṛti: Sanskrit Text with Engish Translation of M. N. Dutt, Index of Ślokas and Critical Notes*. Varanasi: Chowkhamba Vidyabhawan.

Sharma, R. S. 1980. *Śūdras in Ancient India: A Social History of the Lower Order down to circa A.D. 600*. Delhi: Motilal Banarsidass.

Shastri, Ajay Mitra. 1998. *The Sātavāhanas and the Western Kshatrapas: A Historical Framework*. Nagpur: Dattsons.

Sircar, D. C. 1965. *Indian Epigraphy*. Delhi: Motilal Banarasidass.

Shimada, Akira. 2013. *Early Buddhist Architecture in Context: The Great Stūpa at Amarāvatī (ca. 300 BCE–300 CE)*. Leiden-Boston: Brill.

Trautmann, Thomas R. 1995. *Dravidian Kinship*. New Delhi: Vistaar Publication.

Wagle, Narendra. 1995. *Society at the Time of the Buddha*. Bombay: Popular Prakashan.

6

Local Coins and Local Rulers

The Early Deccan

Kasala Jashwanth Prasad

Introduction

In this chapter, we examine how local coins can enable an understanding of the social formation of the early Deccan. Local coins are those coins that were issued by local chieftains, who bore names or titles such as Gobhada, Samagopa, Mahāsenāpati, Mahātalavara, Mahārathi, Sada, Kura, and so on, and ruled several localities of the early Deccan from the middle of the second century BCE to the third century CE. These coins were some of the first on the subcontinent to have names and legends of local rulers inscribed on them, which provide details about these rulers that are not known to us from any other source of information. These rulers were distinct from the well-known kings of the Sātavāhana dynasty. (See Plates VI–VIIIb, this volume.) It is critical to assess the role these chiefs played prior to Sātavāhana rule, while coexisting with their rule and, in some areas, while succeeding them. In each of these phases, the nature of the local polity reflects different trends. We identify these coins as an unconventional source that can be used to reinterpret the polity of several localities of the Deccan, and their interrelation with the larger Sātavāhana empire. This enables us to gain a deeper understanding of the historical landscape, which is not usually discussed in dominant political narratives of the region.

Scholars[1] who have so far studied these local coins as a source material have done so to either trace their individual political identities, or to show how they can be used as a corroborative source while writing the history of the region. Numismatic data of this kind which has been closely looked at till date only offers us scholarly insights regarding who these coins can be attributed to, and to some extent, helps us ascertain the chronologies of these ruling groups. Some of these local coins were found along with other excavated material at different sites across the Deccan. It has been observed that usually the minting of these coins was not done under royal patronage, and therefore we have numerous instances where persons occupying a subordinate position have also issued and minted coins in their names (Shastri 1987). Therefore, these coins are unique because the long period of their existence has not been influenced by the changing trajectories of power at the pan-regional level, and this raises fundamental questions that necessitate a re-examination of the nature of the polity in these parts.

Geographers, archaeologists, and historians have hitherto defined the Deccan in terms of its sub-regional spaces and their specific geo-cultural zones, based on their material and physical features (Sankalia 1979: 98–99; Singh 1993: 698–846; Subbarao 2011: 14). The geographical roots of diversity in the Deccan provide essential insights into how these sub-regions have evolved over historical time. Emphasising the diverse physiographic features of the Deccan, Parasher Sen has highlighted the material particularities of its four distinct sub-regions, namely the southern Deccan (constituting most of present-day Karnataka region, followed by the upper areas of the Krishna-Tungabhadra valley and the Mysore plateau), the eastern Deccan (roughly comprised of present-day Andhra Pradesh state with fertile coastal plain areas), the central Deccan (marked by present-day Telangana state and its hilly plateau region), and the western Deccan (represented by the state of Maharashtra and its hilly *ghāts* alongside strategic passes) (Parasher Sen 1999: 160). The above sub-regional classification of the Deccan has been adopted in this study as we consider it a convenient way to describe the distinct characteristics of the various coins that were found in different localities. It most significantly enables us to highlight difference and particularity that can further be assessed to discuss the nature of the polity that came up in these diverse sub-regions of the Deccan.

Explanations of the early historical period in the Ganges plains have given us chronological parameters that do not neatly apply to other regions of the subcontinent. Thus, there is a need to move away from an epicentre located in the Ganges valley and recognise that these historico-cultural changes have always remained uneven all over the subcontinent, across different spatial units. With this recognition in mind, we observe that the spatial and temporal parameters of the Deccan throw up different definitions of the early historic phase in this region. B. D. Chattopadhyaya has coherently articulated one such definition while elaborating on the transition to the early historic period in the Deccan. He writes:

> The change cannot be viewed either in terms of a gradual evolution from the megalithic culture or in terms of a wholesale north Indian impact because in early historical phase, the Deccan has absorbed some elements which are unique and non-indigenous to both north and south. To understand the historical spatial composition of the Deccan, it is important to locate the nuclear areas of the Sātavāhanas and to examine how they were related to the 'localities' of the pre-Sātavāhana phase (Chattopadhyaya 2003: 39–47).

This understanding of the early historical period in the Deccan is apt for the subject matter that we propose to highlight in this chapter. It enables us to focus on how the criteria of the 'historic' emerges in the different 'localities' of the Deccan, which in any case were part of the specific geographic sub-regions.

The criteria used to understand the transition to the early historic phase in India usually includes such common indices like the emergence of urban centres, coinage, and scripts for writing, alongside other essential material changes signified by pottery, metal technology, and the like. In the Deccan, excavated material pertaining to the Megalithic and the early historic phases[2] are not always found to be clearly distinct from each other. They have been found to coexist at places, and often overlap. In specific sub-regions and localities, this lack of clarity often leads to problems in dating these two cultural phases—the Megalithic and the early historical cultures—and the material remains of these phases are then placed during the same periodical time frame. The issue is further complicated when the early historic phases are called 'Sātavāhana'. It is noticed that in some sub-regions of the Deccan, material remains like the coins that we propose to highlight in this chapter have been found at stratigraphic levels that pre-date the rise of the Sātavāhanas in the Deccan. The question that arises then is whether the existence of these coins should be located instead in the Megalithic period, which is generally understood as a pre-urban phase of human evolution.

This process of transition, and the ambiguities that the material evidence throws up, have earlier been articulated by Sudarshan Seneviratne. Within his broader concerns to understand the processes of state-formation in Andhra and Kalinga, Seneviratne has used the theory of 'secondary state formation' to formulate the processes that led to the transition from the Megalithic to the early historic phase. He emphasised first on the internal processes of change emanating from the Megalithic society, and then on the external influences, primarily defined by the Mauryan presence in some parts of the Deccan (as evidenced by the presence of the Aśokan inscriptions) that led to the formation of the early state in these regions. Seneviratne writes: 'The process of secondary state formation in Kalinga and Andhra was an outcome when the autochthonous forces combined with the consequences resulting from a period of political subordination to the "metropolitan states"[3] of the Mauryas and the Sātavāhanas' (1981: 54–69). This analysis points to a critical feature, that is, the creation of a 'ranked' society',[4] already present during the Megalithic phases, which was a precursor to the rise of a stratified class-based state society when a ruling class with control over the means of production emerged. Thus, this explanation of transition has helped us to understand the nature of power visible in local polities even before the rise of the Sātavāhanas.

Several localities with ruling chiefs were found distributed in the sub-regions delineated above. The distribution of their coins did not necessarily reflect a systematic pattern. We have defined local polities as small political ruling groups that have left tangible evidence of their rule and political prominence in these localities.

Scholars have used several names for these local polities, such as ruling families, lineage groups, social groups, etc. For instance, B. D. Chattopadhyaya has opined that these localities were very similar to *janapadas*, thus implying a certain type of proto-state formation in the early historic Deccan (Chattopadhyaya 1987: 728). This study is framed to first and foremost describe these coins in some depth, as they were found in the four sub-regions of the Deccan, to address a fundamental question: Can these coins, hitherto understood only marginally to corroborate the magnitude of the Sātavāhana empire, now enable us to provide a different picture of the trajectories in which power played itself out in smaller territorial units? That these units were not always autonomous further complicates our analysis, as this then throws up the deeper question of how the Sātavāhana state was built and maintained over time, in relation to these centres of power that are reflected through this coinage.

Local Chiefs—Pre-Sātavāhana Times

Eastern Deccan

Coins of the Sada chiefs were pre-eminent in the eastern Deccan before the rise of the Sātavāhanas. Though we notice the distribution of Sada coins all along the long stretch from Srikakulam (Mukhalingam) to Nellore (Padugupadu) (Prasad 1993b: 53), they were mostly concentrated in the Vaddamanu area located 34 kms northeast of Guntur (Sastri 1992: 1) and adjacent to Amaravati, which was a famous early Buddhist centre. It has further been noted by scholars of Sada coins (Prasad 1993a: 333) and Talavara coins (Reddy and Reddy 1993: 42–43) that Śiva Sada extended his authority further south towards the Bapatla–Ongole–Chandavaram localities by overthrowing the local rulers called the Talavaras, and thus executed a territorial expansion.

Prasad informs us that when Edward James Rapson, one of the first scholars to record Sada coins in his catalogue, reported a hoard of twenty-three coins found in the Krishna-Godavari region, he classified them in the category 'name-uncertain'. But later scholars have ascribed them to Sada rulers. It was the unearthing of thirty-one square- and round-shaped, cast and die-struck, heavy lead coins of the Sadas in the excavations at Vaddamanu that unveiled the names of eight Sada chiefs (Prasad 1993b: 53). The first Sada chief was identified through two heavy single-struck lion-type coins that had on their obverse a heavy lion[5] with an open mouth and curled tail and tree in railing[6] while the reverse was blank (ibid.). The legends on both coins read *raño siri mahāsada(sa)* and *ma ha sadasa,* and therefore, scholars have unanimously attributed them to the earliest known ruler of the Sadas, called Raño Siri Mahā Sada. Eight coins of Sada chief Asaka Sada, bearing the legend *raño siri asakasada* (Kasturi Bai 1986: 15), were reported from the Vaddamanu area, and a stray Sada coin of Asaka Sada with the legend (*raño*) *siri asakasadasa* was found at Dharanikota (Prasad 1993a: 44). Careful observation of all the Sada coins have brought to light their common features—the obverse usually comprised of a heavily built lion with an open mouth, and a tree in railing adjacent to the lion, while the reverse was either faded or left blank (Kasturi Bai 1986: 17). Further, excavations at the Amaravati *stūpa* not only yielded Sada coins, but also unveiled inscriptions that mention them. Based on this, scholars have re-examined the chronology of the Amaravati stūpa in relation to the Sadas and the Sātavāhanas. Based on the Vaddamanu excavations, the early Sada kings were dated to 40 BCE (Shimada 2005: 42). However, mention of a Sada king called Aira Mana Sada in the Velpuru inscription led D. C. Sircar to date this king to the first half of the second century CE on palaeographic grounds (Kasturi Bai 1986: 20).

Based on the opinion of scholars, we may consider the chronological list of Sada rulers as Siri Sada, the earliest known Sada ruler (according to the scholarship of Kasturi Bai, and more recently, Akira Shimada), followed by Mahā Sada, Asaka Sada, Śiva Sada, and Śivamaka Sada, thereby comprising a total of five local chiefs (Prasad 1999: 333). The founder of the Sada dynasty, Siri Sada, was called the lord of Kalinga and Mahishka and he belonged to the Mahāmeghavāhana family line (Kasturi Bai 1986: 20). Siri Sada was the ruler of Mahishkamandala, which is said to constitute the Krishna-Godavari region. His important contribution lay in having shifted his capital from Kalinganagara to Dhanyakataka (Prasad 1999: 333).

Based on the Bhattiprolu and Vaddamanu inscriptions dated to the third century BCE and the second century BCE, respectively, there is some consensus among scholars that prominent local rulers Kubiraka and Somaka, mentioned in these inscriptions, had ruled over the Krishna-Guntur region after the retreat of the Mauryas, and were then succeeded by the Sada chief, Siri Sada (Kasturi Bai 1986: 21). The chronology of the Sada rulers confirms that they ruled the eastern Deccan for one-and-a-half centuries before the region was annexed by the Sātavāhanas under Vasisthiputra Pulomavi. The most recent dating of the Sadas has been provided by Akira Shimada, who holds that Sada rule had begun in the eastern Deccan from 40–30 BCE and continued up to 90–100 CE.[7] The stability of their rule confirms the following major point that enables us to analyse the transition from pre-state to state society in the Deccan. The Sadas, like other local rulers in the various localities of the Deccan, laid the foundation for the rise of various institutions—social, economic, and cultural—which were the forerunners of the institutions of the early historic period when the Sātavāhanas established their pan-Deccan empire.

Central Deccan

Local polities emerged in the central Deccan, where no direct conclusive evidence of Mauryan contact has been reported. Krishnasastry had excavated many sites in this sub-region to suggest that the material culture found clearly shows a difference between that found in the Megalithic phase, and the early historic phase. This was based on excavations conducted at the sites of Kotilingala and Dhulikatta, where evidence of forts have been reported alongside other material remains, along with a large amount of iron artefacts (Krishnasastry 1983: 126). Further, the most interesting data to emerge from the Peddabankur excavations were structures that alluded to certain social groups, such as blacksmiths or *karmaras*, and carpenters or *taskans* (ibid.: 158).

In the midst of these finds, the central Deccan has yielded important evidence of coins with the names and legends of local rulers, thus suggesting an entrenched polity (that is, a well-established polity ruled by local chiefs) that had enough resources to support their existence and endeavours. In Kotilingala, the focus of the central Deccan, located in the Karimnagar district of Telangana, coins have been found that revealed the names of various pre-Sātavāhana local chiefs, such as Gobhada, Siri Kamvaya, Siri Narana, Samagopa, Mahātalavara, and Mahāsenāpati Sagamana. Thirty-one coins found on the surface layer and four coins excavated from the stratified layers at Kotilingala have been attributed to Gobhada, the earliest local ruler at Kotilingala. A Gobhada coin found in the sixth stratified layer bore the legend *(ra)ño gobhada sa* in Brāhmī characters (Parabrahma Sastry 1994: 27). Scholars suggest that the word 'Raño' implies they were independent and not a subordinate of any larger ruling polity (Raja Reddy 1992: 26). Overall, according to stratigraphy and palaeography, scholars have dated Gobhada coins to the late second century BCE (Parabrahma Sastry 1978: 13–14), i.e., between 125–100 BCE (Bajpai 1979: 38–46). Gobhada coins were known for certain symbols minted on them, such as a bow-and-arrow signifying the identity of the ruler and a tree in railing that indicates his affiliation to the Buddhist faith (Raja Reddy 1992: 26).

Samagopa, or Svamigopa, was the next prominent ruler who issued coins made of copper, lead, and potin (Parabrahma Sastry 1994: 29). According to both Parabrahma Sastry and P. L. Gupta (1978), Samagopa coins were mainly of two types, bow-and-arrow type and tree-and-bull type (Parabrahma Sastry 1978: 14–16). The earliest Samagopa coin bearing the legend *rañosamagopasa* was found in the sixth stratified layer of excavations at Kotalingala. According to scholars, Samagopa ruled during the 100 BCE–75 BCE (Bajpai 1979: 38–46). Both Samagopa and Gobhada have been considered to rule before Simuka Sātavāhana, the progenitor of the Sātavāhana dynasty (Parabrahma Sastry 1978: 12–16). Parabrahma Sastry is of the opinion that Simuka had overthrown Samagopa and other contemporary local rulers and had established

Sātavāhana rule in the Karimnagar area of central Deccan during 50 BCE (ibid.: 17).

There are divergent opinions among scholars concerning the identity of Gobhada and Samagopa. Some suggest that they served in the administration of the Mauryas, while others consider them the descendants of the Sunga family, who later became independent rulers at Kotilingala after the Mauryan retreat (Parabrahma Sastry 1978: 17). However, it is clear that unlike the contiguous region of the western Deccan, local units of power played a significant role in the political spectrum of the central Deccan. Though it is difficult to assess the spatial extent of their suzerainty, going by the locations where their coins were found, one can concur with B. D. Chattopadhyaya (2003: 39–47) that they ruled over small and clearly specified janapada-like entities that foreshadowed the rise of a full-fledged state, based on a stratified society.

In the contiguous sub-region of the western Deccan, unlike in the central Deccan, there is emphatic evidence of contact with north India in the form of finding Northern Black Polished Ware (found in Nasik) that goes back to as early as 400 BCE. Though uninscribed coins were found at Nasik, Pauni, and Bhokardan dated 100 BCE–50 CE (Shastri 2001: 339), uninscribed cast copper and die-struck coins dated to an even earlier period, namely second to third century BCE, were also found in these places (Shastri 1982: 2). It is pertinent to note that they do not bear the names and legends of local chiefs. It is only much later that in the western Deccan, we notice inscribed coins of local chiefs such as Satyabhadra and Damabhadra in the Wardha and Nagpur districts of Maharashtra. Based on palaeography, it can be suggested that they existed before the rise of the Sātavāhanas (ibid.: 4). The period of transition, from the Megalithic cultural phase to the early historic, in different sub-regions of the Deccan thus suggests different trajectories of economic expansion and political organisation of power.

Regarding this pre-Sātavāhana phase in the Deccan, we conclude that though the polities were not built on a fully stratified society, they wielded power which can be best described as 'chiefdoms', of chiefs who clearly had the ability to issue coins in their names, indicating a certain political configuration of power. Being relatively small entities with limited state apparatus and administrative structure, some of these local polities were later subsumed into the Sātavāhana empire while others were not totally obliterated by them; these latter polities continued to rule in their localities albeit in a subordinate position. Numismatic sources continue to provide us with interesting evidence that shows that at varying points in time, local rulers in sub-regions of the Deccan had a contemporaneous existence and relationship with the Sātavāhanas. It is for this reason that a precise view of the chronology of the Sātavāhanas acceptable to all scholars eludes us. Nonetheless, we have to accept that the Sātavāhanas grew to provide strong political and administrative institutions that clearly reflected an expanded economic and social set-up.

Local Chiefs and the Sātavāhanas

Despite a lot of scholarly investment in the Sātavāhanas as a dynasty, scholars have been divided on the chronological framework of their rule. Some of this ambiguity arises because an earlier group of scholars had used the 'evidence' from some of the *Purāṇas*, which had mentioned varying numbers of Andhra kings that ruled over these parts. This scholarship also used the early Sātavāhana inscriptions to conclude that the Sātavāhanas ruled immediately after the Mauryas, and suggested a long chronology of Sātavāhana rule. More recently, a majority of scholars have supported what is called the shorter chronology for Sātavāhanas, as they recognise the existence of local polities right after the Mauryan retreat and before the area was controlled by the Sātavāhanas. Thus, numismatic sources have become significant in support of the latter view, suggesting that their rule began from around the mid-first century BCE and declined by the early third century CE.[8] In the sub-region-wise description of such local rulers, the eastern Deccan gives us no conclusive evidence of the presence of local rulers since the time the Sātavāhanas arrived here at a later period, after putting an end to Sada rule (the Sadas had reigned in pre-Sātavāhana times). However, in the western Deccan the Kura rulers, and in the southern Deccan the Mahārathis have left enough numismatic evidence to indicate that they were coterminous with Sātavāhana presence. The central Deccan too has evidence of prominent local rulers like the Mahātalavaras, the Mahāsenāpatis, and the Mahārathis, who were contemporaries of the Sātavāhanas.

Central Deccan

In central Deccan, firm archaeological evidence involving religious and secular structures unearthed at Peddabankur, Kotilingala, and Dhulikatta clearly mark the early historic period proper (Krishnasastry 1983: 123–124). In the midst of these remains, coins of the Mahātalavara chiefs have been found here, as well as those from other localities of this sub-region. It is significant to note that three different types of Mahātalavara coins—horse, elephant, and *nandipāda* (taurine, or bull's hoof)—probably issued by three different chiefs, were reported from Kotilingala, which have been dated to the first century BCE (Parabrahma Sastry 1994: 37). Fourteen Mahātalavara coins were reported from Sangareddy, and Jangaon (including Devaruppalain) districts of Telangana by D. Raja Reddy and P. Suryanarayana Reddy (1991, 1993). They display typical features like the obverse with a horse facing right (sometimes left), a circle with the Ujjain symbol, and tree in railing, bearing the legends *mahātalavarasa*, *mahātalavarasamajasamikasasivasebakasa*, *(mahātalavarasa) siri kumara sebakasa*, *mahātalavarasasiripudasa* while the reverse of these coins display three and six arched hills with crescent[9] as their common features (Reddy and Reddy 1991: 71–80, 1993: 42–43). A hoard of forty Mahātalavara coins found at Phanigiri in Suryapet district of Telangana also displays horse-type lead coins, which are additionally accompanied on the obverse by a *śrīvatsa* or *triratna*[10] symbol, and on the reverse are the characteristic three-arched hill, crescent and wavy lines surrounding it. Of the forty coins, eighteen bore the legend *balakutasamahātalavarasa*, two had the legend *mahātalavarasasa (mikasasivasebaka)*, nine simply had *mahātalavarasa,* three only have *talavara*, and the remaining eight did not show clear legends that could be deciphered (Subrahmanyam et al. 2008: 23). A palaeographic analysis of these coins revealed that those bearing the legend *mahātalavarasa* were dated earlier than the ones with a long legend *mahātalavarasam ajasamikasasivasebakasa* (Reddy and Reddy 1991: 77). A further analysis of the long legends by scholars suggests that the term 'sebaka' alluded to the title of the Mahātalavara chief, while the term 'majasamikasa' was considered the name of the territory controlled by the chief. Similarly, the term 'balakuta' could also be associated with the name of the territory controlled by the chief. Palaeographic analysis has further dated the Phanigiri Mahātalavara coins between the first century BCE and the first century CE, and excavators of this site have identified them as belonging to the subordinates of the Sātavāhana rulers (Subrahmanyam et al. 2008: 25–26).

The Mahāsenāpatis were the other prominent local chieftains who were contemporary to the Sātavāhanas, and whose coins have been found at Kondapur, Kotilingala, and Sangareddy in the central Deccan. The Kotilingala Mahāsenāpati coins were of the *swastikā* type with the legend *mahāsenāpatisagamanasa* inscribed on them, which Parabrahma Sastry (1994: 37) has dated to between the first and second centuries CE based on palaeographic grounds. Kondapur, on the other hand, has revealed one elephant-type potin coin with the legend *ka (u) satakisirimahāsenāpatisa*, and two horse-type lead coins with the legends *rajno kana bhadasamanasevamahāsenāpati savasathipu(tasa)* and *mahasenapatisaharanakasirimahagamakasa* (Siddiqui 1994: 15–17). A careful look at the legends of the horse-type Mahāsenāpati coins reveals that one of the rulers, named Kana Bhada Mana carries the metronym Vasathi. The other ruler's name was Haranaka, and he also bore the title Mahagamaka, which suggests that he was initially a chief of a village; however, this interpretation is not very clear. Other typical features noticed on these three Mahāsenāpati coins from Kondapur are the consistent use of the swastikā symbol on the obverse while on the reverse, a variety of symbols like an upraised arrow, *chaitya* with three, six and ten arches, tree in railing with leaves and wavy lines, and so on are displayed. Scholars have dated these Mahāsenāpati coins from Kondapur to between the second and third centuries CE, which indicates that the Mahātalavara chiefs of Kondapur had flourished while being the contemporaries of the Sātavāhanas, but Mahāsenāpatis continued to exist even after the end of Sātavāhana rule (Siddiqui 1994: 17). Sangareddy too has yielded three Mahāsenāpati lead coins with the above-mentioned common features, except that these coins had taurine symbols on the branches of the tree, and one of the coins bore the symbol of a lion facing left. The legends on these coins were partly deciphered as *senapa (thisa), (saga) mana siva (sa) da, (saga) mana si (va),* and based on words like Senapati and Sagamana, scholars have confirmed them to be Mahāsenāpati coins (Reddy and Reddy 1991: 71–80). Though no clear dates have been given to these coins, their common features and minting techniques enable scholars to consider them contemporaries of the Sātavāhanas.

The Mahārathis were the next significant local chieftains whose presence can be ascertained through their coins in the central Deccan, and also in other sub-regions of the Deccan. Their coin types were divided into three distinct groups: (*i*) bull-type Mahārathi coins prominently found in the western Deccan, (*ii*) chaitya-type Mahārathi coins evidenced in the eastern Deccan, and (*iii*) lion or elephant-type Mahārathi coins bearing the Ujjain symbol and with features similar to the Sātavāhana coins from the central Deccan (Siddiqui 1966: 59). Interestingly, these Mahārathi chiefs of the central Deccan do not have a presence in the Kotilingala–Karimnagar area, which had a rich display of local coins from pre-Sātavāhana times. Siddiqui has observed that the Mahārathis of the central Deccan had matrimonial alliances with the Sātavāhanas, as evidenced from the long legends minted on their coins, which include names such as 'sātakarṇi' and 'sadakana' as prefix and suffix. A good number of Mahārathi coins were found at Kondapur, with legends like *mahārathisa* and *sātakanimahārathisadakana.* A lead coin with the legend *mahārathisivaka (ta) nasa* (Rao 1957: 184) from Nelakondapalli in Khammam district has, after palaeographic analysis, led scholars to date it as contemporaneous to Sadakana Kalalaya Mahārathi, who in turn was considered a contemporary of the Sātavāhana king, Sātakarṇi I (ibid.: 186; Siddiqui 1966: 58). There is a prolific presence of Mahārathi coins in and around Hyderabad.[11] Most have been dated between the first and second centuries CE (Siddiqui 1987: 94). Overall, there were similar minting techniques and symbols on the Mahārathi and the Sātavāhana coins. It is interesting to note that the Mahātalavara and Mahārathi local rulers were politically prominent across different localities of the central Deccan, when compared to the Mahāsenāpati rulers who had a limited presence. Further, while the former were contemporaries of the early Sātavāhana rulers who ruled between the first century BCE and the early decades of the Common Era, the latter continued their existence into much later periods between the first and second centuries CE.

Western and Southern Deccan

In the western Deccan, the Kuras were the prominent local chiefs who had a presence at Brahmapuri in Kolhapur district, Maharashtra, which was a well-known early historic site. Here, a hoard of eighty coins was excavated in the midst of other archaeological features of Sātavāhana times (Deo 1975: 39–40). The common features on Kura coins were symbols of a bow with arrow on their obverse, while the reverse had several symbols such as a tree, chaityas with different arches, a crescent, a swastikā, etc. The legends on these coins have unveiled the names of three Kura chiefs. They are Vasisthiputra Vilivayakura, Mathariputra Sivalakura, and Gautamiputra Vilivayakura. Among the hoard of eighty coins, thirty-two coins were independent issues made by Vasisthiputra Vilivayakura (six), Mathariputra Sivalakura (twelve), and Gautamiputra Vilivayakura (fourteen), while the remaining forty-eight were restruck by the succeeding Kura chiefs.[12] The restriking of Kura coins is probably indicative of the successive rulers' adherence to the authority of the early rulers of the Kura royal family. The identity of the Kura chiefs and their subsequent relations with the Sātavāhanas has been much discussed by scholars. M. Rama Rao had supported the earlier views of scholars like

R. G. Bhandarkar (1884), according to whom the Kura chiefs functioned as subordinates of the Sātavāhanas, and the title 'raño' before their legends indicated that they initially operated as independent rulers from Kolhapur before Gautamiputra Sātakarṇi subdued them (Rao 1955: 63–68). However, after the death of the Sātavāhana ruler Vasisthiputra Pulomavi, the Kuras rid themselves of their subordinate status and once again declared independence, before being subdued by another powerful Sātavāhana king, Yajña Sri, who took the Kolhapur region under his control (ibid.: 69–71). That they exerted their independence illustrates the determination with which local rulers preserved their individuality, despite the dominance of the Sātavāhanas.

When we turn to the southern Deccan, we see that the Mahārathi chiefs were prominent during Sātavāhana rule. A typical archaeological picture of the early historical period in this sub-region is found at Veerapuram in Kurnool district, Andhra Pradesh, which displays a material culture that has been identified with the 'Sātavāhana' level of habitation[13] found at other such sites in the Deccan (T. V. G. Sastri et al. 1984: 24–25). Here, a hoard of thirteen elephant-type Mahārathi coins were excavated (Kasturi Bai 1991: 34–48). While the symbols found on the coins of the early Mahārathi rulers of Veerapuram were six arched hills and trees that were carved, later Mahārathi rulers minted the Ujjain symbol of the Sātavāhanas, clearly indicating a certain allegiance to them (Sastry 1991: 68). Based on the palaeography of their legends, six Mahārathi rulers were placed in a chronological sequence as Mahārathisa Mahāhathi, Mahārathiputa Siva, Mahārathisa Siva Mahāhathi, an unidentified Mahārathi, Mahārathisa Khadapori Hathi, and Mahārathisa Siva Khada (Kasturi Bai 1991: 34–48). Kasturi Bai (ibid.: 47–48) has suggested that after the reign of prince Kumara Haku Sri, son of Sātakarṇi I, the Mahārathis of Veerapuram, who were till then subordinate to the Sātavāhanas, finally became independent rulers and continued to rule the region until 200 CE, when the last Mahārathi ruler, Mahārathisa Siva Khada, was overthrown by the Sātavāhanas, and the Mahārathis once again became subordinates to the latter.

Four Mahārathi coins were reported from Anantapur district, Andhra Pradesh with their obverse bearing an elephant facing left, while their reverse had symbols of a tree with branches. Except for one that had an unclear legend, the others had *maharatisasivasa*, *(maha) ratisa*, *(maha) ratisasiva (sa)* (Reddy and Reddy 1992: 31–32). There is some resemblance with the coins of the previously discussed chief Mahārathisa Siva Mahāhathi of Veerapuram. It is generally accepted that the Mahārathis of Anantapur were contemporaries of the Sātavāhanas and enjoyed a subordinate status (Kasturi Bai 1991: 47–48). In the Chittaldurg–Chandravalli region of Karnataka, a hoard of twenty-two Mahārathi coins that portrayed four successive generations of Mahārathi rulers were found. Their titles have been deciphered to indicate Sadakana Kalalaya Mahārathi, Sadakana Kanha Mahārathi, Sadakana Chatakanha Mahārathi, and an unidentified Mahārathi ruler (Rao 1954: 198). They shared the other typical features of Mahārathi coins (ibid.: 200). Rama Rao has concurred with the earlier interpretation of Rapson, who had opined that Kalalaya of the coins was the same as the name engraved on the Naneghat inscription of Sātakarṇi I, indicating that these chiefs were clearly contemporaneous to the early Sātavāhanas.[14]

Though earlier scholarship has understood these local rulers as the subordinates of the Sātavāhanas, it is to be noted, based on the above descriptions, that in different time periods these rulers reigned as independent rulers. In still other cases, it has been suggested that while maintaining a cordial relationship with the Sātavāhanas, they acted as their royal officers. Important officers in the Sātavāhana administration included the *mahātaraka* who monitored the king's household, the *mahāsenāpati* or commander-in-chief of the king's army, among others (Hanumantha Rao 1976: 34). In this interpretation, local chiefs were seen as playing an integrative role since they had been incorporated into the administrative structure of the Sātavāhanas. For instance, Mahāsenāpati chiefs of the central Deccan were thought of as the guardians of the Sātavāhana rulers while serving as subordinates of this dynasty, as they were usually placed in charge of the bordering *ahāras*[15] so as to protect the kingdom from attacks by the Śakas (ibid.: 36). On the other hand, more recent scholarship views the role of the Mahāsenāpatis in terms of their functioning as part of a feudal hierarchy. They were assigned the critical task of writing the land charters, along with Sātavāhana officers called *amātyas* and *pratihāras* (ministers/advisers to the king; most important position in the Sātavāhana administration)(Sharma 1968: 203). In other words, the Sātavāhanas delegated to them certain tasks, primarily because these groups were the owners and controllers of land (ibid.: 210).[16] However, we observe that it is not easy to follow either of these views simplistically and uniformly. There are instances cited earlier in the chapter where the Mahāsenāpatis ruled as independent chiefs. In contrast to them, the Mahātalavaras and Mahārathis of the central Deccan invariably carried the name Sātavāhana along with their titles in long legends on their coins, indicating their subordinate status. A contrary view suggests that the very fact that coins were issued by these local rulers indicates a decline in the power of the Sātavāhanas (Mangalam 1999: 361). Hence, there seems to have been constant instability and changes in the sovereign status and occasional shifts in the power of these local polities that coexisted with the Sātavāhanas in the Deccan. The political landscape, thus, was never devoid of assertion by local polities, which made their presence felt by issuing their own coins rather than merely re-issuing Sātavāhanas coins or restriking them.

Overview and Conclusion

The study of local coins as a prominent source has primarily indicated how local rulers defined their identity through issuing coins with their own symbols and legends, highlighting the particularity of their own areas of control. This does not mean that they were not influenced by the palaeography and minting techniques from outside their zones of control. In fact, common features show a dynamic interaction between the local elite who negotiated their sustenance vis-à-vis other, similar power centres.

A significant aspect affecting all these local rulers was the overall economic change that swept the Deccan during the period when these polities thrived. They had to necessarily participate in these economic changes, which we can glean from the way social groups—political and economical—participated in trade, while also making donations to the Buddhist Saṅgha, as evidenced in inscriptions found mainly in eastern and western Deccan. The inscriptions prolifically refer to diverse professional groups through terms such as *gahapati*, *sethi*, *vāniya,* and a host of others alluding to merchant, trading, and artisan groups. When and where in the early Deccan such groups began to emerge is also linked to how the local polities were integrating themselves within the larger socio-economic order of the times.

One category of early Deccan inscriptions included the official Sātavāhana inscriptions of western Deccan, found at Junnar, Nasik, Kanheri, and Mahad, which record a good number of land donations made by lay devotees along with donations of villages by some professional groups such as merchants (Ray 1986: 98, 100). The gifting of these villages to monastic institutions and *brāhmaṇas* implies the expansion of the rural economy, which necessitated that the state take control of the newly occupied areas that may have hitherto been under the control of local rulers. The other set of inscriptions, commonly called 'label inscriptions', were donative in nature and were recorded with the donor's name, the names of his family members, his native place, and the religious centre where these donations were made (for an in-depth engagement, see Ghosh 2015). Both the western and eastern Deccan label inscriptions, significantly mention the *gahapatis, sethis*, and other groups such as the Mahārathis and the Mahābhojas. The inscriptions of the Mahārathis and the Mahābhojas alluded to some of the local elites who had issued coins in their names. The ability of all the afore-mentioned professional groups to make donations was based on their wealth, accrued both from land and trade. All trading activities were, however, organised around private guilds that remained largely independent of the political administrative structure of the local polities and the Sātavāhana state. They integrated into the network of the socio-political order of the time by paying taxes, and were thus incorporated into the complex economic system of monetised exchange.

Further, the proliferation of economic institutions across the whole region led ultimately to the expansion of a well-stratified social structure, moving beyond kinship ties (Ray 1986: 90). These socio-economic changes were prominently seen in urban centres, which proliferated during the early centuries of the Common Era all over the Deccan and went hand-in-hand with the expansion of Buddhism in the region (ibid.: 160). The urban centres emerged in different ecological sub-regions of the Deccan, and thus varied in their size and the extent to which they dominated the countryside, especially in areas that were controlled by local polities (Parasher Sen 1999: 159). During the same period, the use and circulation of gold and silver Roman coins in the early Deccan reflected a vibrant trade and commerce in the growing markets and urban centres (Turner 1989: 51). Thus, we notice that prosperous local trade routes across the Deccan, starting at port towns like Bharuch, Sopara, etc., and passing through places like Ter, Bhokardan, Pauni, Kondapur, Nellakondipalli, and Yelleshwaram to reach the monastic institutions, supported by mercantile groups all along the eastern coastline, was something that many of the local political authorities benefitted from. At another level, the introduction of Roman coins with high quality metal enhanced social and economic status in the local gift economy (Bondada 2015: 415). Scholars have pointed out that more than the rampant circulation of Roman coins in the Deccan, the impact that this circulation had on the minting of coins by the local rulers is more noteworthy. For instance, the lead coins of Kura chiefs and Mahārathi chiefs of the western Deccan were known to be made of imported metals of high quality (Ray 1994: 78).

We have shown how, in the period between the Megalithic phase of habitation to what has been called the early historic period in the early Deccan, there was a critical transitional phase that can only be effectively highlighted if we give credence to evidence that emanates from coins issued by local chiefs. These coins emerged in the different sub-regions of the Deccan, and their distribution varied across sub-regions during both pre-Sātavāhana and Sātavāhana times. Their existence and particularity were impacted by different socio-economic and institutional changes that contributed to our overall understanding of the ever-evolving social formation in early historic Deccan. Each phase in this evolution was marked by heterogeneity. Variations in the type and form of megaliths[17] across the Deccan do not challenge the supposition that the Megalithic social set-up was more like what anthropologists have called a rank-based society that had yet to undergo diversification of economic activity, a clear social stratification, and centralised political control. However, developments in the subsequent transitional phase saw the presence of heterogeneous spheres, along with an expansion of settlements and emerging local ruling groups with independent or semi-independent status, which impacted the general growth in the historical development of the early Deccan. These local ruling chiefs had issued coins in their names that clearly indicated their power and significance. In some sub-regions of the Deccan, this was preceded by the presence of the Mauryas, which suggested some form of control exerted by them as evident from the presence of several Aśokan edicts, especially in southern and eastern Deccan.

Studies of lineage-based societies have provided insights that help us to place the nature of these local polities within the broad spectrum of an evolutionary socio-political change that ancient societies undergo. In the context of north India, Romila Thapar has provided a relevant understanding of lineage as a 'corporate group that is made of unilineal kin with a formal system of authority' (Thapar 1984: 10). According to her, lineage is made up of an extended family comprising three to four generations, a feature visible among the Sada rulers of the eastern Deccan, whose extended family of many generations had exhibited considerable authority over this sub-region. The same pattern of political control cannot be observed in the central Deccan, as their name endings indicate that they belong to a small kin-based 'corporate' group. Clearly, these centres of local political authority had the basic preconditions that facilitated their transition to the early historic, but that also needed some significant institutional processes of change to take place. In this context, the work of Uthara Suvrathan, who has analysed the politico-institutional changes in the early historic urban centre of Banavasi in southern Deccan, is instructive. She elaborates that these changes happened when internal strategic political changes occurred in the local ruling families, and their contact with external developments such as Buddhism brought in ideas and people from elsewhere in the subcontinent to this locality, which triggered social and economic change (Suvrathan 2014: 89–142). Similar internal influences such as socio-political changes within the local ruling families and external influences such as Buddhism impacted the local rulers of the central and the eastern Deccan by gradually changing their internal politico-institutional structures. In fact, the period delineated above, when these pre-Sātavāhana chiefs ruled, was coterminous with the spread of both Buddhism and Jainism in the Deccan. In the eastern Deccan, especially, there is strong epigraphic and art-historical evidence that shows how a variety of social groups were impacted by these new ideas that ultimately led to an opening up of society to various kinds of external influences.

Despite such external stimulus in the Deccan, the internal evolution of local polities proceeded unabated, exhibiting individuality and difference in the way the region responded to the growing socio-economic and ideological change. A gradual but firm expansion of trade, the spread of the Brāhmī script, and most emphatically, the spread of Buddhism defined the economic and ideological landscape of early historic Deccan, which was also marked by the rise of the new pan-Deccan ruling elite, namely the Sātavāhanas. We have noted above how local ruling groups continued to survive during the early historic period, negotiating their individual relationship with the Sātavāhanas. Their survival indicates that most of the local ruling groups had a strong economic base, even though their territories may have been annexed by the Sātavāhanas. The internal processes of change seen in the expansion of the rural settlements and emergence of towns and urban centres in all sub-regions of the Deccan not only impacted the rise of the Sātavāhana dynasty as a full-fledged state, but also led to mechanisms by way of which the local polities were integrated into their empire from time to time, only to reassert their independent status after the decline of the empire. Over the *longue durée*, then, the Deccan saw both internal and external processes of change that impacted the way social formation emerged here, albeit without diminishing the role of local chiefs in the creation of the polity, economy, and social order that defined the Deccan of early historic times. A study of their coins has enhanced our understanding of the changing social formation with their temporal and spatial specificities throughout the Deccan.

Notes

Acknowledgements: This chapter is based on my M.Phil dissertation submitted to the Department of History, University of Hyderabad in 2018 under the supervision of Professor Aloka Parasher Sen. I am indebted to her for her valuable suggestions and constant encouragement.

1. The local coins have been studied prominently by Ajay Mitra Shastri (1982), P. V. Parabrahma Sastry (1978, 1994), I. K. Sarma (2000), and others. We have discussed their views in detail during the course of this chapter.
2. Megalithic and early historic phases in the Deccan were represented by different chronological time frames for different sites. Considering the fact that emergence of a new culture does not necessarily imply the end of the previously existing culture, the rough time frames for Megalithic phase are 600 BCE–300 CE, and for early historic phase are 200 BCE–300 CE.
3. The term 'metropolitan state' was used by Romila Thapar (1987), specifically to denote the controlling centre of the Mauryan state.
4. A ranked society possesses a dualistic character where there exists a special ruling stratum even before the total disintegration of tribal relations.
5. After a thorough analysis of the symbols on the coins, scholars identified that the lion symbol minted on these Sada coins was heavy compared to other lion symbols on the coins found in the Deccan. From the legend it was clear that 'rano' is a word, which was synonymous to 'raja'. Since Mahā Sada was the first Sada ruler (according to Prasad), it can be presumed that with such a 'heavy lion' symbol, he wanted to indicate his sovereign status as an independent ruler.

6. 'Tree in railing' is a symbol connected to the Bodhi tree in whose shade Buddha was enlightened. Tree in railing is considered to be one of the dominant symbols in Indian numismatics. Trees are shown with railing and without railing on ancient coins. The idea of minting coins with tree in railing became popular with the spread of Buddhism and the royal patronage ascribed to it.
7. While re-examining the chronology of the Amaravati *stūpa*, Shimada has extensively analysed the numismatic data and stated that Sivamaka Sada was the last Sada ruler who ruled for twenty years, and the Sada dynasty declined under his rule during 90–100 CE (Shimada 2005: 38).
8. The various views on the chronology of the Sātavāhanas are discussed in Parabrahma Sastry (1994: 20–24), Raja Reddy (1992: 2), Shimada (2005: 42), and have most recently been summarised in Subbarayalu (2014: 40).
9. Three arched hills and six arched hills are the usual symbols represented on coins right from the times of Mauryas and Shungas as a representation of Buddhist chaityas. Following the path of these prominent dynasties, the local rulers too minted on their coins the symbols of three arched and six arched hills. Some coins also display ten arched hills. As far as the Deccan is concerned, we have noticed only three, six, and ten arched hills. The crescent refers to a moon which is displayed on the top of the hill. The crescent symbol is found in popular usage on ancient Indian coins across the world. It is considered to be an astronomical symbol indicating either the sun or the moon.
10. The śrīvatsa and the triratna, symbols look almost similar. While the term 'śrīvatsa' is associated with Brahmanism, 'triratna' is a word associated with the three jewels of Buddhism. They look like the *trishul* (trident) symbol.
11. Two swastika-type and two lion-type coins with legends *mahāratipputa (sadakani) satahagasa* (Reddy and Reddy 1992: 29–30) and *sadakanajayahamahāratisa* (ibid.: 31) were reported from Sangareddy, two bull-type bearing the legend *mahārathisa* were reported from Zaheerabad, and two more were reported from the adjoining areas of Hyderabad with legends *harathiputasa* (Siddiqui 1966: 57) and *mahārathiasaghosasa*. The latter legend, according to Siddiqui, was an officer or subordinate of the Sātavāhanas (Siddiqui 1987: 95).
12. For example, the coins struck by Vasisthiputra were restruck by the next local chief, Madhariputra, and the coins that belonged to both these rulers were then restruck by the third Kura chief, Gautamiputra (Rao 1955: 58–80).
13. This phrase refers to stratified levels in excavations that coincide with the Sātavāhana rule.

14. Rama Rao points to Wheeler's dating of these chiefs to late 50 BCE (Rao 1954: 199, 201, 203).
15. Hanumantha Rao suggests that the Sātavāhanas had geographically divided their dominions into various āhāras, which were ruled by governors known as amātyas (Hanumantha Rao 1976: 36).
16. R. S. Sharma informs us here about the general usage of the word '*maha*' as a prefix to the names of various local chiefs as indication of feudal hierarchy (Sharma 1968: 210).
17. The word 'megalith' can be decoded as 'mega' meaning big/large and 'lith' meaning stone. These large stones were erected as monuments under which the people of that period buried their dead.

References

Bajpai, K. D. 1979.'Some Rare Early Coins from Central India and Andhra Pradesh'. *The Journal of the Numismatic Society of India* XLI(I–II): 38–46.

Bhandarkar, R. G. 1884. *Early History of the Dekkan: Down to the Mahomedan Conquest*. New Delhi: Second Asian Educational Services.

Bondada, Gautam. 2015. 'The Role of Monetary Networks in the Trade between India and the Roman Empire'. *Sudasien Chronik—South Asia Chronicle* 5: 400–427.

Chattopadhyaya, B. D. 1987. 'Transition to the Early Historical Phase in the Deccan: A Note'. In B. D. Chattopadhyaya and B. M. Pande (eds), *Archaeology and History, Essays in Memory of Shri A. Ghosh,* Vol. II. Delhi: Agam Kala Prakashan.

———. 2003. *Studying Early India: Archaeology, Texts and Historical Issues*. New Delhi: Permanent Black.

Deo, S. B. 1975. 'Sātavāhana Archaeology'. *Bulletin of the Deccan College Research Institute* 35(1–2): 37–41.

Ghosh, Nairita. 2015. 'Social Groups in Early Brāhmī Inscriptions of the Deccan'. M. Phil. dissertation, University of Hyderabad.

Gupta, P. L. 1978. 'Kotalingala find of Post-Mauryan Coins'. *Numismatic Digest* II(Part II): 24–33. Numismatic Society of Bombay.

Hanumantha Rao, B. S. L. 1976. *The Age of Sātavāhanas*. Hyderabad: Andhra Pradesh Sahitya Akademi.

Kasturi Bai, M. 1986. 'Sada: A New Dynasty Discovered at Vaddamanu, Guntur District in Coastal Andhra Pradesh'. *The Journal of the Numismatic Society of India* XLVIII(I–II): 14– 23.

———. 1991. 'Archaeological Significance of Coins Unearthed at Veerapuram'. *The Journal of Numismatic Society of India* LIII(I–II): 34–48.

Krishnasastry, V. V. 1983. *Proto and Early Historical Cultures of Andhra Pradesh*. Hyderabad: Government of Andhra Pradesh.

Mangalam, S. J. 1999. 'Coins of the Feudatories and Contemporaries of the Satavahanas'. In Ajay Mitra Shastri (ed.), *The Age of the Satavahanas*, Vol. II: 360–390. Delhi: Aryan Books International.

Parabrahma Sastry, P. V. 1978. 'Unknown coins of Satavahanas and their Predecessors'. *Numismatic Digest* II(I): 10–21.

———. 1994. *Sātavāhana Epoch: A New Light*. Hyderabad: Telugu Goshthi.

Parasher Sen, Aloka. 1999. 'Urban Settlements in the Deccan and Satavahana History'. In Ajay Mitra Shastri (ed.), *The Age of the Satavahanas*, Vol. I, 159–189. Delhi: Aryan Books International.

———. 2007. 'Localities, Coins and the Transition to the Early State in the Deccan'. *Studies in History* 23(2): 231–269.

Prasad, P. R. K. 1993a. 'A New Coin of Asakasada from Amaravati'. *The Journal of the Numismatic Society of India* LV(I–II): 44–49.

———. 1993b. 'Sada Coins in Coastal Andhra'. In A. V. Narasimha Murthy (ed.), *Studies in South Indian Coins*, Vol. III, 53–63. Madras: New Era Publications.

———. 1999. 'Pre-Satavahana Phase at Amaravati—Dharanikota'. In Ajay Mitra Shastri (ed.), *The Age of the Satavahanas*, Vol. II, 327–340. Delhi: Aryan Books International.

Rao, M. Rama. 1954. 'Significance of the Chittaldurg Coins'. *The Journal of the Numismatic Society of India* XVI(II): 197–204

———. 1955 'Coins of the Kura Kings from Brahmapuri'. *The Journal of the Numismatic Society of India* XVII(I): 58–88.

———. 1957. 'A Maharathi Coin'. *The Journal of Numismatic Society of India* XIX(II): 184–186.

Ray, Himanshu Prabha. 1986. *Monastery and Guild: Commerce under the Sātavāhanas*. New Delhi: Oxford University Press.

———. 1994. *The Winds of Change: Buddhism and the Maritime Links of Early South Asia*. New Delhi: Oxford University Press.

Reddy, D. Raja. 1992. *Unique Andhra Coins*. New Delhi: B. R. Publishing Corporation.

Reddy, D. Raja and P. Suryanarayana Reddy. 1991. 'Mahatalavara and Mahasenapati Coins'. In A. V. Narasimha Murthy (ed.), *Studies in South Indian Coins*, Vol. I, 71–80. Madras: New Era Publications.

———. 1992. 'Maharathi Coins'. *The Journal of the Numismatic Society of India* LIV(I and II): 29–33.

———. 1993. 'New Mahatalavara Coins'. *The Journal of the Numismatic Society of India* LV(I & II): 42–43.

Sankalia, H. D. 1979. *Indian Archaeology Today.* Delhi: Ajanta Publications.
Sarma, I. K. 2000. *Numismatic Researches: Critical Studies from Excavated Context.* New Delhi: Agam Kala Prakashan.
Sastri, T. V. G., M. Kasturi-Bai, and J. Vara Prasada Rao. 1984. *Veerapuram—A Type Site for Cultural Study in the Krishna Valley.* Hyderabad: Birla Archaeological and Cultural Research Institute.
Sastri, T. V. G. 1992. *Vaddamanu Excavations: 1981–85.* Hyderabad: Birla Archaeological and Cultural Research Institute.
Sastry, C. A. Padmanabha. 1991. 'Coins of Maharathis in Andhra'. In A. V. Narasimha Murthy (ed.), *Studies in South Indian Coins,* Vol. I, 65–70. Madras: New Era Publications.
Seneviratne, Sudarshan. 1981. 'Kalinga and Andhra: The Process of Secondary State Formation in Early India'. *The Indian Historical Review* VII(1–2): 54–69.
Sharma, R. S. 1968. *Aspects of Political Ideas and Institutions in Ancient India.* Varanasi: Motilal Banarsidass, 2e.
Shastri, Ajay Mitra. 1982. 'Pre-Satavahana and Satavahana Coinage of the Deccan'. *The Journal of Numismatic Society of India* XLIV(I & II): 1–16.
———. 1987. *Early History of the Deccan: Problems and Perspectives.* Delhi: Sundeep Prakashan.
———. 2001. 'Nasik in Early Historical Perspective'. In I. K. Sarma and B. Vidyadhara Rao (eds), *Sri Subrahmanya Smriti: Essays on Indian Pre-history, Proto-history, Archaeology, Iconography, Art, Architecture, Epigraphy, Numismatics, Crafts and Conservation,* Vol. II, 337–343. New Delhi: Sundeep Prakashan.
Shimada, Akira. 2005. 'The Political Setting of the Amaravati Stupa: Recent Studies'. *Journal of Deccan Studies* III(1): 33–46.
Siddiqui, A. H. 1966. 'On a New Maharathi Coin'. *The Journal of the Numismatic Society of India* XXVIII(I): 57–59.
———. 1987. 'Copper Seal of Maharathi Asvaghosa'. *Numismatic Digest* XI: 94–95.
———. 1994. 'Some Mahasenapati Coins of the Deccan'. *The Journal of the Numismatic Society of India* LVI(I–II): 15–17.
Singh, Ram Lochan. 1993. *India—A Regional Geography.* New Delhi: UBS Publisher Distributors.
Subbarao, B. 1958. *The Personality of India.* Baroda: MS University of Baroda.
———. 2011. *Regions and Regionalism.* New Delhi: Critical Quest.
Subbarayalu, Y. 2014. 'First Century BCE to Fifth Century CE: The Satavahanas, the Early Tamil Polities, and Their Successors'. In Noboru Karashima (ed.),

A Concise History of South India: Issues and Interpretations. New Delhi: Oxford University Press.

Subrahmanyam, B., P. Brahmachary, and K. Padmanabha. 2008. *Mahatalavara Coins: A Hoard from Phanigiri, Nalgonda District*. Hyderabad: State Department of Archaeology, Government of Andhra Pradesh.

Suvrathan, Uthara. 2014. 'Regional Centres and Local Elite: Studying Peripheral Cores in Peninsular India (*c*. First to Eighteenth century CE)'. *Indian History* (The Annual Journal of the Archive India Institute) I: 89–142.

Thapar, Romila. 1984. *From Lineage to State: Social Formations of the Mid-First Millennium B.C. in the Ganga Valley*. Bombay: Oxford University Press.

———. 1987. *The Mauryas Revisited*. New Delhi: K. P. Bagchi and Co.

Turner, Paula, J. 1989. *Roman Coins from India*. London: Routledge.

7

CHĀḶUKYAN *PRAŚASTIS*

Historical Consciousness and Identity

Aruna Pariti

DEFINING NOTIONS OF 'HISTORY'

Most modern writings on Indian history began with the erroneous notion that ancient Indians lacked a sense of history, and as such, lacked a historical consciousness as found in the West. For instance, the imperialist historian James Mill, in his foundational *History of British India,* located an explanation for the lack of historical sense in the cultural inferiority of Hindus (Mill 1975: 198–199). Hegel (1956) went a step further and attacked the spiritualism and idealism of Indian society that, according to him, made early Indians incapable of writing history (Inden 1986: 429–436). Similar sentiments about history writing were echoed by nationalists too, such as Bankimchandra when he wrote: 'We have no history! We must have a history' (Chatterjee 1993: 76). However, when the nationalists began writing the history of their own people, not only did they invariably accept the methodological patterns set for them by British scholars, but also often seemed only to quote their British predecessors, especially if it concerned glorifying the past of Indian society. Thus, it is not surprising to find scholars like R. G. Bhandarkar begin the introduction to his *Early History of the Dekkan* with the statement:'India has no written history' (Bhandarkar 1985: i, iv). Therefore, we find that in Hegel's writings on the Orient, or more generally in the writings of Eurocentric empiricists and utilitarian thinkers of the nineteenth century, the pre-modern Indian notion of history could not attain an epistemological status that met the criteria of writing a scientific history as envisaged by these scholars. It is against this erroneous notion of Indians lacking a sense of history that this chapter positions the *praśasti* (eulogy) portions of inscriptions belonging to the Chāḷukyan families, who ruled the Deccan during the early medieval period, to put forth a mode of historical writing that was different from the method defined by colonial writers who understood history writing from within the Enlightenment tradition.

A new scientific outlook for historical writings based on inscriptions was first seen in India with the deciphering of the Brāhmī script by James Prinsep in 1837. This was considered a major breakthrough in the development of epigraphical studies. The epigraphical sources, by virtue of their recording specific events and dates, came to be treated as 'hard core' evidence and more reliable than the literary sources (Subrahmanyam 1998: 382). J. F. Fleet, one of the most prolific imperialist epigraphists, had remarked that 'for our knowledge of ancient political history we are indebted only to inscriptions and not to any history works bequeathed to us by the Hindus' (Parasher Sen 1992: 62–73). This clearly shows the importance of inscriptions as a 'knowledge base' that provides 'authentic' historical information for a later generation of historians writing in the twentieth century. Primarily, the information in inscriptions became the backbone of all historical narratives, and the main source for historians to create the fundamental structures and outlines of political history. This trend continued till the 1960s. More recently, information relating to the functioning of temple institutions, the role of social groups in religious patronage, the agrarian social and economic set-up, and the nature of political structures and state-formation have also been extracted from epigraphic records and occasionally subjected to statistical analysis (Talbot 2001: 13). However, we hold that on account of their unique value as sources, it is essential for the historian to acquire a clear knowledge of the basic aspects of inscriptions, including their traditional content, namely the praśastis. Hitherto, when scholars used inscriptions as 'hard core' evidence, they invariably presented these eulogies within an empiricist framework of dynastic chronology (Subrahmanyam 1998: 382). This made a study of inscriptional eulogies in their totality, according to Daud Ali, 'a particularly underdeveloped domain in the study of South Asian history, which is ironic given their remarkable number' (Ali 2000: 166).

Further, when modern historians attempted to construct Indian history using genealogical material from inscriptions, they left out the mythical, epic, and *Puranic* portions of the praśastis. They only chose the material that was considered relevant, authentic, and verifiable for determining political events or actions of the king and thus, tailored their narrative according to a model of positivist methodological framework. However, we argue that one cannot overlook the mythical portions of praśastis as these reflected the world view of the ruling elite, which was embedded in conceptions of the past from which they derived their identity, just as the modern nation-state turns to history to construct a legitimate past which then defines its identity. In this regard, therefore, this study attempts to scrutinise genealogies afresh in the regional context of the Chāḷukyan families in order to ascertain that a certain historical consciousness did exist in early medieval Indian society, which emerged from the historical processes of constructing specific social and political identities. Thus, this study makes a necessary departure from the existing methods of history writing by giving equal paramountcy to the source as well as the interpretations. In this case, the source we address is rooted in a consciousness of these ruling families that hearkens back to a memory of their cultural past that continued to define them in their present.

Nature of Chāḷukyan Praśastis

Most Chāḷukyan inscriptions contain three important components, namely the Praśasti, the Notification, and the Conclusion (Vijaya 1983: 76–77). The main portion that is, the Notification portion of these inscriptions invariably documented land transactions, though there were also records that contained detailed genealogical information in their praśasti portions, which included mythical, semi-historical, and historical genealogies. Praśastis were in fact found in the preamble section. The text of a praśasti was a historical narrative often composed in Sanskrit and, on many occasions, was eulogistic in nature (Thapar 2013: 549). The main intention of the praśasti was to record the actual events that took place in the life of the king in whose name the grant was issued. It was also to record the important events about the king's predecessors. The genealogical information on the ruling families formed the core of the praśasti. They were also found with dated time, which recorded time in terms of an era or regnal year of the ruling king. Interwoven with the genealogical information were lists of military conquests, high-sounding royal or administrative titles, and political symbols or royal insignia acquired by the king and his ancestors. The social mechanisms of marriage networks that is, family trees mentioning marriage relations with other ruling families, were also mentioned, as these were considered crucial to ascertaining the patterns of inter-clan and inter-family relationships. As we shall discuss below, embedded alongside the genealogical and military information in these Chāḷukyan praśastis were the ideological elements highlighting a Vedic/Puranic and pan-Indian identity, with descriptions of the king and his ancestors in heroic and intellectual imagery derived from ancient texts. This portrayal of the king's image was in accordance with the convention adopted by the medieval court poets, who would elevate their patron to the position of a universal sovereign (Chattopadhyaya 1998: 21–43).

There were certain similarities between the praśastis and the *caritas* (biographies) or *mahākāvyas* (poems). Both contain collective genealogical statements, or shared memories of the past that are based on what Bernard Lewis (1975: 11) calls 'remembered history'. Also, both draw extensively on the *itihāsa-purāṇa* (historical antiquity) tradition, which is based on historical memory that selectively depicts features of the past, some of which are 'imagined'. An important part of this tradition was the fact that it was initially memorised, preserved, and transmitted orally to reflect on the dynastic/genealogical aspects of the ruling elite. These retrievals that is, the writing down of oral traditions, are interesting as most of the political, economic, and cultural life was centred around the royal courts, which naturally wanted to perpetuate elite intellectual traditions (such as courtly traditions where the king would be eulogised by the court poet) (De Casparis 1979: 105). Both praśastis and caritas narrate activities and events of the past, but do so in ways that were meaningful and useful to their contemporary audience (ibid.: 16). Inscriptions, just like medieval court literature, were also forms of discourse that contained representations of the self and the world (Ali 2000: 165–229; De Casparis 1979: 16). Since inscriptions were only representations, it is important to delineate the complex mechanisms through which these images of the past were constructed and used. And for this reason, it is crucial for the historian to recognise the social and political aspirations that these inscriptions, embodied along with the ideology they conveyed (Talbot 2001: 15–16). Thus, by examining, or rather, re-looking at the narratives of the praśastis of inscriptional texts of the Chāḷukyan families, we attempt to analyse notions of the past that the ancient ruling elites had recorded in these sources. However, it may be noted that the contents of the praśastis were not uniform and varied from one family to another in different periods of time and space.

Genealogical Traditions in Chāḷukyan Praśastis

The praśasti portions of inscriptions of the Chāḷukyan families[1] contain three kinds of genealogies. These are the mythical, semi-historical, and historical genealogies. The mythical genealogy dealt with the fabrication of origin myths that mention the lineage (*gōtra*), matronymic and family (*kula*) of these rulers. Implicit in this was the cyclic notion of time that was located in a remote past and associated with mythical elements. The semi-historical genealogies were concerned with the legendary past that referred to the genealogies of the *Candravamśa* and/or *Suryavamśa* families. Since these were embedded in Puranic traditions that referred to the Kaliyug lists of kings, it projected both cyclic and linear notions of time. In the next category were the historical genealogies that dealt with the narration of the king and his ancestors, going back to several generations of rulers, enumerated in sequential order. These, however, belonged to the more clearly discernible immediate past of the king whose praśasti was being written, and thus time was reckoned in linear terms. These different categories of genealogical narratives evinced both changes and continuities in different chronological periods. Concomitantly, this reflected on the way different Chāḷukyan families looked at the past and constructed their identities.[2]

Mythical Genealogies

From the early medieval period (sixth century CE) onwards, the mythical genealogies constituting the gotra, the matronymic and the kula/*vamśa* came to be integrated with the genealogies of ruling families. When the Chāḷukyas came to political prominence replacing the Kādambas, they adopted the mythical genealogies of their predecessors, which began with the mention of the Mānavya gotra. This was followed by the mention of the matronymic, namely Haritaputra, or sons of Harita. Finally, the kula or family (*Chāḷukya kula* and *Satyaśraya kula*) to which the Chāḷukyas claim to have belonged was mentioned. Reference to the Chāḷukya kula or vamśa or *anvaya* (family) through which the family was identified suggests an underlying sense of time that came to be measured in cyclic terms. Further, by adopting the mythical genealogy of the Kādambas, who called themselves the *brahma-kṣatras* (Jaiswal 1998: 63), the Chāḷukyas too indirectly associated themselves with the brahma-kṣatra identity, though this has not been directly referred to anywhere in their records. Interestingly, apart from merely referring to these expressions, there was no further attempt to explain the origin of these mythical personages in the early phases of Chāḷukyan rule.

However, from the eleventh century important changes in the descriptive pattern of mythical genealogies occurred in the praśastis of the Eastern and Western Chāḷukyan inscriptions. The different components of the mythical genealogies were elaborated upon to explain the mythical origins of Mānavya, Harita, and Chāḷukya vamśa. In the inscriptions of the Eastern Chāḷukyas, the Ranatipundi grant[3] of Vimalāditya mentions them as belonging to the double-gotra of Mānavya (that is, *dvipakṣa gotra*), thus, for the first time, linking the Mānavya gotra to the brahma-kṣatra lineage. However, there was no attempt to explain either the origins of Mānavya and Harita, or the meaning of the term 'dvipakṣa gotra'. In contrast, in the inscriptions of Kalyani Chāḷukyas of the western Deccan, the mythical genealogy portion in the praśastis was revamped completely. For the first time, a serious attempt was made to trace the origins of Mānavya, Harita, and Chāḷukya. In this exercise, they tried to connect these three mythical elements through establishing a biological linkage between each of them. Further, the origins of these mythical ancestors of the Chāḷukyas were also genealogically connected to the gods such as Vishnu, Brahma, or the Moon whose origin is not known and therefore, this is seen as an attempt to locate the roots of the family in timelessness, or a-temporality. Thus, for instance, in the Sudi inscription dated to 1114 CE, the mythical genealogy of the Western Chāḷukyas of Kalyani is given in the following way:

> From Viṣṇu's lotus was born Brahmā. From Brahmā was born Ātri. From Ātri has sprung the Moon (Budha) and from Budha has originated Pururavas, who was mentioned as the founder of the Lunar dynasty (*Soma vamśa*). The son of Pururavas was Harita. Harita had many sons from whom sprang the Chāḷukya race (*vamśa*).[4]

Thus, it is apparent that in the initial stages of their rule, the Chāḷukyas co-opted the mythical genealogy from the local memories of earlier rulers, namely the Kādambas. Hence, not only does the notion of cyclic time appear obscure, but the brahma-kṣatra identity, to which most of the ruling elites exerted a claim during the early medieval period, also remained nebulous. On the other hand, from the eleventh century onwards the notion of cyclic time becomes more obvious by the conscious linkage with Brahma and Manu, whose origins were rooted in timelessness. Similarly, the brahma-kṣatra identity of the ruling families was now more explicitly stated. Thus, these different versions of mythical genealogies suggest that the immediate concern of the ruling elite was to construct their identity on the basis of what they imagined and believed was their past.

Semi-historical Genealogies

Another tendency among the ruling elite was to trace their genealogical linkages to the *kṣatriya* families of the epics. These genealogies, according to Romila Thapar, served as important historical records that promised a continuity of succession. Further, she argues that they also came to be treated as socially necessary documents as they helped to locate the family's roots in the most ancient past (Thapar 1996: 302). These semi-historical genealogies in the praśastis were thus a critical source to retrieve a distant past, which enabled them to seek valuable symbols for the legitimisation of their newly acquired power (Chattopadhyaya 1976: 61). This was achieved through the patronage of *brāhmaṇa* scholars well-versed in the itihāsa-purāṇa tradition (Kulke 1995: 237–238). Apparently, these court poets did not invent mythical and semi-historic genealogies per se, but selected, recorded, and preserved only that information from the tradition that interested the ruling elite and was also deeply rooted in the social memory of the people.

Different versions of semi-historical genealogies emerged in the inscriptions of Chāḷukyan families of the western and eastern Deccan from the eleventh to twelfth centuries CE. The Western Chāḷukyan records refer to the Mānavya gotra, Haritiputra, and the Chāḷukya kula, along with the mention of fifty-nine kings of the Chāḷukya family who reigned from Ayodhya. This is then followed by the mention of sixteen more kings who are said to have ruled over Dakshinapatha (the southern states of India). However, interestingly, the names of neither the fifty-nine kings nor the sixteen kings are mentioned.[5] Reference to Ayodhya as the original seat of the progenitors of the Chāḷukyas is significant, as this place is associated with the illustrious family of the Ikṣvākus of the Suryavamśa or solar lineage, and thus connects the Chāḷukyas to a lineage of Puranic antiquity. On the other hand, the Gadag inscription of Vikramāditya dated to 1098 CE states that the race of the Chāḷukyas had emerged from the Moon (Soma), thus connecting the Chāḷukyas with the Candravamśa lineage.[6] The family thus seems to have claimed both lineages. An elaborate semi-historical or Puranic and epic genealogy was found in the Sudi inscription of Vikramāditya VI, dated to 1114 CE.[7] This record mentions that Harita was the son of Pururavas, the founder of the Candravamśa lineage. This is in total contrast to the version found in the Puranic sources, where the origin of Harita was traced to Yuvanāśva, the descendent of the Ikṣvāku lineage of the solar race. Thus, by consciously diverging from the earlier memory of lineage connection, court poets tried to fabricate new legendary genealogical linkages for Harita by reversing the Puranic version.

Fabricating new legendary genealogies of a semi-historical nature was a common and ongoing process. Similar tendencies were found in the inscriptions belonging to the Chāḷukyas of Vengi, where also a detailed Puranic and epic genealogy of the Candravamśa lineage was furnished for the first time in the Ranastipundi grant of Vimalāditya, dated to 1011 CE.[8] This record provides a detailed Puranic genealogy beginning with Lord Narayana up to the heroes of the *Mahābhārata* (that is, the Pāndavas), thus giving a genealogical account of forty-seven kings of the Candravamśa lineage (Pariti 2015: 74–81). Here, the court poet shifts the narration to describe a semi-historic genealogy, referring to one Vijayāditya of Ayodhya and his unsuccessful Deccan conquest. His son was mentioned as Viṣṇuvardhana, and was succeeded by his son, Vijayāditya. This is subsequently followed by the narration of the historical genealogy of the family, commencing from Pulakeśi Vallabha of the Badami Chāḷukyan dynasty. Subsequent rulers of this family followed this version of semi-historical genealogy in all their records.

These different versions of semi-historic genealogies establishing linkages with the solar and lunar lineages were important ways of conceptualising time beyond the present. This construct of time came to be perceived as something powerful and divine, which could be associated with the personal identity of the rulers. They would ascribe to themselves certain characteristics of divinity, and also try to establish a 'pure' kṣatriya identity and enhance their personal glory (Inden 1981: 34–35). The selective appropriation of a mythical and Puranic past became crucial for the ruling elite to redefine their own past, despite the fact that it was more imagined than real. These deliberate inclusions of different versions of semi-historical genealogies in the praśastis happened at a time when the newly emerging local chiefs, ruling contemporaneously with the main Chāḷukyan ruling families, posed a challenge to the political stability of their respective empires. In fact, it was primarily the memory of this past that justified their kingship and thus came to be essentially perceived as charters of validation for the current, sometimes unstable, political situations confronting them.

Historical Genealogies

Genealogies as historical records also embodied dynastic vamśa traditions of the historical past, wherein the names and achievements of the king's ancestors were preserved in a chronological order. It was stated in the *Śāstras* (legal texts) that when an economic transaction in the form of a land grant was done, it was imperative to list in laudatory terms the name of the donor along with the names of his ancestors (Thapar 1996: 105–106). Historical genealogies were written within the parameters of linear time as they strictly followed a sequential order of narration. Historical time was often appended with dated time,[9] which was recorded in terms of an era or regnal year of the ruling king.

In the initial years of rule of the Badami Chāḷukyas and the Chāḷukyas of Vengi, the historical genealogy was simple, bearing names not exceeding more than three generations of a king's predecessors, namely his great-grandfather, grandfather, and father, respectively.[10] This also indicates that time cycles were short as ancestors were few. Further, the use of eras, in particular, the Śaka era, was also limited. Gradually, the historical genealogies became lengthy. The praśastis of the Badami Chāḷukyas began with the founder of the dynasty and continued up to the king who issued the grant, with regnal year and era mentioned in each case. A typical example, for instance, is the Vokkaleri inscription of Kīrtivarman II, in which the historical genealogy began with Pulakeśi Vallabha followed by his son Kīrtivarman, and then his son Satyāśraya. The list goes on like this up to the reign of Kīrtivarman II, in whose time the record was written.[11] The Eastern Chāḷukyan inscriptions also give lengthy lists of ancestors along with the number of years each ruled, extending this information to as many as thirty generations. These tendencies emphasised a linearity of time by providing actual details within a chronological framework, to firmly establish the family's authenticity in its historical context.

By the eleventh century, along with the invention of elaborate mythical and semi-historical genealogies, the court poets fabricated lengthy historical genealogies. Variations were discerned in the records belonging to the Eastern Chāḷukyas of Vengi and the Western Chāḷukyas of Kalyani. In the Eastern Chāḷukyan tradition, the historical genealogy began with the mention of three generations of kings of the parent branch, namely the Badami Chāḷukyan dynasty. This was then followed by a mention of the full list of kings belonging to the Eastern Chāḷukyan dynasty, up to the king issuing the record.[12] This clearly highlights the conscious attempt to establish links with the preceding Chāḷukya families in order to partake in their greatness not only to enhance the purity of the lineage, but also to allude to the power connected with them. In contrast, in some records of the Western Chāḷukyas of Kalyani, the historical genealogy belonging to the parent branch, namely the Badami Chāḷukyas, were completely enumerated. This is then followed by an account of the kings belonging to the dynasty of the king issuing the inscription, as found in the Kauthem grant of Vikramāditya V[13] (Murari 1977: 72). This attempt to connect with their parent branch through long genealogical linkages was a clear indication of the concern to project the greatness and antiquity of their family history as it became critical to establish social identity and legitimise their political authority.

It is observed that when the praśastis appeared elaborate with lengthy historical genealogies, the reckoning of time became more linear. The development of this tradition was first seen in the Sataluru inscription of Gunaga Vijayaditya III, dated to the mid-ninth century CE from the eastern Deccan.[14] Successors of Gunaga Vijayaditya followed this pattern of historical-time reckoning without reference to the Śaka era. By the eleventh century, there was a prolific reference to the planet Jupiter's sixty-year cycle in the praśastis, indicating an attempt to introduce the cyclic notion of time with the continued emphasis on a linear reckoning of time through the abundant use of eras. Another important change noticed during this period was the introduction of personal eras named after the king, like Chāḷukya Vikrama era, Jagadekamalla era, Bhūlōkamalla era, and so on, in the Western Chāḷukyan inscriptions. These were used not only to express political authority, but also to emphasise the individual greatness of the king and his concern to have a permanent place in history and a special identity. Such recording of time using personal eras introduced precision in the documentation of various details intended to signify family and individual identity, and concomitantly, the rulers' perceptions of the past were articulated as rooted in specific time (through listing the names of their family members at a specific time, and referring to the era, year, month, weekday, and day when the donation was made).

Enhancing Identities in Praśastis

The Temporal Domain—The Regional Context

Intertwined with the narration of genealogies was the listing of military achievements of the ruler and his ancestors. This component of the praśasti sections was often exaggerated and was more imagined than real. However, it is important enough to be mentioned as it enhanced the glory and identity of the king and his ancestors in specific ways. The early praśastis provided only a short note on the suppression of hostile kings by the early Chāḷukyan rulers, thus suggesting their immediate concern for controlling the areas surrounding the core of their kingdom. Furthermore, since their political control was minimal, the early kings used only simple administrative titles like *rāja* and *nṛpa* (king), but to exert their zeal for conquests and territorial expansion, they adopted military titles like Puru Raṇa Parākrama, Raṇa Vikrānta, Śrī Parākrama, Bhaṭṭārakasya, Ripu Narendra, Vishamasiddhi, Makaradhvaja, Raṇamukha, Raṇabhūshaṇa, and so on, which indicated their passion for warfare.[15] After consolidating their power further, a tendency began to emerge among the later Chāḷukyan rulers to present a detailed account of military conquests undertaken both by the king and his ancestors. Exaggerated military titles became few, but now their real and imagined claims of pan-Indian conquests began to be described through hyperbolic statements in order to retrieve the past achievements of the king's ancestors. This can therefore be considered one mode of historical writing that looked at the immediate historical past to enhance the greatness of the family. Undoubtedly, in this process they were selective in referring only to those ancestors who eclipsed the great powers such as the Kādambas, Harsha of the north, the Rāṣṭrakūṭas, the Pallavas, the Chōḷas, the Kāḷachuris, etc. The conquest of Vanavāsi by Kīrtivarman and the victory of Pulakeśi II over Harsha were highlighted in the records of the Badami Chāḷukyas (See Plate IX, this volume). Both incidents were crucial landmarks in the political history of the Chāḷukyan family, since the conquest of the former permanently established Chāḷukyan rule in the Western Deccan, and the latter conquest elevated the Chāḷukyas to an imperial status (Schwartzberg 1978: 181) and provided a landmark memory to be written about and lauded for generations. Similarly, the military achievements of some of the king's ancestors were highlighted but their defeat at the hands of some of the major powers was often found eclipsed, with neither the inscriptions nor the kāvyas recording them.

From the eleventh century onwards, one can see the invention of new traditions to record these achievements. Thus, for instance, in a few records belonging to the Western Chāḷukyas, the Chāḷukyan lineage was explained through the conquests over the Nāḷas, Kādambas, Mauryas, Rāṣṭrakūṭas and Kāḷachuris, without mentioning the original home of the Chāḷukyas. This was clearly an attempt to give them a historical identity traceable to powerful dynasties. Similarly, both the Western and Eastern Chāḷukyan family records came up with an imagined migration theory of a certain Vijayāditya from Ayodhya to the Deccan. Though the military titles were few in these later records, the only title used extensively was Paramabhaṭṭāraka.[16] The court poets involved in writing the inscriptional text apparently consulted the historical records and reproduced them through a clearly selective process to suit the needs of the present time. In fact, some selective memories critical to the making of the family identity, such as the migration of the Chāḷukyas from Ayodhya to the Deccan, were carried into literary texts, particularly in the *Vikramāṅkadeva Carita* by Bilhaṇa. Thus, both these genres of texts attempted to preserve a certain identity and collective memory of the family's past.

To further enhance the greatness of this identity, the poets of the Chāḷukyan courts entwined military conquests with high-sounding royal or administrative titles, and political symbols or royal insignia acquired by the rulers. This was one way of legitimising control, authority, and sovereignty. The symbols of royal insignia were usually inherited by the king from his predecessor, but could also be seized from an enemy, and still further, be bestowed upon him by an overlord in recognition of his services. Cynthia Talbot (2001: 144) regarded these titles (*birudas)* and symbols as a synopsis of the achievements of the lineage, and as a summary of an individual's claim to fame. It was also indicative of their respective status in society. In the early praśastis of the Chāḷukyas, the king and his ancestor came to be referred to by laudatory titles like Śrī Pṛthvīvallabha[17] and Sarvalōkāśraya (Monier-Williams 1979: 907, 1185), apart from the simple administrative titles like Mahārāja, Mahārājādhirāja, and the like. With the expansion of political control by the eighth century, in the Chāḷukyan praśastis, epithets like Jagadekāṅtaḥ, Rājalōkāśraya, Bhūpateḥ, and Samasta Bhuvanāśraya were more extensively inserted.[18] These eulogistic titles of the king and his ancestors were further accompanied by mention of the political symbols and royal insignia acquired through defeating the kings of north India. For instance, the Badami Chāḷukyan inscriptions mention Vinayāditya's acquisition of *pāḷidhvaja* (flags and banners), *Gaṅga-Yamuna, dhakka* (double war drums), and *mahāśabdas* (important utterances) after defeating the kings of the north, thus linking them to pan-Indian symbols of authority.[19]

It is interesting to note that references to such high-sounding royal or administrative titles of the ancestors were completely absent in the praśastis from the eleventh century onwards. Instead, only personal titles of kings, indicating the king's 'imperial' authority, were started from the reign of Vikramāditya V of the Kalyani Chāḷukyan family. From then onwards, the names of all the kings came to be suffixed with epithets such as Tribhuvanamalla, Trailōkyamalla, Jagadekamalla, Bhuvanaikamalla, and Bhūlōkamalla (Fleet 1896: 435). Thus, the objective of identifying the king through these personalised grandiloquent titles, rather than the dynasty, was suggestive of an attempt to manifest the king as an apparent controller of the universe. Thus, he was sometimes equated with ruling *cakravarti-kṣetra* (universal territory), which included the entire Bharatavarsha or even the world, and the emphasis would now be on his individual identity. Further, during this later period, it was mentioned in these praśastis from the eleventh century that political symbols came to be obtained through the favour of gods and goddesses. Thus, for instance, according to the records of the Western Chāḷukyas of Kalyani, they were supposed to have obtained the *śvētātapatra* (white umbrella) through the favour of Goddess Kauśiki, *mayūrapiṃchha* (peacock's tail) and *kuṅthadhvaja* (spear flag) through the favour of Lord Kārttikeya, and the boar-crest from the holy Nārāyaṇa.[20] On the other hand, the records of the Eastern Chāḷukyas mention that a certain Viṣṇuvardhana Vijayāditya, after appeasing the Gods Kumāra (Skanda), Nārāyaṇa (Viṣṇu), and the divine Mothers (Mātrigaṇa), obtained the white parasol (śvētātapatra), the single conch (*aikaśaṃkha*), the five mahāśabdas (*pañca mahāśabda*), the flags in row (*pālikētana*), and so on.[21] In analysing the pattern of royal titles and political symbols referred to in the praśastis of Chāḷukyan families, we conclude that during the rise and expansion of territorial control, it became important for the state to eulogise past achievements, as these became crucial markers of validation of their political authority. On the other hand, when political control was in a stage of disintegration, it created the need to legitimise authority not by referring to actual events of the past, but by seeking divine intervention through which the greatness of the family identity could be enhanced.

Marriage linkages became another crucial mechanism to ascertain familial identity and establish a pattern of inter-clan and inter-family relationships. The praśastis of Badami and Vengi Chāḷukyas revealed that they entered into matrimonial relationships with such families as the Bappuras, the Sendrakas, the Kāḷachuris, the Pallavas, the Rāṣṭrakūṭas, the Alūpas, the kings of Kaḷiṅga, and the Paṭṭavardhanis (Sastri and Venkataramanayya 1982: 209). These rulers were overpowered by the Chāḷukyan rulers at certain periods in time. These marriage networks thus asserted a 'pan-regional' identity of the Chāḷukyan elites by perpetuating social relationships, especially with those families which had common lineage and ancestral patterns. On the other hand, the Chāḷukyas of Kalyani aligned with the Cheḍis and the Raṭṭas, and subsequent records also frequently mentioned that these alliances contributed to the consolidation of their kingdom during the initial stages of its growth. This Chāḷukyan family identity was firmly entrenched because of the establishment of vertical social relationships with their subordinates. In contrast, the marriage alliances of the Eastern Chāḷukyas with the Chōḷas brought about the new rule of the Chāḷukya-Chōḷas in the eastern Deccan, which led to a transformation of the Chāḷukyan identity due to the expansion of horizontal social relations outside their primary areas of control (Aruna 2000: 72–73).

The Ideological Domain—Pan-Indian Linkages

The praśastis are also emphatic in providing pan-Indian linkages to define the identity of Chāḷukyan families on the basis of certain well-founded ideological and cultural traits in the beliefs they adopted and the world view they propagated. This further provided another layer of identity that became intrinsic to the assertion of their greatness. Daud Ali has differentiated this part of the narrative component in praśastis, which defined the metaphysical notions of the past and its philosophical components based on a Puranic world view as a 'meta-narrative' (Ali 2000: 165).

Adopting the norm for ancient monarchs, the Chāḷukyan families performed various Vedic sacrifices. The Badami Cliff inscription[22] of Pulakeśi I mentions him as the performer of an *aśvamēdha* (horse sacrifice), a clear signal that announced his sovereign authority, which would not be objected to by contiguous rulers. He is also credited in later inscriptions with the performance of other Vedic sacrifices, such as the *vājapeya*, *pauṇḍarīka*, *bahusuvarṇa*, *agniṣṭōma*, *agnichayana*, *rājasūya* sacrifices,[23] which his own inscriptions were silent about. It is interesting to note that subsequent kings of the Badami Chāḷukyan family did not perform Vedic sacrifices, but nonetheless took pride in referring to Pulakeśi I as a model of cosmic and divine authority, thereby emphasising their succession from a divine source of authority, which gave them a singularly different identity from other local and regional players. However, it is worth mentioning that the scions of the Badami Chāḷukyas in eastern Deccan preferred to substitute the individual identity of Pulakeśi I with the family identity 'Chāḷukyas' as the performer of numerous aśvamēdha sacrifices (*aśvamēdha-yājinam Chāḷukyānām kula-jaladhi-samudbhūta*).[24] Thus, there was a deliberate effort to centralise the notion of the 'Chāḷukyan family' as an impeccable source from which the divine authority of the king emanated, thereby emphasising a more distant and 'imagined' past than the immediate past, as noticed in the inscriptions of the Badami Chāḷukyas. This variation, noticed within the family traditions of both the Badami and the Vengi Chāḷukyas, points to the attempts made by the latter to maintain an individual identity distinct from its parent branch.

As is well-known, the above sacrifices could not be performed without the cooperation and support of the brāhmaṇas, who had a monopoly on Vedic knowledge. The early medieval period had seen a proliferation of grants and *agrahāras* (villages granted to brāhmaṇas), given to them for the spread of Vedic learning. They became the chief source for affirming the authority of the king, thus underscoring the brahma-kṣatra relationship (Richards 1981: iv). During the initial stages of the formation of the Chāḷukyan kingdom, the king relied largely on the brāhmaṇas for the enactment of certain religious practices of pan-Indian importance, like the conduct of Vedic sacrifices in order to assert his kṣatriya or kṣatriya-like identity, which was an identity on which the Chāḷukyans had no claim originally (Pariti 2015: 221). To emphasise kṣatriya identity further, the kings were also bestowed with personal attributes of the epic and Puranic heroes, who like them had military prowess, diplomacy, righteousness, generosity, and so on.[25] Besides valour and righteousness, the king was extolled for his generosity and gift-giving, a quality that came in for praise in the praśastis; and here again, the king was compared to these heroes.[26] Therefore, overall, these royal eulogies described the king as apparently possessing all those qualities that were possessed by the major epic and Puranic heroes,[27] well-known to the people through the oral traditions of folklore and the epic.

Scholars like Daud Ali have pertinently observed that most of the early medieval praśastis and kāvyas, as well as the carita literature, had a common source, namely the Puranic histories. Local elites explicitly looked back to the broader and more universal histories of the Purāṇas to write the genealogies of their patrons and describe their greatness (Ali 2000: 170). In such constructions of the past, therefore, memory was socially constructed to present a sense of identity (Cappelletto 2003: 242) that was distinctly different from the others. In drawing on the pan-India tradition and projecting themselves as being on par with heroes from the epics and the Purāṇas, there was also an attempt to create an overarching identity that would be acceptable to a larger number of people, and not simply their adversaries. The stories of the great kings and heroes of the ancient Indian tradition of the epics and *Purāṇas*, largely popularised through oral tradition and rooted in social memory, became the basis for court poets seeking to further enhance the image of the king in order to solicit his subjects' respect. These images were also necessary to establish an effective moral authority and distance themselves from the local rulers.

Apart from the retrieval of a cosmological connection that was added to the enhanced identity that the king and the king's family constructed, references in some praśastis project the king as the upholder of *dharmic* knowledge, as a governor and protector of his subjects, in accordance with the laws laid down in the *Dharmaśāstras*. The cosmological linkages pertinently conveyed that the king represented the macrocosmic symbol of unity, order, power, prosperity, and well-being for the cosmos as a whole, while simultaneously projecting him as the symbol of his kingdom's unity, order, and prosperity (Inden 1981: 32). Whereas, the latter references as the upholder of dharmic knowledge, were designed to show that the king was equipped with the knowledge of the laws of Dharma (of Manava) (Dowson 2000: 209-210). The process through which pan-Indian linkages were established was complex and varied, involving several strategies, which on the one hand exalted the king to the ranks of divinity and on the other, acted as effective instruments through which the political authority of the king was validated.

Conclusion

We submit in this chapter that praśastis of the Chāḷukyan families may be viewed as 'historical texts' composed by court poets for their patrons to legitimise the political authority of the king, family, and dynasty in power. Therefore, rather than dismissing them as an irrelevant and exaggerated source for history writing, they need to be paid attention to in alternative ways as texts that have embedded in them certain notions of 'history', which were constructed for different reasons of political expediency. In our extensive study of praśastis of the various Chāḷukyan families that ruled over the Deccan during the early medieval period, we have noted that dynastic variations were perceptible in the composition of different types of genealogies, though the mode of expression of their understanding of the past belonged to the same genre. Contrary to the view that ancient Indians lacked a sense of 'history', we have put forth the idea that the past, during the early medieval period, was viewed through modes of historical explanation that varied from the contemporary commonplace notions of history during colonial times. In our descriptions of the different types of genealogies, such as the mythical, semi-historical, and historical, we have first narrated how 'Time' was conceptualised in each as a prerequisite to unravel how history was embedded in these genealogical traditions. The genealogical information presented in the Chāḷukyan praśastis refers to different notions of time, such as mythical time rooted in a-temporality, semi-historical time, and historical time which specifically mentioned dates along with genealogical information. Thus, we concluded that the praśastis presented before us both cyclic and linear notions of time, which are essential for any historical writing as they provide authenticity to the source. The preparation of praśastis necessarily entailed the presence of memory, without which it was not possible to create the lengthy genealogical lists based on the itihāsa-purāṇa and dynastic traditions. Hence, the creators of the praśastis continuously looked back to their sources to provide legitimate authority to the king, as well as create a strong social identity.

The making of identity was an integral part of the way these families viewed their past. We have analysed this in the chapter by highlighting the mechanisms that led to this identity formation in two sets of contingencies—the regional and the pan-Indian, the former referring to political identity and the latter to ideological identity. The first was the ever-evolving regional context that meant that the genealogical tradition found in the Chāḷukyan praśastis had to compulsorily enumerate the military achievements of the king and his ancestors, and their military, royal, and administrative titles and political symbols to assert their existence as formidable powers. Such information became more prolific when the kingdoms were expanding their political power through conquests. Land grants were recorded on copper plates using hyperbolic statements of praise, and these plates were also often used to disseminate ideas about the pre-eminence of the king and the greatness of his family's identity in the far-off newly conquered regions. Cementing of these political and economic ties was done effectively through marriage alliances so that identity formation acquired a clear pan-Deccan stamp.

The literate brāhmaṇas in the courts of the various Chāḷukyan rulers at this time ensured that their singular family identity was differentiated from other competing powers in the region. We then moved on to explain that this could only effectively be done by using ideological mechanisms of various kinds. One important mechanism was to project the image of the ruler and his family by incorporating the itihāsa-purāṇa traditions into the praśasti. Comparisons with gods and persons of eminence from the epics were made to confer enhanced attributes to the rulers, and thus differentiate them from their contemporaries since their social identity was given an origin that went beyond their 'real' origin, located in their local and regional actuality. By highlighting certain qualities of the king and his ancestors, and the selective process adopted in drawing comparisons with the heroes of the itihāsa-purāṇa tradition, the court poet was careful to adopt a cautious approach to highlight only those aspects of the ancient text that helped to legitimise the past. The legitimised past was not the historical past, as Chattopadhyaya points out, but an idealised past, which was then presented as a panacea for the tensions of the present by projecting the rulers as superior to their contemporaries (Chattopadhyaya 2002: 119). Hence, court poets under the Chāḷukyan kings often took recourse to the memory of tradition as the representation of the past and used it as a mechanism to legitimise the present (Heesterman 1979: 61-62).

Pertinently, while drawing on tradition the ruling elite adopted well-established means of protecting this identity by supporting Vedic learning, following the *Dharmaśāstra* traditions, and furthermore, created a well-grounded notion of their pan-Indian identity. The *Śruti* and *Smṛti* as found in the Vedas and *Dharmaśāstras* were a critical part of the remembered tradition. According to Sheldon Pollock, the axiom on which the afore-mentioned literary production rested, particularly in the classical and the medieval phases, seemed to be 'that the improvement of any given practice lies, not in the future and the discovery of what has never been known before, but in the past' (cited in Aktor 1999: 260). It was in this manner that the 'remembered' past, in the form of the eternal Vedas and śāstras, were presented as models of truth and righteousness, and hence were credited with epistemological power, which had become authoritative by virtue of its age (ibid.: 258–260).

We have thus gone on to show that from a local individual identity emerged a regional identity of the Chāḷukyas, which was finally evolved to establish their identity at a pan-Indian level. The historical context in which royal eulogies in the inscriptions were produced reflected a clear tendency to refer to a past culture that was based on an unflinching belief in a pan-Indian tradition. Here, tradition was used to 'represent (and re-present) the past' because tradition was invariably used by the Chāḷukyas to legitimise their past. This past was rooted in the cosmic notions of time (that is, circular time), which by its very definition was final and immutable, and therefore seemed to offer a fixed yardstick as a reference against the ever-shifting present (Heesterman 1979: 61–62). Thus, these mechanisms of collating different sources of the past and composing a praśasti show that a different mode of history writing existed during the early medieval period under the Chāḷukyan families. These histories were composed by the *brāhmaṇas,* the *kāyasthas,* and the Jainas, who belonged to the literate class and were patronised by the kings. In fact, the written text, whether in the land grants noted in the inscriptions or in the mahākāvya that was commissioned by the king, was mainly based on what these literate elite, in the process of creating a text, felt about their patron. Hence, there was always a tendency for this information to be formulaic, though the court poet also indulged in the invention of new traditions to idealise the king. Nonetheless, these consciously chosen traditions throw light on the way the dominant groups chose to remember their past. Therefore, a study of the praśastis shows that 'history' as a mode of remembering, recording, and manipulating for political and ideological purposes was present in the early medieval period, and that it provided social identity and self-esteem to the ruling elite in their handling of contemporary local concerns.

Notes

Acknowledgements: This paper is based on my Ph.D thesis titled 'Genealogy as a Source for Writing Social History—The Case of Chāḷukyan Families', completed under the erudite supervision of my research guide, Professor Aloka Parasher Sen, to whom I am always indebted. With her encouragement and continuous support, the thesis has now been published under the title *Genealogy, Time and Identity: Historical Consciousness in the Deccan* (2015).

1. In this chapter, we discuss three major Chāḷukyan families—the Chāḷukyas of Badami (also called Badami Chāḷukyas), the Chāḷukyas of Vengi (also called Eastern Chāḷukyas), and the Kalyani Chāḷukyas (also called Western Chāḷukyas). The trajectories of their rise to power, conflicts with contiguous ruling dynasties, and the periods of their respective rules have been prolifically researched and well understood by several scholars, who provide us with a clear narrative account of their political history (Dikshit 1980: 99; Krishna Rao 1973: 47–49; Murari 1977: 35, 72, 155; Parabrahma Sastry 1974: ix–xiv; Ramesh 1984: 83–84; Suryanarayana 1986: 13–21; Venkataramanayya 1950: 163).
2. A detailed description of these different genealogies has been provided in my book (Pariti 2015).
3. *Epigraphia Indica* (henceforth *EI*) 1900–1901: 348–361.
4. *EI* 1919–1920, XV: 106.
5. *Indian Antiquary* (henceforth *IA*) 1887: 15–24. It may be noted that *Indian Antiquary*, edited by Jas Burgess, Vols III–XX (1874–1890), was reprinted in 1985. It is this edition that has been used for all references to this journal.
6. *EI* 1919–1920: 348–364.
7. Ibid.: 105–108.
8. *EI* 1900–1901: 348–361.
9. Historical time refers to the names of rulers presented in a sequential order. But it is not necessary that their regnal years are mentioned. Dated time on the other hand, mentions the exact time period of the rule of a king recorded in terms of an era (like Chāḷukya Vikrama era),

the regnal year, exact date on which the grant was executed by the king and so on.

10. *EI* 1909–1910: 105.
11. *IA* 1879: 23–29.
12. *EI* 1900–1901: 348–361.
13. *IA* 1887: 15–24.
14. 'Sataluru Copper Plates of Gunaga Vijayaditya III', *Journal of Andhra Historical Research Society,* V, 1930: 101–116.
15. *IA* 1874: 306; 1877: 87; 1878: 163-164; 1884: 137–139; 1890: 7–20; and *EI* 1905–1906: 236–241; 1925–1926: 1–5; 1925–1926: 55–58; 1947–1948: 37–41.
16. *EI* 1896, IV: 204–208; 1919, XV: 80–83, 100–103; and *IA* 1884, XIII: 248–250.
17. *IA* 1882: 68.
18. *EI* 1900–1901: 1–12; 1947: 41–47; 1955–1956: 74–80; and *IA* 1877: 72–75.
19. *IA* 1880: 133–135; *EI* 1947–1948: 125–131.
20. *IA* 1887: 15–24; *EI* 1913–1914: 303–315.
21. *EI* 1900–1901: 348–361; *IA* 1885: 48–55.
22. *EI* 1947-1948: 4-9
23. *IA* 1874: 305-306; 1880: 293-296; 1890: 7-20
24. 'Pedda-maddali Plates of Jayasimha I —Eastern Chalukyan king' *IA* 1884, XIII: 137–139; 'Pulibumra Plates of Jayasimha I—Eastern Chalukyan King' *EI* 1927, XIX: 254–258.
25. In projecting the prowess of the king, he was compared to Bhīma (Dharmānuja or Kaunteya or Vṛkodara) (*South Indian Inscriptions* [henceforth *SII*] 1892: 31-36) for his impetuosity (*EI* 1894-1895: 1-7), Yudhiṣṭhira and Arjuna/Pārtha in courage (*SII* 1892: 31-36), Bībhatsu (Arjuna) (*IA* 1890: 303-311) and Rāma (an invincible conqueror) (*EI* 1925-1926: 1-5), Manmadha (who had put an end to war by destroying his enemies), Sūrya (who destroys darkness), and Bhārgava (destroyer of several enemies) (*EI* 1900-1901, VI: 348-361) for possessing terrible prowess.
26. In this regard, the king was compared to Karṇa, who took delight in charity, was liberal as Śibi (*EI* 1907-1908: 200-206), the son of Uśināra, and was equated with Kāmadhenu, (*IA* 1891: 15-18), i.e., the cow of plenty. Similarly, he was also likened to Airāvata (Indra's elephant) in his acts of excessive and liberal donations (*dāna*) (*EI* 1927-1928: 258-261).
27. *IA* 1891: 15-18.

References

Aktor, Mikael. 1999. '*Smṛtis* and *Jātis*: The Ritualisation of Time and the Continuity of the Past'. In Daud Ali (ed.), *Invoking the Past: The Uses of History in South Asia*, 258-279. New Delhi: Oxford University Press.

Ali, Daud. 2000. 'Royal Eulogy as World History: Rethinking Copperplate Inscriptions in Cola India'. In Ronald Inden (ed.), *Querying the Medieval: Texts and the History of Practices of South Asia*, 168–229. New York: Oxford University Press.

Aruna, A. 2000. *State Formation in the Eastern Deccan*. New Delhi: Bharatiya Kala Prakashan.

Bhandarkar, R. G. 1985 [1895]. *Early History of the Dekkan: Down to the Mohammedan Conquest*. New Delhi: Asian Education Services.

Brough, John. 1946. 'The Early History of the Gotras'. *Journal of Royal Asiatic Society* Part 1: 32–43.

Cappelletto, Francesca. 2003. 'Long-Term Memory of Extreme Events from Autobiography to History'. *Journal of Royal Anthropological Institute* 9: 241-259.

Chatterjee, Partha. 1993. *The Nation and its Fragments: Colonial and Postcolonial Histories*. Princeton: Princeton University Press.

Chattopadhyaya, B. D. 1976. 'Origin of the Rajputs: The Political, Economic and Social Processes in Early Medieval Rajasthan'. *Indian Historical Review* III(2): 59–82.

———. 1998. *Representing the Other? Sanskrit Sources and Muslims*. New Delhi: Manohar Books and Distributors.

———. 2002. 'Confronting Fundamentalisms: The Possibilities of Early Indian History'. *Studies in History* 18(1): 103-120.

De Casparis, J. G. 1979. 'Inscriptions and South Asian Dynastic Traditions'. In R. J. Moore (ed.), *Tradition and Politics in South Asia*, 103–127. Delhi: Vikas Publishing House.

Dikshit, D. P. 1980. *Political History of the Chāḷukyas of Badami*. New Delhi: Abhinav Publications.

Dowson, John. 2000. *A Classical Dictionary of Hindu Mythology and Religion*. New Delhi: D. K. Printworld (Pvt.) Ltd.

Fleet, J. F. 1896. *The Dynasties of the Kanarese Districts of the Bombay Presidency from the Earliest Historical Times to the Musalman Conquest of A. D. 1318*. Bombay: Government Central Press.

Heesterman, J. C. 1979. 'Power and Authority in Indian Tradition'. In R. J. Moore (ed.), *Tradition and Politics in South Asia*, 60-85. New Delhi: Vikas Publishing House.

Hegel, George. 1956 [1899]. *The Philosophy of History*, J. Sibree (trans.). New York: Dover Publishers.

Hultzsch, E. (ed.), Rao Bahadur, and H. H. Krishna Sastry. 1892. *South Indian Inscriptions*, Vols I, V, X. Madras: Archaeological Survey of India.

Hultzsch, E., Lionel D. Barnett, G. S. Gai, D. C. Sircar, V. Venkayya, and J. F. Fleet (eds). 1898-1963. *Epigraphia Indica*, Vols III–XXXXI. Calcutta: Archaeological Survey of India.

Inden, Ronald. 1981. 'Hierarchies of Kings in Early Medieval India'. *Contributions to Indian Sociology* 15(1–2): 34–35.

——. 1986. 'Orientalist Construction of India'. *Modern Asian Studies* 20(3): 429-436.

Jaiswal, Suvira. 1998. *Caste: Origin, Functions and Dimensions of Change*. New Delhi: Manohar Books and Distributors.

Jas Burgess (ed.). 1985. *Indian Antiquary* (1874–1890), Vols III–XX. Delhi: Swati Publications.

Krishna Rao, B. V. 1973. *History of the Eastern Chāḷukyas of Vengi, (AD 610–1210 AD)*. Hyderabad: Andhra Pradesh Sahitya Akademi.

Kulke, Hermann. 1995. *The State in India, 1000–1700*. Delhi: Oxford University Press.

Lewis, Bernard. 1975. *History: Remembered, Recovered, Invented*. New York: Simon & Schuster Inc.

Mani, Vettam. 1984[1975]. *Puranic Encyclopedia*. Delhi: Motilal Banarsidass.

Mill, James. 1975[1817]. *History of British India*, Vol. I. New Delhi: Associated Publishing House.

Monier-Williams, Monier. 1979. *Sanskrit to English Dictionary*. Delhi: Munshiram Manoharlal.

Murari, Krishna. 1977. *The Chāḷukyas of Kalyani*. Delhi: Concept Publishing Company.

Parabrahma Sastry, P. V. 1974. 'The Chāḷukyas of Vemulavada'. *Inscriptions of Andhra Pradesh Series No. 8. Karimnagar District*. Hyderabad: State Department of Archaeology and Museums, Government of Andhra Pradesh.

Parasher Sen, Aloka. 1992. 'Epigraphy as a Tool for Writing Social History'. *Journal of Epigraphical Society of India* XVIII: 62–73.

Pariti, Aruna. 2015. *Genealogy, Time and Identity: Historical Consciousness in the Deccan*. New Delhi: Primus Publications.

Ramesh, K. V. 1984. *Cāḷukyas of Vatapi*. Delhi: Agam Kala Prakashan.

Richards, J. F. 1981[1978]. *Kingship and Authority in South Asia*. New Delhi: OUP.

Sastri, K. A. N. and N. Venkataramanayya. 1982[1960]. 'Eastern Chāḷukyas of Vengi'. In G. Yazdani (ed.), *Early History of the Deccan*, Part VII, 469–512. New Delhi: Oriental Books Reprint Corporation.

Sastri, K. A. N. 1955 [1994]. *A History of South India*. Delhi: Oxford University Press.

Schwartzberg, J. E. 1978. *A Historical Atlas of South Asia*. Chicago: The University of Chicago Press.

Subba Rao, B. 1958. *Personality of India: Pre and Proto-historic Foundation of India and Pakistan*. Baroda: Faculty of Arts, Maharaja Sayajirao University.

Subrahmanyam, Sanjay. 1998. 'Reflections on State-making and History-making in South India, 1500–1800'. *Journal of the Economic and Social History of the Orient* 41 (3): 382–416.

Suryanarayana, K. 1986. *History of the Minor Chāḷukyan Families in Medieval Andhradesa*. Delhi: B. R. Publishing House.

Talbot, Cynthia. 2001. *Pre-colonial India in Practice: Society, Region, and Identity in Medieval Andhra*. New Delhi: Oxford University Press.

Thapar, Romila. 1996[1978]. *Ancient India Social History*. Delhi: Orient Longman.

———. 1997. *Time As a Metaphor of History: Early India*. Delhi: Oxford University Press.

———. 2013. *The Past before Us: Historical Traditions of Early North India*. New Delhi: Permanent Black.

Venkataramanayya, N. 1950. *The Eastern Cāḷukyas of Vengi*. Madras: Vedam Venkataraya Sastry & Bros.

Vijaya, N. R. 1983. 'Evolution of Praśasti in the Inscriptions of the Eastern Chāḷukyas'. Proceedings of Andhra Pradesh History Congress, Warangal Session VIII, 76-77.

8

Seeking History in Fragments

Aloka Parasher Sen

> *The modernist historian follows a line of reasoning from his sources and evidence to a historical reality hidden behind the sources.... In the postmodernist view, evidence does not point towards the past but to other interpretations of the past....*
>
> (Ankersmit 1989: 145–146)

Setting the Stage

An overemphasis on the written word and thereby, on textual sources, has been the hallmark of ancient Indian history writing. This proved fruitful when focusing on those areas and regions of the subcontinent that had produced literature in antiquity, even though this literature provided minimal historical facts and were in no way like the historical chronicles of the past found in other ancient societies like Greece, Rome, or China. An overuse of the Sanskritic heritage of India's past was an unconscious byproduct of early nineteenth-century attempts to 'discover' ancient texts as ostensible sources for writing the new colony's history. It is a fact that the 'modern' study and interpretation of early India was built on a deep study of philology, particularly comparative Indo-European philology, to which Sanskrit was central. The construction of what is popularly known as 'Classical India' owes much to these early attempts of philologists and Orientalists, beginning from the eighteenth century (Thapar 1978). Several interventions in the last three decades of the twentieth century have raised questions about the limitations of doing historical research on pre-modern India in a contemporary India, since the former has been strangulated by the methodological avenues unleashed by Indological discourse. In *Imagining India*, Ronald Inden (1990: 36–49) used some of the insights provided by Edward Said and articulated that the knowledge of ancient India was draped in 'essences', especially those that characterised it in 'caste' and 'religious' terms. In not highlighting ancient India's political and economic agencies, the Orientalist discourse distorted the picture of Indian society and at the same time denied Indians agency in their own history. However, our present concern is not to delineate a history of how 'Indological' studies came into being nor narrate its successive critiques (Lariviere 1994: 18).[1] In this chapter, the challenges prevalent in the researching of India's early past, as indicated above, shall be juxtaposed with the history of localities and, by default then, of traditions known through small and often fragmentary pieces of information. The chapter suggests that we need to move away from the notion of meta-histories based on apparently pan-Indian sources when, in fact, it is a variety of sources at the local level that should engage our attention.

Since our geographic focus is on regions south of the Vindhyas, a conscious attempt is made to not look at the region's ancient past only in terms of written sources available from outside the region. Further, despite this awareness, a central point in our argument is that we no longer need to compartmentalise the various seminal traditions of the Indian subcontinent, traditions which may not necessarily be part of the dominant Sanskritic tradition. They need to be looked at in terms of networks, each dynamically interacting with the other to retrieve from the religious, the material (that is, material remains accessed from archaeology), and the cognitive texts (that is, fragmentary information accessed from local inscriptions that reflect on local imaginations), the textures of history of the marginal social and regional groups that asserted a difference from and yet was linked to a larger whole. We propose that the emergence of these networks (such as various oral, non-written networks of information known to local societies that connect with each other)—their sustenance and mutation—lends a better framework for not only writing regional and local history, but also enables us to hold various fragments together rather than highlight them only as unique, often unexplained pieces of historical debris that accidentally became available to us in their extant form. Even more important is the recognition that especially for the last several decades, history as a discipline in India has moved away from its traditional definition of being part of literature-based studies alone. Historians of ancient India in particular now place equal importance on archaeological sources and also draw on contemporary theories emanating from anthropology, linguistics, and cultural studies. This has clearly been witnessed in the emergence of gender history, history of environment and everyday life, and the history of marginal groups.

In citing Ankersmit (1989) in the opening epigraph, we wanted to emphasise that there is an increasing realisation today that not all historians are talking of history from within the same scope of understanding its purpose and intentions. Today, in most social science and humanities research, there is unanimous acceptance that retrieving a single 'truth' in the garb of absolute objectivity is next to impossible, since we must account for the operation of power which defines relationships between classes, castes, peoples, and countries. In the present context, where we address questions around the use of a fragment and seeking history from it, we must necessarily take cognisance of this issue raised by Ankersmit. It clearly advocates that the 'source' is generated in modern historical interpretations from time to time, and this then becomes the basis of future studies on the subject. Those historians who, irrespective of their ideological dispensation, look for the existence of 'pure facts' in the distant past, make a common plea with reference to ancient India—that 'proper facts' are absent in its early textual sources. In our present endeavour, this has led us to look for 'facts' of the past in the non-textual domain, and see if these can be correlated with the written material available in specific contexts.

Fragment as Source

The question in focus for us in this chapter is the 'fragment'. The fragment must also be considered a source. For very ancient periods of world history, fragments are seen as legitimate sources of information, primarily because of the scarcity of sources for these periods, when they are used to supplement information or corroborate existing information that enables us to get a fuller picture of the historical artefact (Sherwin-White 1983: 265–270). This is a different kind of use of the fragment in history than what we want to suggest. For the present purpose, we use the literal meaning of the word 'fragment'. As a noun, 'fragment' means 'a part broken off or detached'. Elaborated, one could use it in the sense of, for instance, the 'scattered fragments of the broken vase'. It could very well be understood as 'an odd piece, bit, or scrap'. However, we do not retrieve its meaning as a verb, which means 'to break (something) into pieces or fragments; cause to disintegrate'. This meaning would be found in such examples as 'outside influences soon fragmented the Mayan culture'.[2] This latter use would highlight its negative connotation as a wilful agency to divide things, create disunity, split into smaller parts, and so on, which is not what we wish to highlight in order to bring to centrality the 'fragment' in history. We shall thus focus on examples of fragments in the context of them being present in our midst as isolated pieces of information, apparently unrelated to a larger discourse. The examples we take do not always represent broken or missing pieces, but rather that their presence has been forgotten due to their location and unique symbolism. So let us see how a fragment can be treated as source.

The idea of understanding and using the fragment in history caught our imagination when we participated in an excavation that revealed many objects seemingly not connected to each other.[3] An earlier excavation at the same site had been interpreted to suggest that the site was a Buddhist one, even though several structures and material remains stayed outside that label. The new excavations further led to contrary interpretations at the same site, and this therefore raised the issue of how the 'source' was handled by the excavators in the two rounds of excavations (Parasher Sen 2014: 89–107). Some of them were mere fragments, but nonetheless sources of history, albeit of a different kind. Our concern then became: How should we reconcile our tools of interrogating the past with the ideology/world view inherent in these sources we use to write this history? Furthermore, the excavators provided a different meaning to the same objects, based primarily on the location where they were found. Around the same time, we came across a book by Fariello and Owen, who write: 'Regardless of scale, form, or function,'.....their (objects that appear in fragments) 'meaning is couched in a non-verbal language to be received and perceived tactfully and visually'(Fariello and Owen 2005: 155) and, we would add, to be written into history on the merit of their own logic rather than being simply listed peripherally, as part of a meta-narrative focusing on the dominant. And this is the line of argument we would like to pursue.

A good example of a fragment is an ivory statuette from the ancient Deccan that travelled thousands of miles to be found at Pompeii, Italy in 1938, and is now housed in the Museo Nazionale, Naples (See Plate X, this volume). At 24 cm, this statuette is a small item, but almost all scholars have noted that it is distinguished by its fine craftsmanship. The statuette depicts a woman whose head is delicately carved and her whole figure exudes a sense of composure. She has been dated to 79 CE, the year Mount Vesuvius erupted and buried the city of Pompeii. The statuette was found in one of the most densely populated areas of Pompeii in a cache of fine craft goods (Moeller 1976: 76). She stands naked with her head, neck, arms, and legs richly adorned. Her raised arms indicate that she is arranging her hair. On each side she is flanked by a smaller, childlike figure. The latter have been identified as her attendants as they appear to be carrying items for her toilet (Parker 2008: 165). A protrusion extends from the left side of her head, as if it were a continuation of her hairstyle. Earlier scholars saw this as the handle of a mirror, but more recently it has instead been considered the leg of a small piece of furniture. This explanation would be plausible if, as Wheeler suggests, the two smaller figures and the vertical hole that extends from the top of her head to the waist are taken into account, which could indicate a possible intention of the sculptor(s) to have the image viewed from three angles (front, back, and side) since the statuette seems to be rested on something because of this vertical hole (Wheeler 1954: 135). Scholars had earlier identified this image as that of Lakshmi, or the goddess of good luck, fertility, and prosperity, and it is suggested that this provides a 'glimpse of the wide multicultural links of Pompeii' (Beard 2008: 24). Other scholars suggest that it 'was a cult object of an Indian craftsman living in Pompeii' (Moeller 1976: 76, footnote 17). This house, where the statuette was found, has come to be labelled as 'The House of the Indian Statuette' (Beard 2008: 24). On its Indian origins there is no dispute, as its style closely matches the statuary of the Sātavāhana times (first century BCE to third century CE) in general. Further, two closely comparable ivory statuettes of the same period have been found at Ter (Tagara) and Bhokardan (Bhogavardhana) in present-day Maharashtra (Deo and Gupte 1974: 188).

It is tempting to dismiss these statuettes as mere accidental finds and casually place them within the larger story of the unfolding of the Graeco-Roman trade contact across the Indian subcontinent;[4] however, this is not our intention. Our focus here is on an artefact as a fragment found within the Mediterranean world, which we suggest could have been part of a large array of objects that may not necessarily have emanated from the material and systematic trade transactions of the time. These rich material and documentary remains from both sides of the ancient world could have very well existed outside the scope of the meta-narrative elaborating on the economic dimensions of the contact. They could signify many things—they could be objects of pleasure, aesthetics, mystical power, functionality, and so on—that would more holistically highlight the contact between peoples during a period that provided little written description of these matters. Mary Helms (1991), in her comparative work, distinguishes between craft goods and raw materials, both of which the Romans had a vivid sense of; they also had an appetite for artefacts produced in distant places. With reference to the latter, Helms pertinently distinguished the way the Romans viewed Egypt and India based on the nature of the evidence found. In our discussion, based on Helms's work, it would be pertinent to point out that India emerges as an origin of individual choice made by Roman traders/travellers as opposed to Egypt, which was a contiguous region and with which contact was common and frequent. It would be no exaggeration to say, in general, that the Indian origins of any particular item added value to it in Roman eyes, but those who travelled with these objects came from various social and geographical backgrounds. It is generally accepted that goods regarded as distinctly Indian by the Romans carried with them a sense of the exotic. We know on empirical grounds that as a rare piece, the statuette was something that definitely came from the subcontinent; it could not have come from anywhere else. Parker suggests that instead of seeing such objects 'through the lens of commodities', we see how they in fact 'act(s) as a sober reminder of the indivisibility of the imaginary and the real Indias'[5] (Parker 2008: 165). There were intricate cultural meanings attached to them. The ivory figurine may have just been taken back to revel in its aesthetic beauty, in an attempt to appreciate an alien land's cultural ethos. Unlike cotton, linen, and the like, as well as spices and aromatics in the monsoon trade which had their medical and religious uses, this did not have a utilitarian purpose. Many craft goods from the Mediterranean have also been found on the subcontinent. At Brahmapuri near Kolhapur, Maharashtra, we have the discovery of a bronze Graeco-Roman statuette of Poseidon, a trefoil-shaped (a graphic form with three overlapping rings, from the Latin *trifolium*, or three-leaved plant) bronze vessel, possibly a chariot, a spouted bronze jug, and its imitations in fine red clay, which have been found on the floor of the Sātavāhana houses (Lamb 1929: Plate XLVI, A; Sankalia and Dikshit 1952: 154; Wheeler 1951: 345–381). These have been the subject of intensive investigations, much of which struggles with the issue of whether these goods were imported in their current form or produced locally, and whether from local or imported materials. In the present context, we do enter these debates, but to simply point out that it was not merely a one-way travel for unusual objects.

Arjun Appadurai and several other scholars have suggested that in most of these cases, we can merely speculate about the life-histories of individual artefacts, but we need to go down that path so that a possible biography of these can begin to emerge (Appadurai 1986; Gosden and Marshall 1999: 168–169). These biographies of the small and the fragmentary tell us different stories and divert us from the singular monolithic histories in narratives that focus primarily on the big and monumental alone. The fragment of the ivory statuette therefore cannot be fit into the usual narrative of the Graeco-Roman trade with India. At the same time, it does not tell us enough about how it fit into the cultural exchanges between the two ancient societies. It does, however, open up the possibility that Greek and Roman traders, along with others who accompanied them, must have done much more than merely remaining confined to their narrow economic tasks. It was perhaps due to their intermingling with the population at large in the specific areas of their activity that they found time to make friends, buy mementos to take home, and generally discover for themselves the exotic and aesthetic world that they had heard about before they embarked on their journey to the Indian subcontinent. The statuette thus indicates these sensibilities and also provides us with a window to look at historical interactions beyond the material. Human curiosity is not bounded and, in this sense, fragments of various kinds enable us to broaden our scope of bringing in the minute and small into historical discourse, which would otherwise fall by the wayside, their potential unharnessed.

The Fragment and Reconstructing Historical Identities

> *....I detest writing....what is written has an importance that is denied to the spoken....It is one of the white world's ways of destroying the cultures of non-European peoples, the imposing of an abstraction over the spoken relationship of a people.*
>
> (Means 1992: 41)[6]

Social History: Absences

The social history of early India, which first began with British administrators-turned-scholars and Orientalists, focused little on the lower orders and marginal peoples, or for that matter on women as subjects of history. Instead, attempts were made to essentialise Indian society in terms of 'caste', which was seen as irrational in terms of modern ways of organising society. Early ethnographic studies, also done under colonial rule, provided the first vivid descriptions of the subordinate and marginal groups, especially their everyday life, customs, and habits, but at the same time, also gave them new names and defined structures of comprehending them. Contemporary concerns of 'uplifting' the condition of women and the lower orders in Indian society began with the writings of social reformers and nationalist leaders within the confines of their particular agendas—either 'modernising' Indian society or providing new spaces for their respective political struggles. However, in historical studies on early India written during the first half of the twentieth century, these social groups were either absent, or at best mentioned in a peripheral manner. This was primarily because they represented the dark underside of Indian society (especially, issues around the condition of the downtrodden low castes), hardly necessary to the foreground, as it went against the tenor of the time, when leaders were attempting to project a glorious heritage of the country in order to construct a sense of nationalism derived from the same. However, a direct concern with writing about the subordinate emerged first in the work of historians, who used historical materialism as a tool for the scientific enquiry into the social and economic past. Thus, after Independence, for the first time, separate monographs or studies on the lower orders were written—on slavery, on the so-called 'untouchables', the *śūdras,* and so on—highlighting issues such as forced labour and peasant subjection. However, as stated above, the larger concern of such studies was to understand the totality of the agrarian or urban systems, emphasising on the mode of production. In the process, the subordinate emerged in an indirect way as the object of study. Supposedly, their history could only be told in terms of the rules of the dominant sections, and how such rules were inflicted on them. Therefore, though most of these descriptions added to our knowledge of the oppressed in society, the explanations emanated from the texts of the dominant.[7]

This was because, irrespective of ideological positioning, in terms of method, the thrust of scientific research was to use and construct 'authentic sources', and the subordinate or marginal did not emerge clearly in these 'authentic' constructions. Therefore, their absence from history was taken as legitimate and natural. This gets reflected in many books on the social history of ancient India. Well into the twenty-first century, one of the most common ways in which society in early India is described is:

> Indian social structure is made up of four stratified *varnas*...the system (including sub-*varna* classes) formed during the ancient period...the most important characteristic is that the system has stubbornly survived in the present day, *despite the fact that we do not notice it readily in everyday life* (Yamazaki 2005: xiii; emphasis mine).

This quote is from one of the most recent comprehensive publications on ancient Indian society. His perspective emerges from the repeated use of the *Dharmaśāstra*, *Arthaśāstra*, and other literary sources, including Buddhist literary sources to write a social history of early India. Yamazaki explains the rationale behind this in these words:

> ...no historical works, such as official chronicles, were recorded (or if recorded were scattered and lost) during the period in question, forcing us to turn to...religious and theoretical sources as the *only* alternative, despite their obvious flaws (biases) and lack of uniformity, in obtaining an idea about how ancient Indian society actually functioned (Yamazaki 2005: xiii; emphasis mine).

Beyond the use of conventional sources, Yamazaki aimed to study ancient Indian society by 'approach[ing] reality' by comparing the 'orthodox' *brāhmaṇa* view with the 'unorthodox' Buddhist view. In his hypothesis, the idea that the Buddhist texts depict social reality has inherently been accepted as axiomatic in its binary opposition to the theoretical view found in the Brāhmaṇical *Dharmaśātra*. We, however, need to emphasise that both are views from literature.

During the 1970s and 1980s, history writing continued to be dominated by the use of Sanskrit and Pali texts. However, there was also, for the first time, the emerging emphasis on inscriptions, coins, and archeological material as sources of information. Regional angularities (that is, specific regional conditions that were not found elsewhere and looked odd in the larger historical discourse) were sought to be explained and brought to order within the larger logic of the apparently pan-Indian sources. Nonetheless, the growing concern in the past three decades with writing about those silent in the sources on ancient Indian history has gained ground and broadened the ambit of history writing.

The question being raised today is whether multiple histories can be authentic histories. Sociologists, anthropologists (Gupta 2000: 2–9), and social historians who have reported on the origin myths of the śūdra and the so-called 'untouchable' communities explain their respective origins in rather positive ways, which differ radically from the Brāhmaṇical view of the origin of castes. These communities view their position as based on 'a mythic historical act of injustice and betrayal' (Converse and Sharma 1994: 644). A recent account of the 'untouchable' (here, a cobbler) invokes rather pragmatic circumstances that help to 'deny the family's low caste origins; ascribing its misfortune to the "British" in contrast to other myths that blame Brahmins or gods for inventing the caste system' (Jadhav 1994: 712). These oral narratives of the self-perception of these communities contradict the 'official' documents and perspective, such as the Brāhmaṇical legal texts. However, these accounts are not entirely free of contradictions, either, and further, were still interlinked with the larger discourse of caste. Nonetheless, a multidisciplinary thrust of historical research led to it moving away from understanding the past in terms of universal criteria that brought to focus only those who were empowered. These studies opened up new vistas of information and interpretative dimensions that could enable a writing of the excluded, with a deep examination of the intricacies of how the material world interacted with the play of power.

Purnaghata and 'Caste'

To highlight the disparities and inequalities that were present in ancient Indian society is one thing, but a more pertinent issue is how to write into history accounts of those who are absent from dominant sources. How can ancient Indian sources enable us to engage with these issues so as to provide a more varied representation of the past, and be so textured that they can bring in the voices of those who were apparently passive recipients of the written word? We now move on to focus on using a fragment as source, as it is available in a particular local and regional context to provide an alternative way of seeking the history of society in its totality.

As our first example, what we propose to discuss below emerges from the scope provided by inscriptions and materials of art history. Uma Chakravarti writes: 'alliances between master and servants also figure commonly in the Indic story corpus suggesting a certain ambiguity in handling the master-servant relationship as merely hierarchical' (Chakravarti 1993: 52). Though not focusing on 'stories' as alluded to by Chakravarti above, the fragment as source that we shall highlight as an example in this chapter comes from a paper we published in 2007 (Parasher Sen 2007: 47–90), which states that there was a shared social space provided by those moments and periods in time when social groups/individuals participated in a complex environment of ideological and economic transactions. Hitherto, the fragmentary inscriptional data central to the present analysis has mainly been used as corroboratory evidence. We did not exclusively base our research on the latter so as to write an alternative social history, but our aim was to write one that could be understood as coexisting with the dominant narrative of history, pointing to another way in which social identities were asserted beyond the conventional ways known to us.

These fragmentary label inscriptions provided us with interesting names of people in varying contexts—some were travellers, preachers, traders, and so on. This data has been usually deciphered and kept aside since there is no connected narrative inherent in them to elaborate upon. However, we have argued at some length (Parasher Sen 2007: 47–90) that it is this type of data found in regional and local contexts that throws up issues of diversity and agency that the apparently pan-Indian textual traditions fail to provide us with. An important location where a diversity of proper names had emerged in large numbers was in the early inscriptions from Buddhist sites in regions immediately south of the Vindhyas, namely the Deccan, dated to roughly between the second century BCE and fourth century CE (Ray 1986: 20–29). In Chapter 5 (this volume), an analysis of the way these names occur at the various sites/locations in this region noted that cutting across caste lines, many lay followers of the new faith recorded their names as donors, builders, scribes, a variety of craftsmen, traders, and merchants. In many cases, these names did not enable us to ascertain their original 'caste' affiliation. In the western Deccan, amidst several references to the names of *gahapatis, vaṇijas, sethis,* etc., there were names of gardeners, garland-makers, goldsmiths, ironmongers, ploughmen, and so on, who asserted their identity in terms of the places they hailed from. Though they hailed from the less privileged sections of society, they also gave donations to the Buddhist Saṅgha and, in the process, asserted their individual identity. In the eastern Deccan, however, emphasis on kinship identity was more apparent. Thus, even in the context of an example from Amaravati wherein the craftsman belonged to the lowly caste of a leather-worker, the kinship identity was asserted. This example refers to a gift by a leather-worker called Vidhika, son of the *upajhaya* (teacher) Nāga belonging to the *carmakārajāti*, which was generally understood to be ritually impure. It draws our attention because he donated a slab with an overflowing *purnaghata* (auspicious vase) along with his mother, his wife, his brothers, his son, his daughters, and other relatives and friends (See Plate XI, this volume):

> *Camakārasa nāgaupajhayāputasa vidhikasa samatukasa sabhayakasa sabhatukasa*
> *Putas ca nagasa samadhutukasa sanatinitabaindhavasa deyadhamma Punaghatakapato*
>
> (Lüders' 1920, Ins. No. 1273: 151–152).

Another interesting example of a gift is by one Attha, the *kāmika* (labourer) from Sanchi, but there are no other details provided

(Lüders' 1920, Ins. No. 181: 28). Besides labourers, engravers or scribes, excavators, architects, and sculptors of the cave sites, who were essential for the construction and maintenance of cave settlements, have left behind their identities through their names. Their existence points to a critical mass of human population around these sites, with whom the pilgrims, monk inhabitants of the Buddhist cave sites, and the merchants/traders must have interacted for the purpose of using their skills and knowledge. They were in fact the creators of the data we have thus far discussed. Clearly, this data is found in fragments in these localities, and in their prolific association with the Buddhist ethos and symbols. That these reveal the professions of people, with little or no indication of their caste identity, reflects a picture far removed from the way didactic texts describe them.

In the interesting example of the *carmakārajāti* at Amaravati, we get the sense that even a low-caste person had the agency to make donations and participate in the normal activities that other social groups were involved in at the time. Today, very few know that the symbol of the purnaghata had been accepted as an emblem that defined the letterhead for official correspondence in the former state government of Andhra Pradesh, where this Buddhist heritage site of Amaravati is located. With an increasing number of Dalits now being drawn to Buddhism, and more importantly, because such information lies outside the usually defined descriptions of the social order, it has to be necessarily highlighted. It is reported that a replica of this purnaghata was made by the tourism department of the former government of Andhra Pradesh to bring to light the significance of this historical artefact to a large number of people, and thereby create a greater scope to present a more inclusive history. It is thus possible to carefully research on different types of fragments, especially those that reflect on social identities that were neither rigid, nor static over periods of time, as the normative textual traditions would have us believe. Lower orders in society also had access to other ideological moorings (such as Buddhism), and highlighting this enables us to have a more realistic view of how social groups engaged with each other in a dynamic way.

Temple Sculptures and 'Tribe'

Subaltern historians of the colonial period emphasised on 'history from below' and used different types (oral traditions, stories, popular writing) of sources creatively, and thus democratised the content of history. For the ancient period, this is only possible if one revisits the question of the excluded 'other' in Indian civilisation and its relationship to the 'self'.'Indigenous peoples', 'women', and 'low-caste communities' had histories, but they did not always have monumental literary texts that could be attributed to them. From the perspective of research and teaching,[8] one was engaged in an alternative reading of their histories, which could be furthered with the help of methods gleaned from the writings of James Scott and Michael Adas (Haynes and Prakash 1991: 1–22). They advocated viewing the history of ordinary and subject peoples in terms of their long-term and everyday activities, rather than only in terms of their confrontation with a single source of authority. This is possible if we do not view the dominant and the subordinate as occupying two autonomous spaces. Power and resistance, these scholars argued, were so entangled in history that separating them and analysing one without the other would be very difficult. Accordingly, it was possible to see the resistance of ordinary people as disturbing the agendas of power, not only in periods of dramatic confrontation but also in spheres of the everyday. Therefore, in order to recover the lost histories of the subordinate and the marginal, it was important to highlight how new forms of domination and power were articulated from time to time. This method provided an interesting point of contestation, which emanated from the absolutely subordinate and marginalised peoples. Recovering this past for very early periods of the country's history thus meant making use of the tools of history writing in more open ways, namely to contextualise the meanings of stories, incidents, and their interpretations through visual imagery, which can then allow us to write about subordinate and marginal groups as not merely peripheral to the historical narrative.

As an example, we took up a narrative (Parasher Sen 2001: 28–49) of sectarian 'Hindu' belief found in the *Purāṇas* and studied how this belief was transformed at the regional and local levels. In this study, our concern was with explicating that the understanding of the 'self' did not take place in a vacuum but in the context of the great diversity of the 'other', which enriches the dominant perspective through regional influences in the way the myth is remembered from time to time, without destroying the core of its ideological system. At the same time, we argued that communicating with the 'other' enabled the growth of a whole array of expressive modes, rituals, and symbols, which acted as a binding factor for a continuing dialogue between the 'self' and the 'other'. The example we studied in depth was of the Narasimha *avatāra* of Vishnu and his enigmatic relationship with Chenchu Lakshmi, a daughter of the Chenchu tribe of the Nallamalai forests, in the context of the proliferation of his temples at Ahobilam in southeast Andhra Pradesh. Importantly, several fragments of art-historical information and narratives in the form of stories had to be put together to build a historical visibility for the forest people, who had found no place in legal treatises of the dominant society.

While elaborating these ideas for a paper (Parasher Sen 2001: 28–49), we attempted to connect as sources the memories of the Chenchu tribes as recorded by Fürer-Haimendorf (1943) during the early twentieth century, and take a deeper look at the representations of the Narasimha–Chenchu Lakshmi relationship in the form of sculptures in medieval Hindu temples in the locality of Ahobilam to define the particularity of the worship of Vishnu here. The paper also explored the overall structure and importance of the Puranic myths around Narasimha as an avatar of Vishnu, which were found depicted in this local context. Thus, from the memory of the local inhabitants as recorded in eighteenth and nineteenth-century surveys, we moved back in time to the literary, inscriptional, and archaeological evidence that threw light on the historical association of this relationship. It is commonly believed that

> The lord of the temple (at Ahobilam was) .... an ancient tribal deity worshipped from countless ages by the tribes in the Nallamalai hills—more particularly the Chenchus. It is thus that the consort of the Lord is the famous Chenchu-Lakshmi, wooed into holy wedlock by the Man-lion incarnation of Vishnu (Sitapati 1982: 1).

This story was set against the backdrop of the myth of Prahalada and Hiranyaksipu, epitomised as the good and bad *asuras* and known from the *Purāṇas*. The historicity of this narrative was captured in the artistic and sculptural intensity of people in the past, as they tried to represent these myths.

Archaeology has provided us with important sculptures of Lord Narasimha with Chenchu Lakshmi, which explicitly show the close link that this hunting tribal community had with the dominant religious beliefs at Ahobilam. None of these sculptures, however, have received any sanction from the *Āgamaśāstras*, and therefore do not fit into the normal iconographic tenor of the other sculptural art of the place, and so have by and large been ignored in narrations of art history. At Upper Ahobilam, Lord Narasimha is seen wooing Chenchita in a sensitive sculpture found on one of the four central pillars of the *mukhamaṇḍapa* (the front part of a temple) of the main Narasimha Swamy temple built by Harihara II of the Vijayanagara dynasty in 1395 CE. This sculpture shows the Lord and Chenchita standing on a platform. While Narasimha has his palm between her neck and breast in an attitude of wooing, Chenchita is seen looking straight at the viewer, holding a bow in her hand (see Plate XII, this volume). Another fascinating sculpture is found in Lower Ahobilam on a pillar in the *rangamaṇḍapa* (the part of a temple where performances are staged) of the Narasimha temple, dated on stylistic grounds to Vijayanagara times. The outstanding feature of this sculpture is that it shows the Lord in a particularly beseeching mood, while Chenchita is seen clearly as outwardly angry and adamant. Lord Narasimha has his mouth open and is seen holding her chin, trying to appeal to her, while she seems unaffected by this. She is seen holding a bow in her left hand (Narasimhacharya 1989: 395–396). There are a couple of other sculptures only of Chenchita, sporting the bow and arrow in dynamic postures on the pillars of temples in Ahobilam, which explains that this motif had become very popular among artists to have been depicted in the temple so liberally.

A significant aspect of these sculptures is that they are not found in the main parts of these temples where, in fact, Lakshmi is depicted as the so-called Adi Lakshmi, the 'original' (Adi) consort of Lord Narasimha. Therefore, the question that arises is: Why was the wooing of Chenchu Lakshmi so significantly portrayed in these temples and so vividly remembered through oral memory in the form of legends? Chenchita, as the other woman, is certainly loved by Lord Narasimha, but she has been incorporated into the pantheon clearly on a level below that of Lakshmi. Local traditions, of course, have a different story to tell. It is believed that after killing Hiranyaksipu, the Lord forgot to return to his original abode and also forgot about his bride Lakshmi. She, however, decided upon a method to be with him and took birth as the daughter of a Chenchu chief. It took Lord Narasimha a little time to meet her, and then they were married (Lakshminarayana 1991: 24). In this narrative, the Chenchu girl is the true Lakshmi herself. However, the impressions of anger that she displays indicate that the incorporation of the Chenchus into the dominant religious ideology was not a smooth process. That the Narasimha–Chenchita legend continued to be embedded in the oral traditions of the non-literate societies of the hunting-gathering communities of the Chenchus is of some significance in unfolding the history of the locality.

In this example, we see the interplay of myth, history, art, and literature that enabled us to articulate that the so-called tribal 'other' in a local situation was not only in dialogue with the dominant Brāhmaṇical/Hindu discourse, but also ultimately led to the barriers between the periphery and the centre to be dissolved because stories such as that of Lakshmi's rebirth brought together the dominant idea of Lakshmi and reconciled it with the Chenchita. Also, the Chenchus continue to have special ritual rights in these temples and thereby, they have not only transformed the form

Lakshmi took at Ahobilam but also defined the ritual practices here. Thus, the periphery came to define the so-called centre of ideological practices. In the process, several boundaries around belief, ritual, and artistic representation broke down. In the ultimate analysis, then, it was the necessities of 'practical life' that demanded that a dialogue be continued with the social 'other' in order to sustain the dominant notion of the 'self', as explained below. A study of the historical traditions of tribal societies living along the Eastern Ghats reveals considerable reciprocal interchange between them and the state (Murty 1994: 205–218). The study observes that in many areas of knowledge—procurement of forest produce, understanding and controlling its ecology—civilised society was dependent on the forest dwellers. They thus saw themselves as powerful peoples controlling the forests, though they were different from the village peoples. It was power, not morality, that formed the motivating force of myths, and only devotion could overcome the thirst for power. On the part of the Chenchu tribe, some successfully merged with the mainstream, while keeping their individual identity alive. We have argued in this chapter that there were different types of Chenchus, not all of whom accepted the above Narasimha–Chenchu narrative. Today, the Chenchus of Andhra Pradesh find mention in the list of 'tribes' which seek affirmative action in education and employment, through policy and constitutional guarantees of the Government of India. Presenting their history at the micro-level not only provides value to their ways of perceiving reality, but also emphasises that their skills and cultural inputs in the past were of great relevance to the advancement of society and to the definition of what we understand as the Indian civilisation today.

Conclusion

> *Each moment was both mundane and sacred. There was a notion of space in terms of place, locale, region and country and the universe.... The two together provided the basis of multiple identities and local distinctiveness.*
>
> (Vatsyayan 2005: 42)

This quote enables us to highlight not only the spatial and temporal contexts of these examples, but also how the institutional parameters of the Buddhist and Brāhmaṇical/Hindu faiths, respectively, underwent changes at different sites, which provided us with the particular data we needed to illustrate our argument. Her elaboration forms the critical basis of our understanding of *parampara* or tradition in the Indic context:

> Tradition or *parampara* at its best connotes a flow, a vertical transmission in time and a spatial spread horizontally. It does not constitute a frozen, static object or even a corpus of values and behavioural patterns. When the dynamics of the flow is sustained, we recognise it as world-view and lifestyle, distinctive but not static....India throughout its history has known the movements of transmission as also moments of rigidity and fixity (Vatsyayan 2005: 41).

In contrast, contemporary studies on the different regions of the Indian subcontinent in historical time draw on ancient sources, but rarely locate the textual references within the broader world view of where the text originated or the religious group/s that produced them. Inscriptions as documents produced by different levels of state power in various localities have come to be commonly used to refer to regional particularities on taxation, land tenure, local self-government, and so on, without engaging with the broader socio-ideological factors of its production. The study of the political, the economic, the social, and the religious is carried out in separate compartments; similarly, the study of the textual and the epigraphic has also hitherto been treated as segments, thus denying us a comprehensive view of a dynamic and ever-changing regional and social milieu, which would be far removed from the didactic and normative traditions that Orientalist and Indological discourses on early India have regarded as the pan-Indian social fabric.

First, in order to move beyond existing methodological avenues, we have suggested that it is imperative to factor in the small and fragmentary into the historical narrative, while not rejecting the textual in an absolute sense. Second, to look closely into the minute, we need to stand on the local ground and connect various local entities to create an integrated space of the Indian subcontinent. And finally, wherever possible, we must bring in the oral tradition and cultural practices of communities that had no major textual traditions so as to create more inclusive histories, and thus create an intellectual space for the marginal and excluded groups to visualise their own historical pasts.

In the case of the unique ivory statuette that we discussed above, the aesthetic value was intrinsic to the object and had to be emphasised. We held that contact between peoples concomitantly went beyond mere material impetus. But in the ultimate analysis, we are dealing with human beings—their desires, curiosities, compulsions, and joys—people who, in the contexts that they lived in, were also embedded in ideological and social relations. Understanding the 'other' within an overarching world of competition and money was equally relevant and pertinent, if not absolutely essential to cultural well-being. Subsequently, fragments, as short inscriptions or non-conventional art-historical images, alongside texts, provided a more complex picture of the way the ideology of exclusion underwent changes in its necessary contact with regions away from its origin and initial articulation. More firmly, we submit that 'in keeping with any culture of pluralism where multiple contradictory worlds co-exist as central features of everyday life' (Jadhav 1994: 712), denial of the 'other' was not a norm. Indeed, it necessarily could not be so. In the present-day Indian context, when the status of hitherto lower orders in society is changing, we emphasise that historians need to break the impasse by taking a serious look at fragments of information from a variety of sources. Though these fragmentary sources do not present a continuous narrative account of their existence, they forcefully throw up data that tends to question the world view of the dominant. In order to pursue these sources, intensive research into the different regions of the subcontinent is a necessity. It also simultaneously means a shift from 'text' (literary) and 'India' (the totality) to the 'scripts' (epigraphic) and 'material' (archaeological) as objects of study in the 'region' and 'locality'.

It is well known that writing this past is deeply entwined with the way we perceive and live our present, and so history needs to be positioned as an enabler to retrieve and recover horizontally an expansive past, which is also vertically deeper and socially more inclusive. At one level, we were able to highlight the contrast between the prescriptive notions that denied social groups the right to status (such as the carmakāras who took to Buddhism because they were denied proper status according to the *Dharmaśāstras*), and spiritual emancipation and the practice of these methods through social interactions and mobility. Religious context does not remain static in time and place. At another level, we also wanted to emphasise that the trajectory of how a faith evolves has much to do with its practice, and most importantly, how its institutional base developed in different contextual situations. This could only be done by taking a deeper look at the regional and local dimensions of religious history, which the fragments we addressed drew us to.

Notes

1. Lariviere had labelled these critiques of 'Indological discourse' as 'Orientalist', 'Essentialist', and 'Distortionist' to make a fervent plea for the relevance of the study of Indology without belittling the written word, as it was based on scientific methods of interrogation.
2. These meanings of 'fragment' have been accessed at https://www.dictionary.com/browse/fragment (accessed December 2021).
3. I participated in the excavations at the site of Kondapur, Medak District, Telangana in seasons 2009–2010, which were conducted under Superintending Archaeologist Dr G. Maheshwari (Excavation Branch), Archaeological Survey of India, South Eastern Circle.
4. Innumerable studies have been done on this aspect of the Indo-Graeco-Roman trade. For a review of some of the works, see Gupta (2005).
5. The two Indias could refer to India as an imagined space for Romans, who never actually visited the country, whereas the other India could be India perceived as a real space, by those Romans who traded and accessed goods from there.
6. Russell Means was of the Oglala Lakota Tribe, USA and articulated these sentiments in the context of how Native American traditions were destroyed subsequent to the large-scale migration of Europeans into America.

7. The above has been elaborately discussed in Parasher Sen 2007: 1–80 (Introduction).
8. This has reference to the preparation of Parasher Sen (2004), and the teaching of an optional course on 'Marginality and Privilege in Early India' at the University of California, Berkeley (1992) and at the University of Hyderabad (1993–2006).

References

Ankersmit, F. R. 1989. 'Historiography and Post-Modernism'. *History and Theory* XXVIII(2): 137–153.

Appadurai, Arjun. 1986. *The Social Life of Things: Commodities in Cultural Perspective*. Cambridge: Cambridge University Press.

Beard, Mary. 2008. *Pompeii: The Life of a Roman Town*. London: Profile Books Ltd.

Chakravarti, Uma. 1993. 'Women, Men and Beasts: The *Jatakas* as Popular Tradition'. *Studies in History* 9 (1, n.s.): 43–70.

Converse, H. S. and Arvind Sharma. 1994. 'An Ancient Sudra Account of the Origin of Castes'. *Journal of the American Oriental Society* 114(4): 642–644.

Deo, S. B. and R. S. Gupte. 1974. *Excavations at Bhokardan (Bhogavardhana) 1973*. Nagpur and Aurangabad: Nagpur University and Aurangabad University.

Fariello, M. Anna and Paula Owen. 2005. *Objects and Meaning: New Perspectives on Art and Craft*. Lanham MD: Scarecrow Press.

Fürer-Haimendorf, Christoph von. 1943. *The Chenchus: The Jungle Folk of the Deccan*. London: Macmillan & Co.

Gosden, Chris and Yvonne Marshall. 1999. 'The Cultural Biography of Objects'. *World Archaeology* 31(2): 169–178.

Grafton, A. 1997. *The Footnote: A Curious History*. Cambridge: Harvard University Press.

Gupta, Dipankar. 2000. *Interrogating Caste: Understanding Hierarchy and Difference in Indian Society*. New Delhi: Penguin Books.

Gupta, Sunil. 2005. 'A Historiographical Survey of Studies on Indo-Roman Sea Trade and Indian Ocean Trade'. *The Indian Historical Review* XXXII(1): 140–164.

Haynes, Douglas and Gyan Prakash (eds). 1991. *Contesting Power: Resistance and Everyday Social Relations in South Asia*. Delhi: Oxford University Press.

Helms, Mary W. 1991. *Craft and the Kingly Ideal: Art, Trade, and Power*. Austin: University of Texas Press.

Inden, Ronald B. 1990. *Imagining India*. Oxford: Basil Blackwell.
Jadhav, S. 1994. 'Comment on the Myths of Origin of the Indian Untouchables'. *Man* 29(3, n.s.): 712.
Lakshminarayana, Sri R. 1991. 'The History and Sanctity of Sri Lakshmi Narasimhaswamy Devasthanam AHOBILAM'. Special Issue on Sri AhobilamKshetram 11(11–12), Jan–Feb: 24–28.
Lamb, Winifred. 1929. *Greek and Roman Bronzes*. London: Methuen.
Lariviere, Richard W. 1994. 'Protestants, Orientalists, and Brāhmaṇas: Reconstructing Indian Social History'. Second Annual Jan Gonda Lecture, Gonda Foundation. Amsterdam: Royal Netherlands Academy of Arts and Sciences. Available at https://www.knaw.nl/shared/resources/actueel/publicaties/pdf/gondalecture1994-Protestants-Orientalist-andBrahmanas.pdf (accessed December 2021).
Lüders, H. 1920. 'A List of Brāmhī Inscriptions from the Earliest Times to about 400 AD, with the Exception of those of Aśoka', Appendix, II Southern Inscriptions'. *Epigraphia Indica*, Vol. X, Sten Konow (ed.), 98–179. Calcutta: Archaeological Survey of India.
Means, Russell. 1992. 'On the Future of the Earth: An American Indian Perspective'. *Patriotic and People Oriented Science and Technology Bulletin* 23(June): 41– 47.
Moeller, Walter O. 1976. *The Wool Trade of Ancient Pompeii*. Leiden: E. J. Brill.
Murty, M. L. K. 1994. 'Forest Peoples and Historical Traditions in the Eastern Ghats, South India'. In B. Allchin (ed.), *Living Traditions: Studies in Ethnoarchaeology of South Asia*, 205–218. New Delhi: Oxford and IBH Publishing Co. Pvt. Ltd.
Narasimhacharya, M. 1989. *History of the Cult of Narasimha in Andhra Pradesh (From 11th century AD to 17th century AD)*, Sri Malola Grantha Mala–2. Hyderabad: Sri Ahobila Math.
Parasher Sen, Aloka. 2001. 'The "Self" and the "Other" in Early Indian Tradition'. In S. C. Malik (ed.), *Rupa-Pratirupa: Mind, Man and Mask*, 28–49. New Delhi: Indira Gandhi National Centre for the Arts, and Aryan Books International.
Parasher Sen, Aloka (ed.). 2004. *Subordinate and Marginal Groups in Early India up to 1500 AD*, Oxford in India Readings: Themes in Indian History. New Delhi: Oxford University Press.
Parasher Sen, Aloka. 2007. 'Names, Travellers and Inscriptions in Early Historic South India'. *The Indian Historical Review* XXXIV(1): 47–90.
———. 2014. 'Unraveling the Reality of a "City" on the Deccan Plateau'. In Adam Kemezis (ed.), *Urban Dreams and Realities: Remains and Representations of the Ancient City*, 89–107. Leiden: E. J. Brill.

Parker, Grant. 2008. *The Making of Roman India*. Cambridge: Cambridge University Press.

Ray, H. P. 1986. *Monastery and Guild: Commerce under the Satavahanas*. New Delhi: Oxford University Press.

Sankalia, H. D. and M. G. Dikshit. 1952. *Excavations at Brahmapuri (Kolhapur) 1945–46*, Deccan College Monograph Series: 5. Poona: Deccan College.

Sherwin-White, S. M. 1983. 'Babylonian Chronicle Fragments as a Source for Seleucid History'. *Journal of Near Eastern Studies* 42(4): 265–270.

Sitapati, P. 1982. *Sri Ahobila Narasimha Swamy Temple*, Archaeological Series No. 56. Hyderabad: State Department of Archaeology and Museums.

Thapar, Romila. 1978. *Ancient Indian Social History: Some Interpretations*. New Delhi: Orient Longman.

———. 2013. *The Past before Us: Historical Traditions of Early North India*. New Delhi: Permanent Black.

Vatsyayan, Kapila. 2005. 'From Interior Landscapes into Cyberspace: Fluidity and Dynamics of Tradition'. In Kamala Ganesh and Usha Thakkar (eds), *Culture and the Making of Identity in Contemporary India*, The Asiatic Society of Mumbai Bicentenary Volume, 39–50. New Delhi: Sage Publications.

Wheeler, R. E. M. 1951. 'Roman Contact with India, Pakistan and Afghanistan'. In W. F. Grimes (ed.), *Aspects of Archaeology in Britain and Beyond: Essays presented to O. G. S. Crawford*, 345–381. London: H. W. Edwards.

———. 1954. *Rome beyond Imperial Frontiers*. Harmondsworth: Penguin.

Yamazaki, Gen'ichi. 2005. *The Structure of Ancient Indian Society: Theory and Reality of the Varṇa System*, Toyo Bunko Research Library 6. Tokyo: The Toyo Bunko.

Glossary

Āgamaśāstras	ritual texts
agnichayana	Vedic sacrifice of 'piling the fire'
agniṣṭōma	Vedic sacrifice in praise of Agni
agrahāra	village granted to a *brāhmaṇa*
āhāra	district
ahimṣā	nonviolence
aikaśaṃkha	single conch
Airāvata	Indra's elephant
ākhyāyika	biography
akrodha	to be without anger
amātyas	minister/adviser to the king; most important position under Sātavāhana rule
ambi	bucket
ampi	water/raft
anatya/anatyayoni	'last born'
anatyāvasāyin	'impure' *jāti*
anvaya	family
ārajavam	to speak your mind and act accordingly
araṇya	habitable forest
āridupadugai	arable land near a river
Arthaśāstra	text on statecraft
āśrama	dwellings of ascetics, stage of life
aśvamēdha	horse sacrifice
āṭavikarāja	king of the forest
aṭavi	wild forest
avatāra	incarnation

āvēsani	architect, also foreman of artisans who led the builders.
bahusuvarṇa	possessing much gold
baṁmaṇni/brāhmaṇī	wife of a *brāhmaṇa*
bhāṇaka	preacher
bhandagarika	in-charge of warehouses
Bhaṭṭārakasya	Venerable One
bhikkhus	Buddhist monks/mendicants
Bhūlōkamalla	Wrestler of the terrestrial world
Bhūpateḥ	Lord of the earth
Bhuvanaikamalla	Sole Wrestler of the world
birudas	titles
Bodhisatta	an Enlightened being on the way to Buddhahood
brahma-kṣatra	rulers having both *brāhmaṇa* and *kṣatriya* identity
brāhmaṇa	priests—first in caste hierarchy
cakravarti-kṣetra	universal territory
Candravamśa	lunar family
Cankam	assembly of poets or Tamil Literary Academy
carita	historical biography
carmakāra/chaṁmakāra	leather worker
chaitya	Buddhist hall of meditation
Chāḷukyakula	Chalukyan family
cheruvu	water reservoirs, lakes
dama	self-control
dāsaka	fisherman
daya	compassion
dhakka/pratidhakkā	drum
Dhamma	policy of King Aśoka
dhaṁmanigāma	pious hamlet
dhaṁñika	corn dealer
dvipakṣagotra	the 'double *gotra*' of a sage who claims lineage from both *brāhmaṇa* and *kṣatriya*

ēri-k-kōppu	field watered from a reservoir
gadhika/gaṁdhika	perfumer
gahapati/gṛhapati	householder, landowner
gāma/grāma	village
gaṇa	followers of Lord Śiva
gāthas	verses
gavendra	owner of the cow-herd
gorocana	pigment
gōṭhī/gōṣṭī	assembly/committee
gōtra	family, race, lineage, kin
hairaṇyaka	un-coined gold, precious metal
hālika-kuḍubika	person who owns and cultivates land
hālika/hālakiya	ploughman
Haritiputra	sons of Hariti
hēraṇikā/hēraṇaka	treasurer
itihāsa-purāṇa	ancient Indian historical tradition
itihāsa	'thus it was'
Jagadekamalla	Sole Wrestler in the world
janapada	habitable territory
jāti	birth, rank, caste, family, race and lineage
Kailāsa	mountain in the Himālayas
kāl	channel
kalam	small boat
kullanai	a water-regulator structure of stone
Kāmadhenu	cow of plenty
kamalavana	garden of lotuses
kamāra	blacksmith
kāmika	labourer
kanakadaṇḍa	golden sceptre
kapiñjala	a kind of small bird
kartthumpu	sluice construction with stones
kāsākāra	brazier
katalkol	sea-induced flood, deluge
kathā	tales

kavirayar	poet
kiḷar	pail for drawing water
kimcuka	kind of orange-red flower
Kirāta	name of a hunting tribe
Kirātapati	Lord of the Kirātas
kōlīkanikāya	weaver
kṣatriya	ruling caste/class—second in caste hierarchy
kṣetra	area, field
kuḍubika	peasant family, owner of land
kula	family
kulārika	potter
kuntha	spear
kuṅthadhvaja	spear flag
kurinci	mountains
kuvai	arrowroot
lohavāṇiyiya	iron-monger
maḍai	sluice gate
Mahābhōja	chief/local ruler
Mahābhōjī	wife of *Mahābhōja*
mahākāvya	poetry
Mahāmāta/Mahāmātra	high official, Prime Minister
Mahārāja	Great King
Mahārājādhirāja	Supreme King of the great kings
Mahāraṭhi	chief/local ruler
Mahātalavara	chief/local ruler
Mahātaraka	one who monitors the king's household
mahāśabdas	important utterances
Mahāsenāpati	military general
maināsँ	a song bird
makaradhvaja	*makara* (crocodile) banners
mālākāra	garland maker
Mānavyagotra	lineage of the sage, Mandavya
maṇikāra	jeweller
marakalam	small boat made of wood

marutam	wetlands
mataku	sluice
mātrigaṇa	demi gods attending upon Siva/ Mothers of three worlds
mayūrapiṃchha	peacock's tail
mleccha	barbarians
mlecchāṭvika	barbaric forest dwellers
mukhamaṇḍapa	front portion of temple
mullai	forests
muni	ascetic
mutthukkuḷippar	people who dive for pearls
nadu	sub-regions
nandipāda	taurine, or bull's hoof
nattukkāl	district channel for water
nāṭya	drama
navai	ship with a flag mast
nēgama/nigama	organisation of traders; also, stands for town
neytal, neithal	coastal regions
nṛpaḥ/nṛpa	king
nulitteruvitta	string-line or straight-line technique of building sluices
odayaṁtrika	workers fabricating hydraulic engines
pādamulika	servant
palai	arid regions
pāḷidhvaja	flags and banners
pālikētana	flags in row
pañcamahāśabda	five important utterances
pāniyagharika	superintendent of water-houses
parampara	tradition
parappu, paravai	sea
paricārakī-kṛta	servants
parinirvānṇa	passing away of Lord Buddha
perumkuḷam	large pond
praśasti	eulogy

pratihāras	minister/adviser to the king; most important position under Sātavāhana rule
pulavar	scholar
Punal Nadu	well-watered land
purnaghata	auspicious vase
Puru Raṇa Parākrama	brave on the battle field
puspaudyān	flower garden
rāja	king
rājamacha	royal minister
rajāmatyas	group of ministers
Rājasūya	consecration ceremony performed by kings
rajavēja/rajvaidya	royal physician
rājyas	kingdoms
Raṇabhūshaṇa	a gem in war
raṇarasika	fond of fighting
Raṇa Vikrāṅta	victorious in battles
rangamaṇḍapa	where performances are staged in the temple
rasa	aesthetic experience
Ripu Narendra	one who is an enemy of kings
ṛṣis	sages/seers
Śabara	name of forest dwelling tribes
śāli	kind of rice
Samasta Bhuvanāśraya	asylum of the whole world
Sangam	assembly of poets or Literary Academy in Tamil
sanyāsis	renouncers
sargabandha	poetry
sarvalōkāśraya	lord of the entire world
sathavāha/sārthavāha	caravaneer
satya	truth
sēla-vaḍhakī	cave builder
senipamukha	chief of the guilds

śeṇī\śrēṇī	guild
sethis	merchants
seṭhin/śreṣṭhin	leader merchant
Śrī Pṛthvīvallabha	favourite of the world
śrīvatsa	symbol of triangular swirl or an endless knot
stūpa	a hemispherical commemorative monument housing sacred relics of the Buddha or other saintly monks/nuns that serves as a Buddhist shrine
śūdras	servants—fourth in caste hierarchy
Suryavamśa	solar lineage
suvaṇakāra/suvanakara	goldsmith
śvētātapatra	white parasol/umbrella
tāpasinī	female ascetic
taskans	carpenters
tilapiṣika	oil millers
timil	hump of a bull, ship
tinai	ecological zones
Trailōkyamalla/ Tribhuvanamalla	Wrestler of the three worlds
triratna	symbol on coins—three jewels of Buddhism
udyān	garden
upadhyayar	teacher
upajhaya	teacher
ūrār	inhabitants of a village
ūrkuḷam	village tanks
vaiśya	traders, merchants
vamśa or anvaya	family/dynasty
vana	garden or forest
vanapālas	forest guards
vaṇija/vanijaka/vāniya	traders/merchants
vaniyinī	wives of merchants

vanyadhānabījadhāninām	burning of chaff of the *śāli* rice, which produced smoke
varāhalāṃchchana	symbol of the boar-crest
varṇa	caste, status group
vasakāra	bamboo worker
vayakkāl	field channels for water
vendan	chief
Vindhyaṭvi	forest of Vindhya
Vishamasiddhi	one who has obtained success in unconquerable straits
Viśvāsāmatyas	most trusted and important advisors of the king
vrātyas	degraded *kṣatriyas*
yajňa	a Vedic sacrifice

Notes on the Contributors

Nairita Ghosh is Doctoral Research Scholar in the Department of History, Jamia Millia Islamia University, New Delhi. Her research interests include studies in paleography, epigraphy, geography, philology, and social history of early India.

Mrinalini is Lecturer in the Department of History, Adarsh P. G. College, Pilani, Rajasthan. Her research involves the *Kāvya* literary tradition, with special focus on the study of the environment, religion, and culture of ancient India.

Aloka Parasher Sen is Professor Emerita in the Department of Sanskrit Studies, University of Hyderabad, Hyderabad. She had earlier served in the Department of History (1979–2018) at the same university. She has written books/monographs extensively on various aspects of the economy, society, religion, and culture of early India, with special reference to the Deccan and is the author of *Settlement and Local Histories of the Early Deccan* (2021) and *Mlecchas in Early India* (1991). She has edited *Social and Economic History of Early Deccan: Some Interpretations* (2019 [1993]), *Kevala-Bodhi: The Buddhist and Jaina History of the Deccan* (2003), among others.

Aruna Pariti is Assistant Professor in, and currently, the Head of the Department of History, University College for Women, Koti, under Osmania University, Hyderabad. She is also Academic Counsellor for MA History, IGNOU, Hyderabad. She has been published widely in reputed journals. She is the author of *Genealogy, Time and Identity: Historical Consciousness in the*

Deccan (6th–12th Centuries CE*)* (2015) and *State Formation in the Eastern Deccan (7th Century* AD*–13th Century* AD*)* (2000).

Kasala Jashwanth Prasad is Doctoral Research Scholar in the Department of History, University of Hyderabad, Hyderabad. He has also taught Indian History at the Vijayavardhini Degree College, Hyderabad and visited Freie Universität Berlin, Germany as Research Intern in 2017.

V. Rajesh is Associate Professor in, and the Head of the Department of Humanities and Social Sciences, Indian Institute of Science Education and Research (IISER) Mohali, Punjab. He is the author of *Manuscripts, Memory and History: Classical Tamil Literature in Colonial India* (Foundation Books, 2014). He is currently working on the intellectual history of progressive literary movements in Tamil Nadu.

Sagnik Saha is Doctoral Research Scholar in the Department of History, University of Hyderabad, Hyderabad, and is currently working as a Guest Lecturer in the Department of Ancient Indian and World History, Sanskrit College and University, Kolkata. His research interests include space and materiality, subalternity, and everyday practices in early Indian history.

Sreekala M. V. is Doctoral Research Scholar in the Centre for Historical Centre Studies, Jawaharlal Nehru University, New Delhi. She specialises in the history of ancient India, and is currently working on environmental aspects in *Brāhmaṇa* literature.

Index